A PRACTICAL GUIDE TO REAL ESTATE INVESTING FOR BEGINNERS

SIMPLE STRATEGIES TO GRASP THE MARKET, INVEST WISELY, AND MANAGE MONEY & RISKS FOR LONG-TERM WEALTH FOR YOU AND YOUR FAMILY

MARI SELLIN

ADMIRANDA PUBLISHING

MARI SELLIN

A Practical Guide to Real Estate Investing for Beginners

Simple Strategies to Grasp the Market, Invest Wisely, and Manage Money & Risks for Long-Term Wealth for You and Your Family

First published by Admiranda Publishing 2025

Cover photo credit: Unboxing Studio.

Interior book design: Mari Sellin.

Paperback and hardback cover: Mari Sellin and @aliatif1050.

Second edition

ISBN: 978-91-989616-7-6

This book was professionally typeset on Reedsy.
Find out more at reedsy.com

Contents

INTRODUCTION 1

LAYING THE FOUNDATION FOR SUCCESS 4

1.1 UNDERSTANDING REAL ESTATE AS AN INVESTMENT 5

1.2 THE PSYCHOLOGY OF A SUCCESSFUL INVESTOR 7

1.3 SETTING REALISTIC INVESTMENT GOALS AND EXPECTATIONS 9

1.4 ASSESSING YOUR FINANCIAL READINESS FOR REAL ESTATE INVESTMENTS 12

1.5 INVESTING IN YOUR PERSONAL AND PROFESSIONAL DEVELOPMENT 14

1.5.1 Educational Resources and Staying Informed 15

1.5.1.1 Educational Programs and Certifications 15

1.5.1.2 Self-Education 16

1.5.1.3 Staying Informed and Continuing Education 17

1.5.1.4 Essential Real Estate Terminology Every Beginner Should Know 19

1.6 HARNESSING TECHNOLOGY IN REAL ESTATE INVESTING 23

1.6.1 Introduction to Available Apps and Software Solutions 24

1.6.2 Utilizing Big Data for Market Analysis 24

1.7 DEVELOPING YOUR REAL ESTATE NETWORK 26

1.7.1 The Importance of a Reliable Network 26

1.7.1.1 Using Social Media to Enhance Your Real Estate Network 28

1.7.1.2 Collaborating with Real Estate Agents and Brokers 30

1.7.2 Evaluating the Right Group for Your Needs 31

1.7.2.1 Introduction to Real Estate Investment Groups 32

1.7.2.2 Best Practices for Active Participation 33
1.7.2.3 Creating Your Own Real Estate Investment Group 33
INVESTMENT STRATEGIES 35
2.1 CHOOSING THE RIGHT PROPERTY FOR YOUR INVESTMENT GOALS 36
2.1.1 Define Investment Objectives 36
2.1.2 Considerations for First-Time Buyers 36
2.2 CHOOSING THE RIGHT NICHE FOR YOU 37
2.2.1 Investing in Residential vs. Commercial Real Estate 40
2.2.1.1 Decision Factors for Investment Choice 40
2.2.1.2 Residential Real Estate Nuances 41
2.2.1.3 Comparative Analysis of Residential Real Estate and Commercial 42
2.2.1.4 Benefits and Challenges of Commercial Real Estate 42
2.2.2 Multi-Family Properties vs. Single-Family Rentals 43
2.2.3 Commercial Real Estate Basics for Beginners 45
2.3 CHOOSING THE RIGHT STRATEGY FOR YOU 47
2.3.1 Short-Term and Vacation Rentals 48
2.3.2 Student Rentals 48
2.3.3 Live-In House Flips 49
2.3.4 House Flipping 49
2.3.4.1 Flipping Properties: A Comprehensive Guide 49
2.3.4.2 Case Study: Successful Residential Flip 52
2.3.5 House Hacking 54
2.3.6 Turnkey Investing 54
2.3.7 Wholesaling 55
2.3.7.1 Introduction to Real Estate Wholesaling 55
2.3.8 Real Estate Development 57
2.3.8.1 Developing Real Estate: From Purchase to Project Completion 57
2.3.9 Buy-and-Hold 59
2.3.9.1 Case Study: Building a Rental Portfolio from Scratch 59
2.3.9.2 Case Study: Overcoming Investment Challenges 62

2.3.10 BRRRR Investing 64
2.3.10.1 The BRRRR Method Explained 64
2.4 FINDING A PROPERTY, MAKING AN OFFER AND NEGOTIATING 67
2.4.1 The Role of Property Inspections and Appraisals 68
2.4.2 Property Inspections 68
2.4.2.1 Physical Inspection is an Essential Part of the Valuation Process 68
2.4.3 Property Appraisal 70
2.4.4 Negotiations 71
2.4.4.1 The Power of Negotiation 71
2.4.4.2 The Investor's Guide to Real Estate Contracts 72
2.4.5 Upon Completion of the Purchase 75
2.4.5.1 Checklist Breakdown 77
2.5 BUILDING LONG-TERM WEALTH STRATEGIES 79
2.5.1 Ethical Investing: Doing Well by Doing Good 79
2.5.2 Sustainability and Green Investments in Real Estate 81
2.5.3 Reflecting on Your Real Estate Journey and Preparing for What's Next 83
2.5.3.1 When to Scale Your Real Estate Investments 84
2.5.3.2 Strategies for Achieving Financial Independence through Real Estate 87
2.5.4 Diversification Strategies of Your Investment Portfolio 90
2.5.4.1 Different Investment Strategies 90
2.5.4.2 Geographical Diversification 91
2.5.4.3 Different Types of Properties 91
2.5.4.4 The Need for Careful Planning 91
2.6 EXIT STRATEGIES FOR REAL ESTATE INVESTORS 93
2.6.1 Refinancing 93
2.6.2 Equity Release Options 95
2.6.3 Real Estate as a Retirement Strategy 96
2.6.3.1 Real Estate for Retirement Income 96
2.6.3.2 Downsizing or Rightsizing in Retirement 97

2.6.4 Estate Planning and Real Estate 97
2.6.4.1 Succession Planning for Real Estate Investors 98
2.6.5 Knowing When to Sell Your Real Estate Investment 100
2.6.5.1 Lease-to-Own: A Win-Win Exit Strategy 103
MARKET ANALYSIS TECHNIQUES 106
3.1 UNDERSTANDING MARKET TRENDS AND ECONOMIC INDICATORS 107
3.1.1 Global Economic Factors Affecting Real Estate 107
3.1.2 Identifying Macroeconomic Indicators 109
3.1.2.1 Utilizing Financial News and Reports 109
3.1.2.2 Impact of Government Policies 111
3.1.2.3 Leverage Market Trends 111
3.1.2.4 Demographic and Social Changes 112
3.1.2.5 Investor Activities and Market Speculation 113
3.1.3 Location Analysis 114
3.1.3.1 Identify Emerging Markets and Using Local Insights 115
3.1.3.2 Identify Key Market Indicators 116
3.1.3.3 The Importance of Understanding Local Events 116
3.2 ANALYZING AND PREDICTING MARKET TRENDS TO YOUR ADVANTAGE 118
3.2.1 Analyze Historical Data 118
3.2.2 Forecasting Techniques 119
3.2.2.1 Leverage Technology and Data Analytics 121
3.2.2.2 Leveraging Social Media for Research 122
3.2.3 Explore Supply and Demand 123
3.2.3.1 Real Estate Market Cycles 123
3.2.3.2 Navigating Market Downturns 125
3.3 TECHNIQUES FOR FINDING UNDERVALUED PROPERTIES 128
3.3.1 Real Estate Platforms 128
3.3.2 Networking 129
3.3.3 Eviction Records 130
3.3.4 Public Records and Auction Sites 131
3.3.5 Driving For Dollars 133

3.3.6 Financial Distress Signals 134
3.4 VALUATION METHODS AND TECHNIQUES 134
3.4.1 Comparative Market Analysis (CMA) 134
3.4.2 Sales Comparison Approach 136
3.4.3 Income Approach 137
3.4.4 Principles in Commercial Investment 141
3.4.5 Cost Approach 141
3.4.6 Calculating Return on Investment (ROI) 142
3.4.7 Rent-to-Value (RTV) Ratio 145
3.4.8 Development Cost 146
3.4.9 Evaluating Property Values with AVM 147
MAKE A DIFFERENCE WITH YOUR REVIEW 152
Unlock the Power of Generosity 152
FINANCIAL MANAGEMENT 154
4.1 FINANCING REAL ESTATE INVESTMENTS 155
4.1.1 How to Invest with Little to No Money Down 155
4.1.1.1 Zero Down Payment with Government Loans 155
4.1.1.2 Government and Grant Programs 156
4.1.1.3 Partnerships and Joint Ventures 156
4.1.1.4 Using Home Equity 156
4.1.1.5 Exploring Alternative Funding Sources 158
4.1.1.6 Understand Wholesaling 161
4.1.2 Traditional Mortgage Options for Beginners 163
4.1.3 Exploring Government Loans and Incentives 165
4.1.3.1 Introduction to Government Loans 166
4.1.3.2 Strategic Use of Government Loans in Real Estate Investing 166
4.1.3.3 Application Process for Government Loans 168
4.1.4 Government Programs and Assistance 169
4.1.4.1 Detail State and Local Grants and Incentives 169
4.1.4.2 Finding Government Programs and Grants 169
4.1.5 Creative Financing Strategies: Lease Options 170
4.1.5.1 Lease Option 171

4.1.5.2 Rent-to-Own 172
4.1.5.3 Legal Considerations 172
4.1.6 Creative Financing Strategies: Seller Financing 173
4.1.7 Sites for Custom Real Estate Agreements 174
4.1.8 Refinancing Options and Strategies 175
4.1.9 Real Estate Investment Trusts (REITs): A Different Approach 178
4.1.10 Essential Investment Terms 180
4.2 TAKING CARE OF EVERYDAY FINANCES 185
4.2.1 Financial Order: The Backbone of Real Estate Investment 185
4.2.2 Keeping Accurate Records: Ensuring Tax Compliance 185
4.2.3 Leveraging Accounting Software in Real Estate 186
4.2.4 The Symphony of Financial Statements and Chart of Accounts 188
4.2.5 Budget and Forecast: Navigating Future Financial Waters 188
4.2.6 Rent versus Costs: Maximizing Property Profitability 189
4.2.7 Your Annual Financial Compass 189
4.2.7.1 Financial Year Wheel 189
4.3 BUILDING AND MAINTAINING AN EMERGENCY FUND 193
4.4 TAX IMPLICATIONS AND BENEFITS 195
4.4.1 Tax Issues and How to Navigate Them 195
4.4.1.1 Staying Informed on Tax Laws 195
4.4.1.2 Strategic Tax Planning 196
4.4.1.3 Visual Aid: Tax Planning Timeline 197
4.4.2 Deductions on Your Real Estate Investments 198
4.4.2.1 Improvement vs. Repair: Navigating Tax Implications 199
4.4.2.2 Vacancy Deductions: Managing Non-Rental Periods 200
4.4.2.3 Taking a Deductible Salary Depends on Business Structure 200
4.4.3 Understanding Real Estate Depreciation 201
4.4.3.1 Different Types of Depreciation 201

4.4.3.2 Depreciation Recapture 203
4.4.4 Maximizing Deduction 203
4.4.4.1 Implementation of Cost Segregation 203
4.4.4.2 Consulting with Tax Professionals 204
4.4.4.3 Tax Credits 204
4.4.4.4 Capital Gains Tax Strategies You Need to Know 205
4.5 FINANCIAL TERMS 207
MINIMIZING FINANCIAL RISKS 212
5.1 THE IMPORTANCE OF DUE DILIGENCE IN REAL ESTATE 212
5.1.1 Conducting Due Diligence: A Step-by-Step Guide 215
5.1.1.1 Understand Local Market Conditions 215
5.1.1.2 Review the Property's Strategic Advantages 216
5.1.1.3 Review Property Documentation 216
5.1.1.4 Evaluate the Financials 217
5.1.1.5 Assess the Property's Condition 218
5.2 INSURANCE 218
5.2.1 Protecting Your Investments from Unseen Circumstances 218
5.2.2 Assessing Coverage Needs 219
5.2.3 Types of Real Estate Insurance 219
5.2.3.1 Title Insurances 219
5.2.3.2 During Construction 220
5.2.3.3 Tenants Insurance 220
5.2.3.4 Insurance for Property Owners 221
5.2.4 Comparing Insurance Providers and Policies 222
5.2.4.1 Cost-Benefit Analysis of Insurance Options 223
5.2.4.2 Websites to Compare Insurance Policies 223
5.2.5 Handling Insurance Claims 224
5.2.6 Integrating Insurance into Risk Management Strategy 224
5.3 DIVERSIFICATION TO REDUCE RISK 225
5.4 NAVIGATING THE LEGAL LANDSCAPE OF REAL ESTATE INVESTING 226

5.4.1 Basic Legal Considerations Every Investor Should Know 227
5.4.1.1 Overview of Property Rights 227
5.4.1.2 Keeping Up with Real Estate Laws and Regulations 227
5.4.1.3 Understanding Property Laws 229
5.4.1.4 Contracts and Agreements 229
5.4.1.5 Protective Legal Documentation 230
5.4.1.6 Navigating Landlord-Tenant Laws 230
5.4.1.7 Dispute Resolution 231
5.4.1.8 Importance of Legal Compliance in Modifications and Construction 231
5.4.1.9 Consulting with Legal Professionals 231
5.4.2 Navigating Zoning Laws and Regulations 232
5.4.2.1 Zoning laws 232
5.4.2.2 State and Local Regulations 233
5.4.2.3 Building Permits 234
5.4.2.4 Stay Updated on Zoning Laws, Regulations, and Tax 234
5.5 PROPERTY SCAMS 236
5.5.1 Protect Yourself from Scams 236
5.5.2 Different Kinds of Property Buying Scams 236
5.5.3 Different Kinds of Rental Property Scams 237
5.5.4 Different Kinds of Property Scams Online 237
5.5.5 Look Out for These Signs 238
5.6 LEGAL TERMS 238
EFFECTIVE PROPERTY MANAGEMENT 242
6.1 EFFICIENT PROCESSES 243
6.2 FINDING AND VETTING TENANTS 244
6.2.1 Marketing 244
6.2.1.1 Residential Tenants 244
6.2.1.2 Commercial and Industrial Tenants 245
6.2.2 Screening Process 246
6.2.3 Having Fair Housing Laws 247

6.2.4 Accurate Documentation 247
6.3 HANDLING TENANT ISSUES AND EVICTIONS 247
6.3.1 Lease Agreements 247
6.3.1.1 Policies 248
6.3.1.2 Maintenance Responsibilities 248
6.3.1.3 Tenant Adaption 249
6.3.1.4 Setting Rents 249
6.3.1.5 Managing Payments 250
6.3.2 Open Communication 251
6.3.3 Evictions and Preventive Measures 251
6.3.4 Valuable and Free Information from Online Resources 252
6.4 MAINTENANCE AND UPKEEP: KEEPING YOUR PROPERTY IN TOP SHAPE 254
6.4.1 Budgeting for Maintenance and Repairs 254
6.4.2 Using Professional Services 255
6.4.3 Develop Useful Maintenance and Investment Plans 256
6.4.3.1 A Seasonal Maintenance Plan for Regular Checks 257
6.4.3.2 Long-Term Maintenance and Investment Plan 262
6.5 APPS FOR PROPERTY MANAGEMENT 263
6.5.1 Reflecting on Real Estate Tech Startups 265
6.5.1.1 The Role of AI in Predicting Real Estate Trends 266
6.5.1.2 Blockchain Technology 267
6.5.1.3 Internet of Things (IoT) 268
6.5.1.4 Have a Strategic Approach 268
6.5.2 Evaluating App Effectiveness through Trials and Reviews 270
6.6 MANAGEMENT TERMS 271
READY TO MAKE AN IMPACT? 276
CONCLUSION 277
REFERENCES 280
About the Author 289

INTRODUCTION

As I stood before my first real estate investment, my heart was a mix of fluttering excitement and gnawing nerves. While promising on paper, the property had some issues that the seller deliberately withheld from me and unexpected repairs that ate into my budget. These lessons were invaluable. I realized that thorough due diligence, realistic budgeting, and a hefty dose of perseverance are essential. I wish to pass these lessons to you as you make your own foray into real estate investing.

Let's face it: stepping into real estate can be daunting. You're not just investing money but also hoping for what might be. Over the years, I've met many who have stood where you stand. From retirees looking to boost their pension to young professionals seeking to escape the rent cycle, each had unique reasons but shared a common goal—to succeed in real estate investing. Their stories, filled with strategies and lessons, are woven through the pages of this book to guide and inspire you.

From my early days as a newcomer, navigating through the complexities of the market, to becoming a seasoned property consultant, my journey has been both challenging and rewarding. Starting with a background in real estate economics, technology, and law, I've spent the last 20 years in various capacities—eight years of employment followed by 12 years consulting for everything from small startups to large established companies. My extensive experience has equipped me with insights that I now share with you, aiming to simplify what can often seem a complex venture.

As the founder of Admiranda Publishing, my mission has always been to empower and educate. This book manifests that mission by helping you understand the nuts and bolts of real estate investing without overwhelming you. Expect to learn how to analyze markets, manage properties, understand financing options, and handle risks—all presented with clarity and a focus on practical application.

This guide is designed specifically for beginners who might feel that real estate is an elite game out of reach. I'm here to show you that it's not only accessible but also immensely rewarding. With the proper knowledge and mindset, the path to real estate investing success is more straightforward than you might think.

We'll tackle common fears and misconceptions head-on, providing motivational insights to propel you forward. Real estate investing is not just about financial gain—it's about building confidence, acquiring new skills, and realizing your potential. This book, divided into six chapters, offers these tools and challenges you to grow and achieve more than you thought possible. The six chapters are:

By the end, you'll have a solid real estate investing foundation and be equipped to make your first investment confidently. Remember, every expert was once a beginner. The journey to mastery begins with a single step, and by turning this page, you're already on your way.

"Success in real estate starts with belief, backed by action" is a mantra I've lived by throughout my career. Let this book be your first action toward a successful venture in real estate investing. Let's get started!

LAYING THE FOUNDATION FOR SUCCESS

"Success in real estate starts with education, grows with experience, and is realized through persistence."

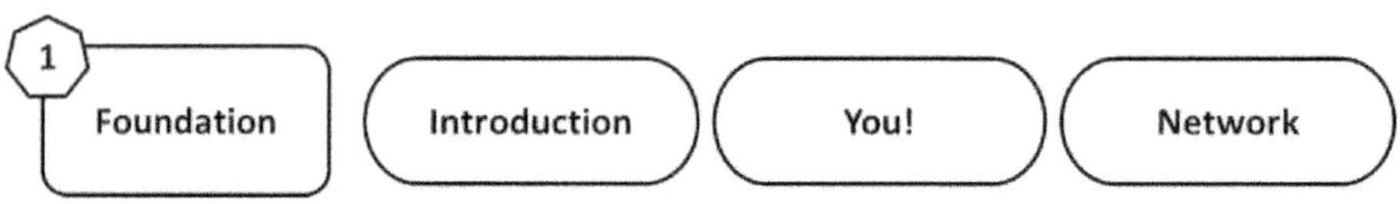

Real estate stands out as a beacon of tangible value in the land of investment—an asset you can see, improve, and utilize in various ways to generate income. Think back to the first time you considered investing. Perhaps it was a moment of realization during a conversation, a seminar, or while reading about the financial successes others have achieved through real estate. This chapter is designed to transform that initial spark of interest into a solid foundation of understanding, equipping you with the necessary tools to navigate the complex yet rewarding landscape of real estate investment.

1.1 UNDERSTANDING REAL ESTATE AS AN INVESTMENT

Historically, real estate investments have provided a compelling argument for those looking to diversify their portfolios. Compared to more volatile markets such as stocks or commodities, real estate typically offers a unique blend of stability, reliable cash flow, and favorable tax treatment. Moreover, real estate values have generally appreciated over time, outpacing inflation and yielding substantial gains for well-positioned investors.

Understanding market cycles is crucial to mastering real estate investment. Each cycle—comprising expansion, hyper-supply, recession, and recovery—presents different challenges and opportunities. For example, during the expansion phase, investors might experience rapid value increases and high property demand. Recognizing the phase of the market cycle can significantly influence your strategy, whether you're deciding to buy, sell, or hold. (Read more in Chapter 3.2.3.) Historical analysis reveals that informed investors who adapted their strategy to these cycles often secured robust returns, mitigating risks during downturns and capitalizing on the upswing.

Economic indicators such as employment, GDP growth, and interest rates are pivotal in shaping real estate markets. For instance, a robust economic environment with solid job growth typically fuels demand for housing, pushing up property values and rental rates. Conversely, rising interest rates calm property markets as borrowing costs increase. Investors can glean insights into how economic shifts profoundly impact real estate by examining past scenarios, such as the housing boom and subsequent correction in 2008. (Read more in Chapter 3.)

Real estate markets can vary dramatically between regions and even within different neighborhoods of the same city. This variability means that local knowledge is power. For example, a city with a burgeoning tech industry may offer lucrative opportunities in residential and commercial real estate sectors due to an influx of workers and companies needing space. Investors conducting thorough local market research can better identify these opportunities and anticipate shifts affecting property values.

Several trends are poised to influence the real estate sector significantly in the future. Demographic shifts, like the aging population in Western countries, will likely increase demand for retirement homes and age-friendly living solutions. Similarly, technological advancements, such as the rise of smart homes, can enhance property values and appeal. Staying informed about these trends through credible sources and expert forecasts is essential for forward-thinking investors. (Read more about real estate markets and trends in Chapter 3.)

The intrinsic value of real estate is closely tied to its ability to generate income through rent or its use in business operations, which provides investors with leverage—using borrowed capital to increase the potential return of an investment. Consider a scenario where purchasing a property with a 20 % down payment and borrowing the remainder at a low interest rate allows you to control a valuable asset that could appreciate in value over time. Moreover, the rental income from tenants can cover mortgage payments and operational costs, leading to a profitable venture as the property value increases.

Real estate's potential for generating cash flow through rental income and its appreciation over time presents a compelling case for its inclusion in any investment portfolio. For example, a well-located property may yield significant rental income, which covers all expenses and provides a healthy return on investment. Over time, as you pay down the mortgage and potentially benefit from property value appreciation, your equity in the property increases, enhancing your financial stability.

However, investing in real estate also involves carefully evaluating risk versus reward. While the rewards can be significant, the risks—such as market volatility, tenant issues, or unforeseen maintenance costs—require careful management. Successful investors mitigate these risks through thorough market research, due diligence, and strategic planning, ensuring their investments are sound and prepared for any challenges. (Read more about risk management in Chapter 5.)

Real estate offers diverse opportunities for investors willing to delve into its intricacies. By understanding the historical context, economic factors, and regional variations and preparing for future trends, you can make informed decisions that balance risk and reward. This foundational knowledge sets the stage for exploring more profound aspects of real estate investment, from financing options to property management, all of which are covered in the subsequent sections of this book.

1.2 THE PSYCHOLOGY OF A SUCCESSFUL INVESTOR

Understanding the psychology behind successful real estate investing is as critical as grasping financial principles. It's about nurturing a mindset that embraces growth and resilience. Throughout my career, I've observed that the most successful real estate investors share a common trait: they possess an unyielding emotional resilience that helps them navigate the ups and downs of market cycles. For instance, during the recession period of the late 2000s, while many recoiled in fear, seasoned investors with a solid psychological foundation saw an opportunity. They understood that real estate cycles are part of a broader economic pattern and maintained their composure, making strategic purchases that would yield significant returns as the market recovered.

Dealing with analysis paralysis—a state where the fear of making incorrect decisions stops progress—is a common barrier for many beginners. The sheer amount of data, forecasts, and analyses can be overwhelming, leading to indecision. To combat this, setting clear, firm decision-making deadlines and simplifying the criteria for investment decisions proves effective. It's essential to perform due diligence and engage in thorough scenario analysis. (Read more about due diligence in Chapter 5.1.) Still, it is equally important to recognize that no investment comes with guaranteed outcomes. Learning to make well-informed decisions within a reasonable timeframe is crucial.

Risk tolerance varies significantly among individuals and directly impacts investment strategies. Understanding your comfort level with risk is pivotal. This self-awareness can guide your investment choices—whether you lean towards conservative strategies involving lower returns and lower risks or more aggressive strategies with the potential for higher returns but also higher risks. Effective risk management starts with this understanding and extends into strategic planning, where diversification plays a key role. You can mitigate potential losses by spreading investments across various property types and markets. This strategy has helped many thriving investors maintain stability during volatile periods.

A long-term investment perspective often distinguishes successful investors from those chasing quick gains. Real estate is generally not a get-rich-quick arena; it rewards patience, persistence, and a forward-looking approach. Consider the investor who purchases properties in emerging neighborhoods, understanding that development projects planned for the next decade will gradually increase property values. Such foresight requires a robust long-term strategy but promises substantial rewards. (Read more in Chapter 2.5.)

Fear of failure is one of the most significant psychological hurdles. Overcoming this fear starts with setting realistic goals and understanding that setbacks are not failures but learning opportunities. Every seasoned investor has faced challenges; however, their continued success often hinges on their ability to learn from these experiences and proceed without apprehension. Embracing this mindset can transform potentially discouraging obstacles into stepping stones toward greater wisdom and confidence in your investment decisions.

Education is another cornerstone of building confidence in the investment realm. Continuous learning about market trends, legal changes, and financial strategies can alleviate anxiety and equip you with the knowledge to make sound investment choices. Whether through formal education, self-study, or practical experience, enhancing your understanding of real estate will bolster your confidence and decision-making capabilities. (Read more about education in Chapter 1.5.1.)

Lastly, the role that a support network provides is essential. Real estate investing, particularly in the early stages, can be a solitary journey fraught with uncertainty. Building a network of fellow investors and professionals provides emotional support and valuable exchanges of ideas and advice. Regular interactions with peers who understand the challenges and complexities of real estate investing can give reassurance and inspire innovative approaches. Many successful investors attribute part of their success to the insights gained and encouragement received from their investment communities. (Read more about developing your network in Chapter 1.7.)

As you delve deeper into real estate investing, remember that developing a solid investor psychology is as crucial as acquiring financial acumen.

1.3 SETTING REALISTIC INVESTMENT GOALS AND EXPECTATIONS

Embarking on your real estate investment adventure requires a grounded, realistic perspective on what can be achieved. Tempering enthusiasm with practical expectations about potential returns, investment timeframes, and the effort needed to navigate this market successfully is essential. Real estate is not a magic bullet for quick wealth but a strategic game that demands patience and persistence. For instance, property flipping may offer quicker financial returns but involves significant risk. It requires a deeper understanding of market timing. In contrast, long-term rental properties might offer more stable passive income streams but require ongoing management and commitment.

Setting SMART (Specific, Measurable, Achievable, Relevant, Time-bound) goals is foundational in real estate investing. These goals serve as your roadmap, guiding each decision and strategy. Consider a specific goal, like purchasing three rental properties in emerging neighborhoods over the next five years. This goal is measurable in terms of the number of properties and the timeline, achievable based on your financial capacity and market research, relevant to your objective of building a profitable real estate portfolio, and time-bound with a clear deadline. By framing your goals within these parameters, you can maintain a clear focus and measure your progress effectively.

Aligning your investment goals with your financial situation is crucial. It requires a realistic assessment of your available capital, debt levels, and income stability. For example, suppose you're currently carrying significant personal debt. In that case, it might be wise to prioritize its reduction before securing a mortgage for an investment property. This alignment ensures that your real estate ambitions do not jeopardize your financial health but complement your overall financial plan.

Different investment strategies may also dictate varying timeframes. As mentioned, short-term investments like house flipping can provide quick returns but often involve higher risks and require a hands-on approach. On the other hand, investing in developing raw land or acquiring long-term rental properties can see a slower return but greater overall profitability and stability. Each strategy comes with its own set of risks and rewards, and understanding these can help you choose the path that best fits your risk tolerance and investment capacity.

It is also vital to regularly review and adjust your investment goals. Numerous dynamic factors, such as economic shifts, interest rate changes, and regional development plans, influence the real estate market. A solid strategy today could become less advantageous tomorrow. Regularly assessing your investment plan allows you to adapt and refine your approach, ensuring it remains aligned with current market conditions and financial goals.

Dispelling common myths about real estate investing is another crucial aspect of setting realistic expectations. Many beginners believe that they need substantial capital to get started or that real estate investments are guaranteed to yield high returns. However, there are various entry points into real estate investing, many of which only require a little upfront capital. Moreover, like any investment, real estate comes with no guarantees—understanding and managing the associated risks is paramount. Effective risk management techniques such as thorough market research, conservative financial forecasting, and adequate insurance coverage can safeguard your investments from unexpected adversities.

Lastly, the importance of diversification must be addressed. As with other types of investments, diversifying your real estate portfolio can help soothe risks and stabilize returns. This might mean spreading your investments across different real estate types —from residential to commercial properties—or geographic locations. Diversification provides a barrier against market instability and ensures that your investments have the opportunity to grow under different economic conditions, thereby stabilizing your financial returns over time. (Read more about diversification in Chapters 2.5.4 and 5.3.)

By setting realistic goals, aligning them with your financial situation, understanding the appropriate timeframes for different strategies, and maintaining flexibility to adapt to market changes, you equip yourself with a robust framework for successful real estate investing. These strategies prepare you to meet the challenges of the real estate market but also position you to capitalize on opportunities that arise, ensuring that your investment efforts yield fruitful results.

1.4 ASSESSING YOUR FINANCIAL READINESS FOR REAL ESTATE INVESTMENTS

Real estate investment can be a mighty and rewarding pathway to building wealth. Still, it's essential to understand how it compares to other investment options like stocks, mutual funds, or simply parking your money in a bank account. Each investment vehicle comes with distinct risk profiles, interest potentials, and demands on your financial liquidity. Real estate typically requires more substantial upfront capital than buying stocks or mutual funds. It involves active management but often provides more stable and predictable returns, especially rental income. Moreover, while the risks associated with real estate are considerable—ranging from market fluctuations to tenant issues—the tangible nature of the asset provides a level of security that paper assets cannot. Real estate also offers potential tax benefits that can significantly enhance overall returns, unlike savings accounts, where interest earnings are taxed as income.

Before diving into the world of real estate, a thorough review and assessment of your finances is crucial. Start by calculating your net worth—total assets minus total liabilities. This exercise helps you understand your financial foundation and how much you can comfortably invest without jeopardizing your financial health. Next, evaluate your cash flow: how much money comes in and goes out each month? Understanding your cash flow is vital in managing the carrying costs associated with real estate, such as mortgage payments, insurance, maintenance, and property taxes. Additionally, assess your debt levels. High-interest debts, such as credit card balances, can undermine your ability to finance real estate deals, weather vacancy periods, or handle unexpected repairs.

Understanding the costs associated with real estate investment is equally critical. These costs go beyond the purchase price of the property. Initial costs can include down payments, which typically vary from 20 % to 30 % of the property's purchase price, and closing costs, which can account for an additional 2 % to 5 %. If the property requires immediate repairs or renovations, these costs must also be factored into your initial budget. Moreover, ongoing expenses such as property management fees, maintenance, property taxes, and insurance must be considered, as they can considerably impact your investment's profitability.

Deciding on a budget for your real estate investments is a fundamental step. This budget should account for the purchase price, initial repair costs, and ongoing property management and maintenance. A contingency fund is essential to cover unexpected expenses such as legal fees or emergency repairs. When budgeting, consider the potential for rental income to cover these ongoing expenses. Your investment's cash flow is vital to a sustainable real estate investment, and positive cash flow is essential to a successful investment.

Financing your real estate investment is another critical consideration. The most common method is a mortgage, which offers the leverage necessary to purchase a property with a relatively small amount of cash. However, mortgages have interest obligations and require good credit scores to secure favorable terms. Hard money loans are another option, typically used for shorter terms and by investors looking to renovate and flip properties quickly. These loans are easier to obtain but come with higher interest rates. For those with it, using private money from personal contacts can offer more flexible terms and potentially lower costs, though it can involve more complex personal agreements. (Read more in Chapter 4.1.)

Finally, the importance of a good credit score cannot be overstated in real estate investing. Your credit score affects your ability to secure financing and your loans' terms and interest rates. Improving your credit score can save you thousands of dollars in interest over the life of a loan. Strategies to improve your credit include ensuring all bills and loans are paid on time, maintaining low credit card balances, and paying down existing debt.

1.5 INVESTING IN YOUR PERSONAL AND PROFESSIONAL DEVELOPMENT

The journey through real estate investing is not just about acquiring properties and managing finances; it's equally about personal growth and professional development. Crafting an individual development plan is a strategic approach that aligns your aspirations with your real estate professional objectives. This plan should encompass various facets, including skill enhancement, effective networking, and leadership development. For instance, enhancing negotiation skills can significantly influence real estate dealings, allowing for better terms and deals. On the other hand, networking opens doors to opportunities that might otherwise remain inaccessible, and cultivating leadership qualities can propel you to make informed, confident decisions that will steer your investments toward success.

Soft skills such as negotiation, communication, and critical thinking are often underestimated in the real estate business, yet they play a crucial role in every transaction and interaction. Effective communication can resolve conflicts, maintain tenant relationships, and negotiate deals that might otherwise falter. Critical thinking lets you analyze complex situations or deals and derive logical, profitable conclusions. Resources such as online courses, workshops, and books tailored to real estate professionals can be invaluable to improve these skills.

Mentorships and coaching are transformative experiences that can accelerate your growth in the real estate sector. A mentor who has navigated the complexities of the market can provide guidance, moral support, and encouragement. They can offer insights into their successes and failures, giving you a clearer perspective on what to embrace and avoid. Whether in person or through structured programs, coaching helps set goals, develop strategies, and improve performance in specific areas of your real estate career. The benefits of these relationships are profound, often leading to quicker learning curves and increased confidence in decision-making.

Balancing the demands of a professional career in real estate with personal life is vital for long-term success and well-being. Getting caught up in pursuing profit and losing sight of life outside work is easy. However, maintaining a healthy work-life balance is essential for sustaining your passion and productivity in real estate investing. Strategies to achieve this balance include setting clear boundaries for work, prioritizing tasks to enhance efficiency, and making time for relaxation and family. Automating certain aspects of your real estate operations, such as using property management software to handle day-to-day tasks, is also beneficial. It frees up time spent with loved ones or on personal development.

Incorporating these strategies into your real estate career improves your professional capabilities. It enriches your personal life, making the journey in real estate investing a more fulfilling and balanced experience.

1.5.1 Educational Resources and Staying Informed

1.5.1.1 Educational Programs and Certifications

The journey to becoming a skillful real estate investor is paved with continuous learning and professional development. Various educational programs are tailored to cater to the diverse needs of investors, ranging from those just starting to seasoned professionals seeking to enhance their expertise. Recognized institutions, online platforms, and real estate schools offer many learning opportunities through courses, workshops, and seminars. These programs cover fundamental topics such as real estate principles and property management, as well as more advanced subjects like real estate investment analysis and legal aspects of real estate. Many of these courses lead to certifications recognized within the industry, such as the Certified Commercial Investment Member (CCIM) or the Residential Accredited Appraiser (RAA), which can significantly bolster an investor's credibility and professional standing.

Obtaining professional certifications in real estate investing is not merely about adding credentials to your name; the benefits extend far deeper. These certifications are a testament to an investor's commitment to upholding the highest standards of knowledge and professionalism. They instill confidence in clients and colleagues, showcasing an investor's dedication to their craft. Furthermore, achieving and maintaining these certifications allows investors to expand their knowledge base, keep abreast of the latest industry trends, and refine their investment strategies. The rigorous training and examinations ensure that certified investors are well-equipped to navigate the complexities of the real estate market with competence and confidence.

Continuing education is a cornerstone of maintaining these certifications and staying competitive in the ever-evolving real estate landscape. Most certifying bodies demand specific continuing education units (CEUs) for certificate renewal. This requirement motivates investors to engage in learning activities continually, be it through additional courses, seminars, or conferences. The purpose of this ongoing education is twofold: it ensures that investors remain knowledgeable about new laws, technologies, and market dynamics, and it helps them to adapt and innovate their practices effectively. In a field where market conditions and legal frameworks change frequently, being well-informed can make the difference between making a wise investment decision and facing a costly mistake.

1.5.1.2 Self-Education

For those who prefer a more self-directed approach to learning, numerous resources are available that can be tailored to individual needs and schedules. Books on real estate investment cover various topics and provide foundational and nuanced insights. Podcasts are another excellent resource, providing the convenience of accessing expert advice and industry news. Platforms like **BiggerPockets.com**[1], for instance, provide educational content through articles and podcasts and foster a community of investors who share tips, challenges, and successes. Online platforms such as **Udemy.com**,

Coursera.org, and **LinkedIn Learning** offer courses on real estate and related fields, allowing learners to progress at their own pace.

Whether opting for structured educational programs that lead to certification or choosing self-directed learning paths, the key is to select resources that best match your learning style, professional goals, and the specific areas of real estate investing that interest you most. Engaging regularly with various educational materials and community resources can dramatically enhance your understanding and performance in the real estate market, turning challenges into opportunities for growth and profit.

1.5.1.3 Staying Informed and Continuing Education

The landscape of real estate investment is constantly developing, influenced by economic shifts, legislative changes, and technological advancements. In such a dynamic environment, the value of expert analysis becomes undeniable. Analysts and industry experts provide insights crucial for understanding current market conditions and navigating investment opportunities effectively. These experts draw upon a vast array of data, experience, and analytical tools to forecast trends and offer guidance that can be pivotal in decision-making processes. For instance, analyzing demographic trends and housing supply data can help investors identify emerging markets with high growth potential before they become apparent to the general market. This kind of foresight is invaluable and can significantly enhance the strategic positioning of your investment portfolio.

However, finding reputable sources for these insights is as crucial as the insights themselves. The internet is awash with information, and distinguishing between credible sources and misleading data is vital. Start by identifying analysts and organizations with a proven track record. Reputable analysts are often associated with established financial or real estate institutions and are frequently quoted in well-known publications. Academic institutions and professional real estate organizations also provide high-quality, reliable research. Evaluating the credibility of these sources can be furthered by examining their methodologies, the transparency of their data sources, and the consistency of their analysis over time. Peer reviews and citations can also indicate reliability in academic and professional publications.

Integrating expert insights into your investment strategy requires a systematic approach. Begin by aligning the information with your investment goals and parameters. For example, if an expert analysis predicts growth in the multifamily housing market in a particular region, assess how this aligns with your investment strategy and risk tolerance. Case studies of successful real estate investments often reveal that the strategic incorporation of expert analysis can lead to informed and, consequently, more profitable investment decisions. Suppose an investor learns from reliable forecasts that a specific suburban area is expected to experience population growth due to a new transportation project. Acting on this information, the investor might purchase residential properties in that area to cater to the incoming population, thus positioning their investment optimally for capital appreciation and rental demand.

To aid in your journey of continuous education and staying informed, a vast array of resources is available. Books like "The Intelligent Investor" by Benjamin Graham and "Real Estate Market Analysis: Methods and Case Studies" by Deborah L. Brett and Adrienne Schmitz provide foundational and advanced knowledge. Websites like Investopedia.com, BiggerPockets.com, and the National Association of Realtors[2] offer up-to-date news, guides, and forums where investors can learn and share experiences. Podcasts such as "The Real Estate Guys"[3] and "Investing in Real Estate with Clayton Morris"[4] offer insights on the go, featuring interviews with industry experts and successful investors. Forums and online communities provide real-time interaction with other investors and experts, which can be invaluable for sharing strategies and staying abreast of the latest trends and legislative changes affecting real estate.

By cultivating a habit of continuous learning and integrating expert insights into your investment strategy, you equip yourself with the tools necessary to make informed decisions and adapt to the ever-changing real estate investment landscape. The pursuit of knowledge is continuous, and in the realm of real estate investing, it is a critical component of sustained success and growth.

1.5.1.4 Essential Real Estate Terminology Every Beginner Should Know

As a beginner in navigating the world of real estate investing, you need to master a new language—the language of real estate itself. Understanding the terminology is the bedrock upon which your investing acumen is built, enabling you to communicate effectively with brokers, agents, and financial advisors and to make informed decisions. Let's start by demystifying fundamental financing terms crucial for every investor.

Amortization is a term that refers to the process of spreading out a loan into a series of fixed payments over time. Each payment includes both principal and interest, initially weighted more towards interest. As time progresses, the portion of each payment that goes toward the principal gradually increases. For example, suppose you secure a 30-year mortgage for a property. The amortization schedule is set to keep the monthly payments consistent throughout the term. Still, the composition of the payments shifts over time from primarily interest to primarily principal. This process makes long-term budgeting easier and builds your equity in the property more significantly with each passing year.

Cash flow, the lifeblood of any rental property investment, measures the net amount of money transferred into and out of a property. It's a vital measure of a property's financial health and is particularly important for rental properties. Positive cash flow is critical for maintaining liquidity and funding operations. Positive cash flow, where the income from the property exceeds all expenses, means that the property is generating a profit. For instance, if your rental income is $2,000 monthly and your total costs (mortgage, taxes, and maintenance) are $1,500, your cash flow is $500 monthly. Negative cash flow, on the other hand, would mean the property costs more to maintain than it earns, signaling potential problems or a need for reevaluation.

The **capitalization rate**, or **cap rate**, is a measure used to assess a property investment's profitability and return potential. It is calculated by dividing the Net Operating Income (NOI) by the purchase price or the current market value. High cap rates indicate potentially higher returns but also higher risk. (See their formulas in Chapter 3.4.3.)

An essential investment term is **ROI**, or **Return on Investment**, which is a straightforward yet powerful method used to analyze the efficiency of an investment or compare the efficiency gains of several different investments. ROI is calculated by dividing the net profit of the investment by the cost of the investment. For example, if you purchase a property for $200,000 and sell it later for $300,000, your net profit is $100,000. Assuming there were no additional costs, the ROI would be $100,000 divided by $200,000, resulting in a 50 % return on your investment. ROI is a critical measurement that helps investors gauge the profitability of their investments. (Read more in Chapter 3.4.6.)

Capital gains are the profits investors realize when they sell an investment property for more than the price they paid. For example, if you buy a property for $250,000 and sell it later for $350,000, your capital gain is $100,000. Understanding capital gains is essential for tax purposes, as these gains can be subject to capital gains tax, depending on the duration of property ownership and other factors. (Read more in Chapter 4.4.4.4.)

Equity represents the value of ownership built up in a property. It is one of the most critical concepts in real estate investing. It is calculated by deducting the outstanding loan balance from the property's current market value. For instance, if your property is valued at $250,000 and you owe $200,000 on the mortgage, your equity in the property is $50,000. This equity can increase in two ways: as you pay the mortgage or the property value appreciates. Understanding equity is vital as it can be leveraged to obtain additional financing or invest in more properties. (Read more in Chapters 2.6.2 and 4.1.1.4.)

In real estate, **leverage** refers to using borrowed capital to increase the potential return on an investment. For example, using a mortgage to finance a property purchase lets you control a more significant asset and potentially reap greater gains on your investment equity.

Refinancing is another critical term that involves replacing an existing mortgage with a new one, usually to reduce monthly payments, secure a lower interest rate, or tap into the property's equity. For instance, if interest rates have dropped since you took out your original mortgage or your credit situation has improved, refinancing could reduce your interest rate and, by extension, your monthly payments. Alternatively, suppose your property has appreciated in value. In that case, you might refinance to access the equity in a cash-out refinance, providing you with capital to invest in other properties or renovations. (Read more in Chapter 2.6.1 and 4.1.8.)

In accounting terms crucial for real estate, understanding how to produce a profit and loss account and a balance sheet is indispensable. These financial statements reflect the reality of your investment's performance. A profit and loss account, or income statement, summarizes your revenues and expenses over a specific period, showing how much profit or loss was made. On the other hand, the balance sheet is a snapshot of your financial position at a particular point in time, detailing your assets, liabilities, and equity. These documents are fundamental for assessing the health of your investment, securing loans, and attracting partners or investors.

Understanding property-specific terms such as lien, easement, and encumbrance is also crucial. A lien is a legal right or interest that a creditor has in the property, usually used as collateral for a debt, and must be paid off when the property is sold. An easement is a non-possessory right to use and/or enter another's real property without possessing it, which can affect property value and usage. Encumbrance refers to any claim or liability attached to a property, such as liens or easements, that may affect the property's transferability and free use until dismissed.

Legal and tax terms are equally essential for navigating real estate investment successfully. Understanding a deed, a legal document that grants ownership of a property, and a title, a legal way to say you own a right to something, is fundamental. For tax purposes, knowing the implications of property taxes, which are annual taxes paid to local governments based on the assessed value of the property, is crucial. Misunderstandings in these areas can lead to essential legal issues or financial losses.

Exploring different types of real estate investments is also beneficial. Residential properties, intended for living purposes; commercial properties, used for business activities; REITs, which are companies that own, operate, or finance income-producing real estate; and crowdfunding, which allows investors to pool money to invest in real estate projects, each offer diverse opportunities and risk profiles. Understanding the nuances of each can help you diversify your investment portfolio effectively. (Read more in Chapter 2.)

Finally, grasping the basics of property valuation is critical. Methods like the comparative market analysis (CMA), which compares a property to similar properties recently sold in the same area, and the income approach, which is based on the income the property is expected to generate, are essential for determining a property's market value. These valuation methods are crucial during the purchase process and vital for assessing the property's potential for appreciation. (Read more about valuation in Chapter 3.4.)

The importance of location must be balanced when it comes to real estate investing. The adage "location, location, location" is accurate as the geographical setting influences property values, investment potential, and rental income possibilities. Factors such as proximity to amenities, economic stability, crime rates, and future development plans in an area can significantly impact the desirability and profitability of a property. For instance, a property located near a new public transport system or in a region with growing employment opportunities is likely to experience an increase in value. (Read more in Chapter 3.1.3.)

Equipped with this essential real estate vocabulary, you are better prepared to continue reading this book and engage in the market intelligently. The terms you will find later are not just words but valuable knowledge to help you make informed decisions that align with your investment goals. They will help you communicate better with industry professionals and empower you to analyze investment opportunities and manage your portfolio effectively.

1.6 HARNESSING TECHNOLOGY IN REAL ESTATE INVESTING

Imagine stepping into a world where the complexities of real estate investing are simplified by cutting-edge technology. You can analyze properties, manage your investments from the comfort of your home, and even close deals. It isn't just a glimpse into the future; it's the reality of today's real estate landscape, significantly influenced by technological advancements. In this chapter, we will introduce and explore how different software solutions and apps are revolutionizing real estate investing, making it more accessible, efficient, and profitable, especially for beginners like you. (You will find more about software solutions throughout the book and in Chapter 6.5.)

1.6.1 Introduction to Available Apps and Software Solutions

The digital age has ushered in a plethora of software solutions designed to streamline every aspect of real estate investing. Whether you're scouting for new properties, analyzing potential investments, managing existing portfolios, or nurturing client relationships, there's a technological tool designed to assist.

In Chapter 3.3, Techniques for Finding Undervalued Properties, there are web pages such as property search platforms like Zillow.com and Realtor.com that provide extensive listings and valuable market data at your fingertips. Some of the platforms mentioned there also have more functions. For example, investment analysis tools like BiggerPockets.com's calculators help evaluate the profitability of potential investments by analyzing cash flow, return on investment, and other critical metrics.

For those managing multiple properties, property management software like AppFolio.com and Buildium.com offers comprehensive solutions that cover everything from tenant background checks to rent collection and maintenance scheduling. These tools save time and enhance the accuracy and efficiency of managing real estate assets. (Read more about them and what to think about when evaluating apps in Chapter 6.5.2.)

1.6.2 Utilizing Big Data for Market Analysis

In real estate investing, 'Big Data' has become a transformative force, revolutionizing market analysis by providing valuable insights into trends, consumer behaviors, and investment opportunities. Big Data enables a granular market understanding, leading to informed and predictive decision-making.

Utilizing this data involves various platforms that aggregate and analyze information. Sources of Big Data in real estate include public records, real estate websites, social media analytics, and government databases. Public records offer property ownership and sales information, while websites like Zillow.com aggregate sales data and market trends. Analyzing Big Data ranges from basic spreadsheets to sophisticated software. Advanced tools like Tableau.com and Microsoft Power BI[5] integrate data from multiple sources, creating visualizations highlighting patterns and correlations. These tools transform vast data into actionable intelligence. (Read more about available software in Chapter 3.2.1.)

Social media tools like Hootsuite.com reveal consumer sentiments, and government databases provide essential demographic and economic data. Social media trends can be analyzed using tools like BuzzSumo.com. (Read more about this in Chapter 3.2.2.)

For instance, if Big Data shows young families moving to a suburb, it indicates a growing demand for family-friendly properties. Investing in such areas could be lucrative. Similarly, analyzing past market cycles and economic indicators can help predict future trends, allowing strategic investment positioning.

Several case studies highlight the potential for substantial returns with Big Data analytics. For instance, investors who used Big Data to monitor urban development could purchase properties before prices rose, resulting in significant returns.

Harnessing big Data in real estate investing gives you a strategic advantage. It enables you to make informed decisions and minimize risks, making you a competitive player. Integrating Big Data analytics into your strategy enhances your ability to identify and capitalize on trends, giving you a significant edge in the competitive field of real estate investing. Big Data is the key to unlocking this potential and staying ahead of the curve.

1.7 DEVELOPING YOUR REAL ESTATE NETWORK

Entering the field of real estate investing can sometimes feel like navigating a labyrinthine marketplace where, at every turn, new challenges and opportunities are introduced. Amidst this complexity, the value of a robust support network cannot be overstated.

1.7.1 The Importance of a Reliable Network

Networking isn't merely about collecting contacts; it's a strategic tool for building relationships that provide support, advice, partnerships, and direct investment opportunities. The trust and mutual benefits fostered through these relationships are the foundation for successful careers.

As you navigate your real estate investment career, cultivating a diverse network of professionals is vital. This network should ideally include real estate agents who can provide valuable market insights and access to potential deals and brokers who are instrumental in facilitating transactions. Certified Property Appraisers also play a critical role by accurately valuing properties and ensuring you make informed investment decisions. Lenders are essential for securing the financing needed to grow your portfolio, while architects can help envision and execute renovations that enhance property values.

Moreover, engaging with partners can help spread risks and pool resources for more significant projects beyond your capacity. Property managers relieve the burden of day-to-day operations, freeing you to focus on broader investment strategies. Lawyers are indispensable for navigating the legal complexities of real estate transactions and ensuring compliance. Bookkeepers and accountants help manage your finances, providing the clarity needed for strategic decision-making. Fellow investors offer a reservoir of shared experiences and opportunities for co-investment, while insurance agents ensure that your investments are protected against unforeseen circumstances. Developers open doors to new projects with the potential for high returns, and handypersons and contractors execute the improvements necessary to increase a property's value and appeal.

Initiating and nurturing relationships with these professionals requires a proactive approach. Attending industry conferences and real estate seminars provides the latest insights and forecasts while offering a platform to connect with experts and peers. Local community and investor meetings are invaluable for building local networks.

When interacting with industry professionals, it is essential to present yourself effectively. Prepare a brief elevator pitch that outlines who you are, what you do, and what you are looking for. Ask insightful questions that demonstrate your interest and deepen your understanding of their expertise and how it could benefit your investment goals.

Following up is the most crucial part of networking. After meeting someone, send a brief, personalized message referencing something specific about your interaction. It keeps the communication line open for future collaborations and information exchange. Regularly engaging with your contacts through updates or queries helps maintain and strengthen these relationships, ensuring that you remain at the forefront of their minds when opportunities arise.

The digital age has expanded the realm of networking beyond physical interactions. Webinars and virtual conferences have become prevalent, offering convenience and a broader reach. Participate actively in these online events, as they are educational resources and networking goldmines. Engaging in real estate forums and online platforms can also connect you with global professionals and investors, which can be particularly useful if you are considering cross-border investments.

Remember, the essence of networking in real estate investing lies in the mutual benefits it offers. By providing value to others, whether through sharing your insights, offering opportunities, or connecting people, you cultivate a network that supports your goals and contributes to the success of others in the community. This reciprocal nature of networking makes it a powerful tool for building a successful and sustainable career in real estate investing.

1.7.1.1 Using Social Media to Enhance Your Real Estate Network

In today's digital era, social media is not just a tool for socializing but an invaluable asset for networking and business growth, especially in real estate. Platforms like Bigger Pockets, LinkedIn, Facebook, Twitter, and Instagram have transformed how investors connect, learn, and conduct business. Each platform has unique attributes that benefit specific aspects of real estate networking. BiggerPockets.com, for example, is tailored specifically for real estate investors and industry professionals, offering a concentrated pool of industry knowledge and networking opportunities. LinkedIn provides a professional setting ideal for connecting with real estate agents, brokers, accountants, and other professionals. At the same time, Facebook groups can be a goldmine for local market information and community-based networking. Twitter offers a platform for real-time interaction and updates on market trends. Instagram can be a powerful tool for showcasing properties and branding your real estate ventures.

Creating content that captivates and engages your audience effectively is crucial in leveraging social media. Start by identifying topics that resonate with your target audience, such as market trends, investment tips, or transformation stories of properties. The frequency of your posts is also essential; consistent activity keeps your audience engaged and helps establish your presence as an active and reliable source of real estate knowledge. Moreover, incorporating multimedia such as videos, virtual tours of properties, and infographics can significantly increase the engagement and reach of your posts. For instance, a well-crafted video tour of a property listing can give potential investors a better sense of the space, boosting interest and interaction.

Building a solid online presence is essential for enhancing credibility and attracting valuable connections. Start by ensuring your social media profile is professional and reflects your real estate expertise. Regularly update your profile with exciting and relevant information and content highlighting your knowledge and industry successes. Engaging actively with your audience is also crucial; respond promptly to comments, participate in discussions, and share relevant content from other users. It boosts your visibility and helps build relationships with your followers, establishing a community of interested prospects and peers.

Social media also serves as a good tool for market research. By following real estate hashtags, joining real estate groups, and monitoring posts from industry leaders, you can gain insights into market trends, consumer behavior, and competitive strategies. This information can be instrumental in making informed investment decisions and staying ahead of market shifts. For example, noticing a trend in posts about a burgeoning neighborhood could prompt further research into the area, potentially uncovering a lucrative investment opportunity before it becomes common knowledge.

Lastly, measuring the impact of your social media activities is vital for understanding their effectiveness and optimizing your strategies. Utilize built-in analytics tools to track your posts' engagement rates, follower growth, and website traffic. With these insights, you can refine your content and engagement strategies, ensuring that your social media efforts contribute positively to your real estate business objectives. By analyzing which types of posts create the most interaction or what times of day yield the highest engagement, you can tailor your social media activities to maximize their impact, driving more meaningful connections and opportunities in your real estate endeavors.

1.7.1.2 Collaborating with Real Estate Agents and Brokers

Establishing strong collaborations with skilled real estate agents and brokers can significantly enhance your strategic capabilities in the complex landscape of real estate investing. These professionals are your navigators and allies in the vast real estate market, equipped with in-depth knowledge and expertise crucial for identifying and securing lucrative investment opportunities. Choosing the right agent or broker involves careful consideration of several vital factors. Selecting individuals with a profound understanding of investment properties and a thorough knowledge of the local market is paramount. This expertise ensures they can provide valuable insights on market trends, property valuations, and investment potential that align with your specific investment goals.

Furthermore, the breadth of their networking reach can open doors to exclusive listings and potentially secret opportunities. Their established relationships with other real estate professionals, local authorities, and community members can facilitate smoother transactions and give you a competitive edge in negotiations. Building relationships with these agents and brokers should focus on long-term engagement rather than transactional interactions. Effective communication is the cornerstone of this relationship. You should clearly articulate your investment objectives, expectations, and preferences immediately. This clarity helps agents and brokers provide tailored services and advice, making your collaborations more effective.

Providing mutual value is also vital; respect their professional expertise, provide timely feedback, and ensure that the relationship benefits both parties. This mutual respect fosters a positive working relationship. It encourages your agents and brokers to go the extra mile in assisting you with your investment endeavors.

These professionals are skilled in crafting deals that maximize your financial outcomes while mitigating risks. Whether negotiating purchase prices, contract terms, or closing costs, their expertise can be invaluable in ensuring that you achieve favorable outcomes in your real estate transactions. Additionally, some real estate agents offer property management services, which can be particularly beneficial for investors who prefer to avoid managing the day-to-day operations of their properties. These agents can handle responsibilities such as finding and vetting tenants, managing leases, and maintaining the property. Utilizing their services can give you more freedom to focus on broader investment strategies and portfolio growth, especially if you own multiple properties or invest in markets outside your local area.

In conclusion, the role of real estate agents and brokers extends beyond mere facilitators of property transactions. They are essential partners in your investment journey, offering expertise, market insights, negotiation skills, and sometimes even property management services. By carefully selecting the right professionals and fostering strong, mutually beneficial relationships with them, you can significantly enhance your effectiveness and success as a real estate investor. This collaboration simplifies your investment process and enriches your understanding and capabilities within the market.

1.7.2 Evaluating the Right Group for Your Needs

Choosing the right investment group is crucial and should align with your investment goals and strategies. When assessing potential groups, consider their focus—some might specialize in commercial real estate, while others may focus on residential properties. The members' experience level is also essential; groups with a mix of experienced and novice investors can offer a dynamic learning environment where knowledge is actively shared.

Another consideration is the group's activity level. Some groups meet weekly, offering regular opportunities for learning and networking, while others meet less frequently. Additionally, the group's geographical focus should align with your areas of interest. Suppose you are interested in investing in your local community. In that case, a local investor club might benefit more than a national group focusing on a broader market.

With their collaborative frameworks, investment groups offer a unique blend of educational and investment opportunities. By choosing the right group and engaging actively, you can improve your real estate knowledge, expand your investment opportunities, and build a network of supportive, like-minded individuals. Being part of a group where others understand your challenges and can provide advice and encouragement is immensely beneficial. This community aspect of real estate investment makes the journey less daunting and more rewarding, providing professional growth and personal connections.

1.7.2.1 Introduction to Real Estate Investment Groups

Real estate investment groups represent a vital resource in this landscape, offering a platform for collaboration, sharing knowledge, and pooling resources. These groups, from local investor clubs to more structured entities like Real Estate Investment Trusts (REITs), provide a community where novice and experienced investors can find support, opportunities, and valuable insights.

A Real Estate Investment Group (REIG) is a consortium of investors who pool their resources to invest in properties much more effectively than they could individually. These groups can vary significantly in structure and focus. Some are informal networks, offering a forum for sharing information and resources without financial commitments. Others, such as Real Estate Investment Trusts (REITs), are formal entities that own, operate, or finance income-producing real estate, offering investors a chance to own valuable real estate that they might not be able to purchase individually. (Read more about REITs in Chapter 4.1.9.)

Local investor clubs fall somewhere in between, often organized by like-minded individuals who meet regularly to discuss market trends, share leads on properties, and sometimes pool funds for joint investment ventures.

The benefits of joining such groups are manifold. Firstly, they provide a platform for shared knowledge and experiences. More seasoned investors offer insights and guidance, which can be invaluable for someone just starting their real estate journey. This knowledge-sharing can accelerate your learning curve dramatically, helping you avoid common pitfalls and better understand the nuances of market dynamics.

Moreover, investment groups often provide access to investment opportunities that individual investors might need help finding on their own. Together, groups can access more extensive, more lucrative properties and undertake more significant projects with better returns. A group's collective bargaining power often means better purchase terms and more market influence.

1.7.2.2 Best Practices for Active Participation

Active participation in your chosen group can significantly enhance your experience and the benefits you derive from it. Contributing to discussions, sharing resources, and volunteering for leadership roles or group projects raise your profile within the group. It deepens your understanding of real estate investing. Engaging in these groups facilitates stronger connections and can lead to opportunities and partnerships that might not have arisen otherwise.

1.7.2.3 Creating Your Own Real Estate Investment Group

If existing groups do not meet your needs or if you see a unique niche or opportunity, starting your own real estate investment group is a viable option. Begin by defining the group's objectives clearly—are you focusing on a particular property type, geographical area, or investment strategy? Once the objectives are set, recruit members who share your vision. Look for individuals who bring various skills and perspectives to the table. Setting up initial meetings, whether virtual or in-person, can help solidify the group's goals and strategies. Managing group activities effectively requires clear communication, defined roles, and, ideally, some form of governance structure to ensure that all members are aligned and accountable.

As we conclude this chapter on developing your real estate network, remember that the strength of your network can be a significant determinant of your success in real estate investing. From investment groups to social media strategies and professional collaborations, each component of your network offers unique benefits and opportunities. By actively engaging and investing in these relationships, you equip yourself with the tools and support necessary to navigate the complexities of real estate investing and achieve your financial goals.

The next chapter delves into advanced strategies for real estate investment, focusing on identifying the niche and strategy that align with your goals and risk tolerance to help you maximize returns and minimize risks.

* * *

The chapter's footnotes

1 To make it easy for you, as a reader, to find good websites and information, you will find "simple URLs" like this directly in the text. Just enter the specified address, such as "Biggerpockets.com." in your browser. If you want to select the full address, you usually add "https://www." or sometimes just "https://". You will find the URLs that are not "obvious" as footnotes.

2 https://www.nar.realtor/

3 https://realestateguysradio.com/

4 https://morrisinvest.com/podcasts/

5 https://www.microsoft.com/en-us/power-platform/products/power-bi

INVESTMENT STRATEGIES

"To know the road ahead, ask those coming back."
-CHINESE PROVERB

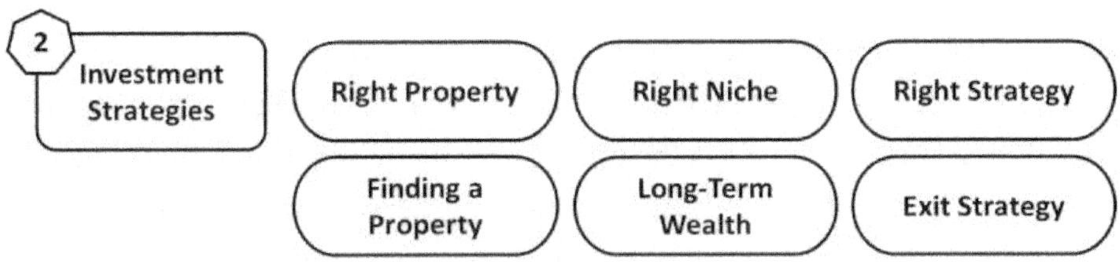

Imagine stepping into a meticulously organized art gallery, where every piece of art is carefully selected to create a harmonious ensemble that resonates with the collector's deepest aspirations. Similarly, crafting your real estate investment portfolio requires a strategic blend of discernment, foresight, and alignment with your long-term financial goals. This chapter is designed to be your curator's guide, helping you select the suitable properties that complement your investment objectives and enhance your portfolio's overall performance.

2.1 CHOOSING THE RIGHT PROPERTY FOR YOUR INVESTMENT GOALS

2.1.1 Define Investment Objectives

Before looking at properties, clarifying what you hope to achieve through your real estate investments is crucial. Are you looking for a steady rental income to provide financial stability? You may enjoy the thrill of flipping properties for a quick profit. Or are you focused on the long-term appreciation of real estate assets that can contribute to a robust retirement plan? Understanding your investment objectives is like setting the destination in your navigation app; it guides every decision.

For example, suppose you aim to generate passive income. In that case, you'll likely focus on properties in stable or emerging neighborhoods that attract long-term tenants. On the other hand, if you're interested in property flipping, your attention might shift towards undervalued properties in areas poised for rapid growth. Each objective shapes your strategies and actions in the market, from property selection to financing and management.

2.1.2 Considerations for First-Time Buyers

For first-time real estate investors, the array of options available can be as daunting as it is exciting. Starting with properties that require less management and potentially offer a higher appreciation might be a prudent strategy. Single-family homes, for example, can be an excellent entry point. They generally require less upkeep than multi-family units or commercial properties. They can be easier to sell when you're ready to realize your investment gains.

Additionally, consider properties that present less complexity in terms of repairs and renovations. A property that needs minor cosmetic updates could offer a quick win and boost your confidence without the daunting challenges of a major fixer-upper. However, it's essential to conduct a thorough inspection and possibly consult with a construction expert to ensure that no hidden issues could turn your investment into a money pit.

For those new to the field, leveraging professional help can make a significant difference. Engaging with a reputable real estate agent who understands your investment goals and knows the local market well can provide invaluable insights and guidance. They can help you navigate the complexities of property selection, negotiations, and transactions, ensuring that your first investment is sound and promising.

Choosing the right property as a beginner is not just about buying real estate; it's about setting a cornerstone for future growth. By starting with manageable, less complex properties and gradually moving to more ambitious projects, you can build a solid foundation of experience and confidence. This approach mitigates risks and enhances your learning curve, preparing you for more complex investments in the future.

As you contemplate your first foray into real estate investing, remember that each property you consider should align with your broader financial strategies and goals. Whether a quaint duplex in a family-friendly neighborhood or a chic condo in a bustling urban center, the right property will resonate with your objectives, offering a balance of risk and reward that suits your financial landscape. By being organized and strategic in your choices, you can ensure that each investment moves you closer to your financial aspirations, much like carefully chosen pieces of art that transform a space profoundly.

2.2 CHOOSING THE RIGHT NICHE FOR YOU

When you embark on the path of real estate investing, one of the first decisions you'll face is selecting the correct type of property to meet your investment goals. This choice is akin to choosing the right tool for a job; every kind of property, from residential to commercial or industrial, serves different purposes and offers varying levels of risk and return. Understanding the distinct characteristics of each can significantly influence your investment success.

Residential properties, for instance, are often the most accessible for new investors. They can range from single-family homes, which are relatively straightforward to manage, to multifamily units like duplexes or apartment complexes, which can generate more significant income but require more hands-on management. The appeal of residential properties lies in their consistent demand—people always need a place to live. However, they can also be affected by economic downturns, where job losses can affect tenants' ability to pay rent.

Commercial properties, such as shopping centers, retail locations, or office spaces, offer another dimension of real estate investing. These properties often come with longer lease terms, which can provide stable, long-term income. However, they require a deeper understanding of business trends, as the success of your investment is closely tied to the economic health of your tenants. For example, investing in retail spaces can be highly lucrative if located in a bustling area with high consumer traffic. However, shifts in consumer behavior, like the increase in online shopping, could impact profitability.

Industrial real estate is a unique niche that includes warehouses, factories, and distribution centers. This sector can be desirable because of the lower competition and long-term leases that businesses often require. The returns can be substantial, mainly if the property is in a strategic location that benefits logistics and manufacturing companies. However, the initial investment and ongoing management costs can be higher, and the success of your investment can be heavily dependent on the industrial and economic policies in place.

Apart from these traditional categories, several other niches within the real estate market might align with your investment goals. Investing in land, for example, offers opportunities either through the development of raw land or by holding undeveloped land in the path of growth and selling it at a profit. Each approach requires a keen understanding of market trends and zoning laws but can result in significant returns if managed correctly.

Exploring alternative real estate investment vehicles can also broaden your portfolio. Real Estate Investment Trusts (REITs) allow you to invest without owning physical properties, offering a way to diversify your investments with less capital and lower risk. Similarly, investing in private notes or mortgage loans can provide regular income with security backed by real estate. For those interested in less traditional routes, tax lien certificates offer a way to earn returns by paying property tax debts, with the potential to acquire property at a fraction of its value if liens are not redeemed.

Crowdfunding platforms have also become popular ways to invest in real estate. These platforms allow investors to pool money together to invest in larger projects, from commercial developments to residential renovations that would be unattainable individually. Each crowdfunding opportunity varies in structure, risk, and potential return, and choosing the right platform and project is crucial for success.

Each real estate niche offers distinct challenges and advantages, and your choice should align with your risk tolerance, financial goals, and the level of involvement you desire in managing your investments. By carefully considering each option and how it fits into your overall investment strategy, you can select the right niche that meets your financial objectives and matches your passion for real estate investing. As you continue to explore these options, remember that diversification within your real estate portfolio can help manage risk and maximize returns, providing you with a robust strategy for building wealth through real estate.

2.2.1 Investing in Residential vs. Commercial Real Estate

When you begin to explore real estate investment avenues, you'll quickly find that your path branches into two broad categories: residential and commercial properties. Each category offers opportunities and challenges tailored to different investment styles and objectives. Understanding these nuances is crucial as you develop a strategy that aligns with your financial goals and risk tolerance.

2.2.1.1 Decision Factors for Investment Choice

Your risk tolerance, financial goals, and market conditions should guide you in choosing an investment strategy between residential and commercial real estate. Residential properties might be more suitable if you desire a more hands-on approach and enjoy interacting with tenants. On the other hand, if you are prepared for a higher initial investment and are looking for longer-term, more stable returns, commercial real estate might be the right choice.

To aid in this decision, consider developing a decision-making framework that evaluates various factors, such as the amount of capital you want to invest, the preferred level of involvement in property management, and your long-term financial objectives. Analyzing market conditions is also crucial; for instance, a thriving urban area with growing employment opportunities might offer lucrative residential and commercial real estate opportunities. Still, the final decision would depend on how these opportunities align with your investment strategy.

In making this decision, it's also wise to consult with financial advisors and real estate professionals who can provide insights based on current market trends and future projections. Their expertise can help you assess each investment type's potential risks and rewards, ensuring that your decision is well-informed and aligned with your financial plan.

As you navigate the complexities of choosing between residential and commercial real estate investments, remember that each type offers unique opportunities and challenges. By carefully considering your financial goals, consulting with experts, and staying informed about market conditions, you can make a strategic choice that aligns with your investment objectives and positions you for long-term success in the real estate market.

2.2.1.2 Residential Real Estate Nuances

Residential real estate is often the first stop for new investors due to its more straightforward entry barriers than commercial real estate. Properties within this category range from single-family homes to multi-unit residential buildings. One of the most significant advantages of residential real estate is its more straightforward management dynamics. Unlike commercial properties, which can involve complex lease agreements and operational logistics, residential leasing is generally more straightforward. However, you must go beyond merely owning properties to excel in residential real estate investing.

Strategies for maximizing returns in residential real estate include engaging in short-term rental arrangements, such as vacation rentals, which can offer significantly higher yields than long-term leases. Platforms like Airbnb have made this more accessible than ever. However, it's essential to be aware of local regulations regarding short-term rentals. Another effective strategy is the lease-to-own arrangement, which can be particularly appealing in markets where potential buyers may need help to secure traditional financing. This approach opens up a new tenant base and provides the potential for a sale at the end of the lease term, often at a premium price.

2.2.1.3 Comparative Analysis of Residential Real Estate and Commercial

Diving deeper into the distinctions, commercial real estate encompasses properties used for business purposes, including retail spaces, offices, warehouses, and more. The dynamics of leasing commercial real estate differ markedly from residential properties. Commercial leases are typically longer, sometimes extending up to 10 or 20 years, providing a longer duration of steady cash flow but also necessitating a higher level of commitment from both parties. Furthermore, tenant relationships in commercial real estate are often more complex, involving detailed negotiations over lease terms, property improvements, and maintenance responsibilities.

The investment horizon also contrasts significantly between the two categories. Residential real estate can be fluid, with buyers and sellers quickly buying and selling properties. Commercial real estate investments are usually longer-term endeavors, requiring a deeper market analysis and a more substantial initial capital outlay but potentially offering higher returns due to the scale and lease structures.

2.2.1.4 Benefits and Challenges of Commercial Real Estate

Commercial real estate is enticing for many investors due to its potential for higher yields and longer lease terms, which provide a regular, predictable income stream. Commercial tenants often pay for many property expenses, including maintenance and property taxes (commonly known as a triple net lease), which can significantly reduce the owner's cost burden.

However, managing commercial properties can be a formidable challenge, requiring a deep understanding of market trends, tenant needs, and regulatory requirements. For example, owning a retail space requires insights into consumer behavior, retail trends, and economic cycles. Similarly, industrial properties necessitate knowledge of logistics, manufacturing trends, and environmental regulations. These factors make commercial real estate management a specialized field, often requiring professional property managers with specific expertise.

2.2.2 Multi-Family Properties vs. Single-Family Rentals

Navigating the landscape of real estate investment requires a nuanced understanding of the various property types available to you. At the heart of this exploration lies the distinction between multi-family properties and single-family rentals, each offering unique benefits and challenges. Multi-family properties, such as duplexes, triplexes, and larger apartment complexes, embody scalability in real estate investment. They allow you to rapidly expand your portfolio within a single location, offering multiple rental incomes from one building and significantly enhancing your cash flow potential. It is in contrast to single-family rentals, where expansion typically means acquiring multiple separate properties, spreading your investments—and often your attention—across various locations.

The scalability of multi-family units also introduces a level of efficiency in property management. For instance, renovating a multi-family property or addressing maintenance issues can be more streamlined and cost-effective than managing several single-family homes. These economies of scale can reduce per-unit expenses and increase your investments' overall profitability. However, this doesn't mean that multi-family investments are without their challenges. The complexity of managing multi-family units is considerably higher. You're not only dealing with more tenants, each with their individual needs and issues, but also more complex building systems, more significant regulatory compliance requirements, and potentially more frequent tenant turnover, particularly in high-demand urban areas.

Moreover, the financial barriers to entering the multi-family investment space can be substantial. These properties typically come with a higher upfront cost than single-family homes, reflecting their potential for higher income generation. Securing financing for multi-family properties might also be more challenging unless you have a proven track record in managing similar investments or a significantly robust financial standing. This is where a solid understanding of economic analysis becomes indispensable. For multi-family properties, you must be adept at calculating and interpreting financial metrics such as the capitalization rate to assess the return on investment. It is based on the income the property is expected to generate. Other crucial metrics include the gross rent multiplier, which provides a rough measure of the value of an investment property by comparing its price with its gross rental income and vacancy rates, which can drastically affect your cash flow projections.

Managing a multi-family property demands a proactive approach to tenant relationships and building maintenance. High tenant turnover can quickly erode your profitability, making tenant satisfaction an essential focus. Regular maintenance checks, timely repairs and upgrades, and, many times, most crucially, open lines of communication with tenants are all critical practices that help reduce turnover and maintain steady rental income. While demanding, these tasks are crucial for preserving your property's value, ensuring your tenants' satisfaction, and stabilizing your income flow.

When considering your real estate portfolio's diversification, incorporating multi-family and single-family properties can offer a balanced approach to risk and revenue generation. Single-family rentals attract long-term tenants looking for stability, often leading to lower turnover and maintenance costs. On the other hand, multi-family properties can provide a higher income stream and opportunities for value addition through property improvements and management efficiencies. Adequate portfolio diversification involves understanding the market dynamics specific to each property type and strategically allocating your investments to maximize returns while mitigating risks.

Let's consider a case study highlighting the successful investment in multi-family properties. Imagine a real estate investor who purchased a rundown apartment complex in a well-located urban area. Recognizing the potential, the investor implemented a series of renovations that significantly improved the quality of the units and the building's overall appeal. By introducing professional management practices, the investor enhanced tenant satisfaction, reduced turnover, and attracted higher-paying tenants. This strategic approach increased the property's value. It maximized the cash flow, demonstrating the substantial benefits that can be achieved through well-executed multi-family property investments.

Navigating the complexities of multi-family real estate investments requires a great understanding of market trends, tenant management, and financial analysis. By mastering these elements, you can enhance your investment strategy, ensure the growth of your real estate portfolio, and achieve your broader economic goals. Whether drawn to single-family homes' charm or multi-family properties' dynamic potential, your success hinges on a deep understanding of each investment's unique attributes and how they align with your investment objectives.

2.2.3 Commercial Real Estate Basics for Beginners

Understanding the spectrum of commercial real estate (CRE) types is indispensable when you contemplate diversifying your investment portfolio within the real estate sector. Commercial properties come in various forms, each serving different purposes and offering unique investment potentials. Office spaces, for instance, range from bustling downtown high-rises to suburban office parks catering to businesses requiring professional environments. Retail locations, including small shops and large shopping centers, are venues where commerce thrives, directly affected by consumer behavior and economic conditions.

Warehouses and industrial sites are critical for companies needing storage, distribution, or manufacturing space. These properties are often located in less central areas where larger plots of land are available and more affordable. Special-purpose facilities, such as hotels, hospitals, and educational buildings, serve specific needs and can be very lucrative. However, they often require specialized management knowledge. Each type of commercial property brings its own benefits and challenges, influenced by location, market demand, and economic trends, making them fascinating yet complex real estate investment strategy components.

For beginners eager to enter the commercial real estate market, the journey begins with thorough market research to understand which type of commercial property aligns with your investment goals. Are you drawn to the steady income potential of office rentals or perhaps the dynamic retail market where consumer trends offer opportunities for high returns? Each choice requires different considerations regarding market demand, location advantages, and tenant agreements. Building a network of experienced professionals, like real estate agents specializing in commercial properties, lawyers familiar with commercial real estate laws, and financial advisors who understand commercial investment strategies, is crucial. These experts provide the guidance and insights necessary to successfully navigate your initial commercial real estate ventures.

Understanding commercial leases is fundamental as they differ significantly from residential leases. Commercial leases are typically longer, sometimes spanning several years, and include terms like triple net leases, where the tenant handles most property expenses. These leases can also include escalations, which are agreed-upon rent increases over the term, and provisions for leasehold improvements, which are modifications made to the property to suit a tenant's needs. Grasping the complexities of these leases is crucial as they directly impact the profitability and management of your commercial property investments.

Investing in commercial real estate also involves recognizing and managing risks unique to this sector. More extended vacancy periods can be a significant risk factor, as finding new tenants for commercial properties often takes longer than for residential properties. The success of your tenants' businesses, particularly in retail and special-purpose facilities, can strongly influence your investment's performance. Economic cycles play a critical role in the commercial real estate market; downturns can lead to reduced business activity, affecting your tenants' ability to meet rental obligations.

Therefore, analyzing market trends is vital. Economic indicators like employment rates, business growth, and retail sales data can signal the health of the market segments relevant to your properties. Understanding these trends helps you anticipate market changes that could impact your investments, allowing you to adapt strategies, perhaps shifting focus between different types of commercial properties or renegotiating lease terms to better align with evolving economic conditions.

The potential benefits of commercial real estate are compelling, offering opportunities for significant returns on investment through capital appreciation and rental income. However, these investments require careful management and a deep understanding of market dynamics to mitigate risks. For those new to commercial real estate, the journey is both challenging and rewarding, filled with learning opportunities that can pave the way to becoming a savvy real estate investor capable of navigating the complexities of this exciting market.

2.3 CHOOSING THE RIGHT STRATEGY FOR YOU

When you embark on the journey of real estate investing, selecting the right strategy that aligns with your financial goals, risk tolerance, and personal commitment level is crucial. Each strategy offers different benefits and challenges. Whether you're looking for quick returns through flipping or building long-term wealth through buy-and-hold rentals, understanding the nuances of each strategy will enable you to make informed decisions and effectively manage your investments.

As you continue to explore these diverse strategies, consider your circumstances, the amount of time you can dedicate to managing your investments, and your comfort level with the associated risks. Real estate investing is not a one-size-fits-all interest; it is a dynamic field that requires adaptability, continuous learning, and a clear understanding of your financial landscape. By understanding and carefully selecting the approach that best fits your objectives, you can optimize your investments for maximum returns and sustainability.

2.3.1 Short-Term and Vacation Rentals

With platforms like Airbnb, short-term and vacation rental properties have become popular investments. These properties often generate higher daily income than traditional long-term rentals but require active management and marketing, especially in competitive tourist destinations.

2.3.2 Student Rentals

Investing in properties that cater to students near colleges or universities can be highly profitable due to the constant demand for housing in these areas. However, student rentals can also come with higher turnover and increased management challenges.

Suppose you have vacant apartments during the summer holidays. In that case, you can rent them out as vacation rentals if they are furnished.

2.3.3 Live-In House Flips

Live-in house flips are a variation in which you purchase a property, move into it, and make improvements while living there. This approach can save on costs such as dual mortgages and provide significant tax advantages. It requires a willingness to live a work-in-progress and a flexible lifestyle, but it can be a highly effective way to increase the value of your investment with lower upfront costs.

2.3.4 House Flipping

House flipping is an appealing strategy for those looking for short-term investment returns. It involves purchasing properties at a lower market price, often because they need repair or renovation, then selling them at a higher price after making necessary improvements. This plan requires a good eye for potential, a deep understanding of property valuation, and an ability to manage renovations efficiently. Successful house flipping also depends heavily on timing and market conditions, making it a higher-risk endeavor that can yield significant returns if executed well.

2.3.4.1 Flipping Properties: A Comprehensive Guide

The allure of property flipping lies in its potential for quick financial returns. Still, it demands acute market knowledge, adept project management, and a keen understanding of property valuation.

The primary step in property flipping is identifying undervalued properties that hold promise for a profitable flip. It involves thorough market research to understand where the best opportunities lie and what types of properties are most in demand. Key factors to consider are the location of the property, its current condition, and the prevailing market conditions. For instance, a property in a desirable neighborhood that requires cosmetic updates may present a lucrative opportunity. In contrast, a property in a less favorable area may not yield the desired return even after extensive renovations.

A checklist for evaluating potential properties might include assessing the building's structural integrity, the condition of major systems like plumbing and electrical, the layout and functionality of the space, and the potential for adding value through renovations. Understanding the zoning laws and potential permitting requirements is crucial, as these factors can significantly affect the renovation timeline and costs. (Read more in Chapter 5.4.2.)

Once you have identified a suitable property, the next step is executing quick, high-impact renovations that will likely increase the property's market value. This phase requires careful planning to ensure that the renovations align with what is attractive in the current market and can be completed within a set budget and timeframe. High-impact areas typically include the kitchen and bathrooms, flooring, fixtures, and curb appeal enhancements such as landscaping or exterior painting.

The staging and selling process is where your efforts come to fruition. Staging involves furnishing the property in a way that highlights its best features and makes it appealing to potential buyers. This step is crucial as it helps buyers visualize themselves living in the space, and demand increases the likelihood of a sale. (See link tips in References.) The selling phase should be strategically planned to coincide with favorable market conditions to maximize the selling price. Working with experienced real estate agents who know and understand the local market and have a proven track record of closing sales can significantly smooth this final phase.

Financial planning is the foundation of successful property flipping. It requires a detailed budget for the purchase price, renovation costs, holding costs such as taxes and utilities, and selling costs, including agent commissions and closing fees. Accurate financial analysis ensures that the total investment does not exceed the property's after-repair value, thereby protecting your profit margins. Strategies for keeping costs down include sourcing materials at a discount, choosing renovations that offer the best return on investment, and efficiently managing the renovation process to avoid delays and overruns.

However, flipping properties is not without risks. Market fluctuations can affect the selling price, unexpected structural issues can arise during renovations, and budget overruns can erode profit margins. Conducting a thorough risk assessment before proceeding with a property flip is essential to mitigate these risks. It includes evaluating the stability of the local real estate market, having a contingency budget for unexpected expenses, and possibly consulting with construction experts to identify potential issues before purchasing a property.

Real-world examples of both successful and unsuccessful property flips can provide valuable lessons. Successful flips often share common themes, such as thorough initial research, well-managed renovations, and effective marketing and sales strategies. On the other hand, flips that go differently than planned often suffer from poor initial property selection, underestimation of renovation costs, or misjudgment of the market. Analyzing these examples helps highlight the importance of meticulous planning and risk management in property flipping. Remember that you may need to hold the property to wait for the market or the right buyer willing to offer the desired price.

In summary, flipping properties offers an exciting opportunity for quick financial gains in the real estate market. It requires a strategic approach from the initial property selection and renovation planning to the final stages of staging and selling. By understanding the market, managing renovations efficiently, and navigating the selling process effectively, you can maximize your returns while minimizing risks. Remember, each flip provides valuable learning experiences, building your skills and confidence for future projects in the realm of real estate investing.

2.3.4.2 Case Study: Successful Residential Flip

Initial Assessment and Purchase

The journey of a successful property flip often begins with a meticulous assessment process. Consider the story of Sarah, a first-time investor who identified a promising property in a transitioning neighborhood known for its potential upside. The property, a dated single-family home, was located near a newly planned public park and had easy access to local schools and shopping centers—an ideal spot for families looking to rent or buy.

Sarah's initial assessment was thorough. She evaluated the property based on several critical criteria: location, condition, and market timing. Knowing the area was on the cusp of becoming a sought-after residential locale due to upcoming infrastructure projects, she recognized the timing was perfect. While needing a cosmetic facelift, the property had solid bones—meaning no substantial structural repairs were necessary, minimizing initial investment risks.

Her purchase strategy was grounded in detailed financial analysis and market research. She negotiated a below-market price by highlighting the cost of needed renovations and presenting a quick closing deal to the eager sellers. This approach secured her a reasonable purchase price. It kept initial investment costs in check, preserving her budget for the renovations needed to maximize the property's value.

Renovation Strategies and Execution

Once the property was hers, Sarah faced turning her vision into reality. Her renovation strategies were clear: modernizing the home while keeping within a strict budget and timeline. She prioritized updates that would significantly boost the property's appeal and value—remodeling the kitchen and bathrooms, replacing old carpet with hardwood flooring, and applying fresh paint throughout the home.

Selecting the right contractors was crucial. Sarah chose to work with professionals her real estate network highly recommended, ensuring reliability and quality workmanship. She maintained a tight schedule, closely managing the renovation process to avoid costly delays. Regular on-site visits and open communication with her contractors helped keep the project on track.

Marketing and Selling the Flipped Property

With the renovations complete, Sarah's focus shifted to marketing and selling the property. She employed several effective strategies to ensure a swift sale at a profitable price. Professional staging was arranged to showcase the home's potential, helping prospective buyers envision themselves living in the space. Strategic pricing was crucial; Sarah set the sale price at a competitive point yet maximized her profit margins based on a comparative market analysis.

She leveraged various advertising platforms, listing the property on social media, famous real estate websites, and local community boards. She also hosted open houses to generate buzz, create a sense of urgency among potential buyers, and attract multiple offers.

Financial Review and Lessons Learned

The financial outcome of Sarah's flip was a testament to her strategic approach. The cost versus profit analysis revealed a significant return on her investment, with the final selling price substantially exceeding her total expenses, including purchase and renovation costs. This success, however, was not without its challenges. Unexpected plumbing issues during the renovation led to unplanned expenses. Sarah managed these by reallocating funds from less critical aesthetic enhancements to essential repairs, ensuring the project stayed within budget.

From this experience, Sarah learned the importance of contingency planning—setting aside a portion of the budget for unforeseen costs. She also realized the value of a solid network, as recommendations from trusted professionals were crucial in managing the renovation efficiently and effectively.

This case study of Sarah's residential flip provides a clear example of how combining diligent market research, strategic planning, and effective execution can lead to successful real estate investments. Her journey offers valuable insights and practical lessons that you can apply to your investment strategies, particularly the importance of thorough initial assessment, strategic renovation planning, effective marketing, and the necessity for financial prudence and flexibility.

2.3.5 House Hacking

House hacking requires purchasing a multi-unit property and renting out the others while living in one unit. This strategy helps offset the cost of your mortgage and other expenses, allowing you to live for free or at a reduced cost while building equity in the property. House hacking is an excellent way for first-time homeowners to enter the real estate market.

2.3.6 Turnkey Investing

Turnkey investing involves purchasing renovation-ready and rent-ready properties. These properties are typically managed by a third party, making them an attractive option for investors who prefer a more hands-off approach. This strategy particularly appeals to those not residing in the same area as their investments or those new to real estate investing who might still need the experience or time to manage properties directly.

2.3.7 Wholesaling

Real estate wholesaling is a strategy where you enter into a contract to buy a property and then sell the contract to another buyer before closing. It allows you to make a profit without ever actually owning the property. Wholesaling requires excellent negotiation skills and a strong network of buyers and sellers, but can be lucrative with minimal capital investment.

2.3.7.1 Introduction to Real Estate Wholesaling

Real estate wholesaling is a compelling strategy for those looking to make a mark in the property market without the hefty capital typically associated with purchasing real estate. At its core, wholesaling in real estate involves you, the wholesaler, entering into a contract to buy a property and then assigning that contract to an end buyer for a higher price. This method serves as an intermediary step, where your role is to identify potential deals, secure them under contract at a price below market value, and transfer these deals to end buyers who are either investors or purchasers looking to capitalize on the property themselves.

The appeal of wholesaling lies in its accessibility. It requires less upfront capital than traditional property investments and can be quickly executed. However, it demands a keen sense of market trends, the ability to find undervalued properties, and strong negotiation skills to secure lower-priced contracts. The process begins with diligent market research to identify undervalued properties or sellers motivated to sell quickly, often due to circumstances such as foreclosure, divorce, or financial distress. This initial step is critical to set the foundation for a profitable wholesale deal.

Navigating the legal and ethical considerations in wholesaling is paramount to ensuring your successful and reputable real estate endeavors. Transparency with buyers and sellers is crucial; clear communication of your intentions and the contract terms must be maintained throughout the process. Understanding and complying with state-specific regulations governing wholesaling activities is essential, as legal requirements vary significantly. Some states may require you to have a real estate license to wholesale properties. In contrast, others may impose specific rules on how contracts are assigned. Consulting with a real estate attorney to understand these nuances can safeguard you against potential legal issues and enhance your credibility in the market.

Embarking on a successful wholesale transaction involves several key steps. Initially, when assigning the contract to an end buyer, you must identify and negotiate a deal for a property below market value, ensuring enough room for profit. Once a property is under contract, the next step is to find an investor-buyer willing to purchase the contract. This buyer typically pays a fee or a percentage of the property's value, which becomes your profit from the deal. Effective marketing strategies and an extensive and solid network of potential buyers are essential for quickly transferring these contracts. Platforms such as real estate investment groups, online forums, and local investor meetups can be invaluable for connecting with potential buyers.

Building and maintaining a robust network of buyers and sellers is fundamental to the success of your wholesaling business. This network provides a steady stream of potential deals and buyer leads, enhancing your reputation in the market. Attend real estate networking events, join relevant online communities, provide consistent value, and maintain integrity in all your dealings. Establishing solid relationships based on trust and mutual benefit can lead to repeat business and referrals, which are often the lifeblood of a successful wholesaling operation.

As you delve into real estate wholesaling, remember that, like any investment strategy, it comes with challenges and risks. Market fluctuations, the urgency to quickly close deals, and the dependence on a network of buyers and sellers can all pose significant pressures. However, with a thorough understanding of the process, a commitment to ethical practices, and a proactive approach to building a solid network, wholesaling can offer a lucrative gateway into the real estate market with relatively low barriers to entry. This strategy allows you to gain valuable experience in the real estate sector. It provides the flexibility to manage your investments with minimal financial commitment, making it an attractive option for new and seasoned investors seeking to expand their portfolios or break into the market. (Read more in Chapter 4.1.1.6.)

2.3.8 Real Estate Development

For those looking for a more hands-on investment, real estate development involves purchasing land and constructing new buildings or renovating existing structures. This strategy can offer high returns but involves significant risks, including higher capital requirements, potential regulatory hurdles, and market vulnerabilities.

2.3.8.1 Developing Real Estate: From Purchase to Project Completion

Real estate development represents a pinnacle of investing endeavors, blending creativity with economics to transform landscapes and build communities. This comprehensive process spans a variety of project types, from residential communities that offer homes to families to commercial complexes that drive business growth and mixed-use developments that combine both elements for holistic neighborhood solutions. Each type of development project caters to specific needs and demographics, offering unique challenges and rewards. Understanding the scope of real estate development is crucial; it's not merely about construction but about envisioning and actualizing a project that meets the needs of a community while providing a return on investment.

Real estate development begins with land acquisition, where strategic selection based on location, market demand, and future growth potential is critical. Following this, obtaining zoning approvals can often be a complex dance of meeting municipal requirements, including environmental impact assessments, public hearings, and multiple levels of bureaucratic approval.

Each phase is critical, laying the groundwork for what will eventually become a tangible asset. For instance, choosing a site for a new residential development involves analyzing demographic trends, local amenities, and transportation infrastructure, ensuring the project will attract residents and hold its value over time.

Once the land is secured and zoned appropriately, the construction phase commences. This stage is characterized by its dynamic nature. It involves architects, contractors, engineers, and numerous tradespeople, all coordinated to make architectural plans a reality. Effectively managing this phase requires a robust understanding of construction management principles, adherence to timelines, and budget control. Any delays or budget overruns can significantly impact the project's overall profitability, making rigorous management practices essential.

Financial structuring is another pillar of real estate development. Large-scale projects often require significant capital, which can be sourced through various financing options such as joint ventures, where multiple investors or companies share the risk and reward; syndications, which pool money from several investors; and construction loans, which are specifically designed to fund the building phase of development projects. The role of financial leverage in these projects is profound, enabling the amplification of potential returns and increasing risk exposure. Effective cash flow management throughout the development phase ensures that funds are available as needed and that the project remains financially viable.

Risk management in real estate development is about foreseeing potential challenges and mitigating them proactively. Common risks include delays in construction due to unforeseen issues like bad weather or supply chain disruptions, cost overruns from budget miscalculations or changes in material costs, and regulatory challenges that may arise if local laws change or the project encounters unexpected legal hurdles. Implementing a comprehensive risk management strategy involves regular project reviews, contingency planning, and maintaining flexible operational strategies to adapt to challenges if and when they arise.

Real estate development is an endeavor that requires a blend of vision, financial acumen, and meticulous planning. Each step, from land acquisition and zoning to construction and final sales, is interconnected, with the success of each phase impacting the overall project outcome. Whether developing a quaint residential neighborhood or a sprawling commercial complex, thorough preparation, strategic financing, and proactive risk management are universal. By adhering to these principles, you can navigate the complexities of real estate development and successfully transform your vision into profitable, functional spaces that meet the needs of their occupants and contribute positively to the community.

2.3.9 Buy-and-Hold

The buy-and-hold strategy involves purchasing properties to own them for the long term. Investors typically earn money through rental income and potential property value appreciation over time. This strategy is ideal for those looking to build long-term wealth and can provide a stable income stream. It requires managing tenants and property maintenance, making it crucial to invest in areas with strong rental demand and potential for growth.

2.3.9.1 Case Study: Building a Rental Portfolio from Scratch

Imagine embarking on a venture to build a substantial rental portfolio from the ground up. This ambitious goal requires a keen understanding of the market, strategic planning, and meticulous management. Let's delve into the story of James, a determined investor who successfully created a thriving rental portfolio, navigating through various challenges and leveraging opportunities to achieve his financial objectives.

Strategic Planning and Financing

James's journey began with a clear strategic plan that outlined his long-term goals: to build a diversified rental portfolio that would provide a steady income stream and appreciate over time. He knew careful planning was essential, especially when selecting a target market. His choice was a region with a growing job market, a steady influx of new residents, and a stable political environment, which promised sustained demand for rental properties.

Securing financing was the next critical step. James explored various funding sources, including traditional banks, private lenders, and real estate investment groups. His strategy was to leverage these sources to maximize his investment capacity while maintaining financial stability. Risk management was integral to his financing strategy. James meticulously analyzed the potential ROI on each property before purchase, ensuring that even if market conditions shifted, his investments could withstand downturns without jeopardizing his entire portfolio.

Acquisition and Property Management

Acquiring properties was conducted with precision. James implemented a rigorous due diligence process for each potential acquisition. He evaluated properties based on location, condition, rental income, and appreciation potential. Negotiations were grounded in thorough market research, allowing him to purchase properties below market value and increase equity from the start.

Once properties were acquired, effective management became the cornerstone of maintaining high occupancy rates and tenant satisfaction. James initially opted to work with a property management company to handle day-to-day operations. However, as his portfolio grew, he brought this in-house to maintain closer control and reduce operating costs. His management team focused on tenant relations, regular maintenance, and proactive problem-solving, ensuring tenant retention rates and well-maintained properties, enhancing their value over time.

Scaling the Portfolio

James's portfolio was scalable through a combination of reinvesting profits and strategically utilizing a 1031 exchange to defer capital gains taxes, which provided additional capital for further investments. He also diversified his portfolio by investing in different types of properties and new geographical areas, which not only spread risk but also opened up new growth opportunities.

Expanding into new markets, however, brought its own set of challenges. Each market had its unique dynamics and regulatory environments. James spent considerable time researching new markets, understanding local laws, and building networks with local real estate professionals. This meticulous approach helped him mitigate risks associated with expansion and capitalize on new opportunities effectively.

Evaluation of Investment Performance

Over time, James's portfolio showed substantial growth. He regularly analyzed financial metrics such as cash flow, ROI, and equity growth. This continuous evaluation allowed James to decide whether to hold, sell, or reinvest in properties. Strategic decisions based on performance metrics significantly impacted his portfolio's success. For instance, properties that consistently underperformed were customized or divested, freeing capital for more lucrative investments.

James successfully built a rental portfolio from scratch and is a powerful example for aspiring real estate investors. It highlights the importance of strategic planning, thorough market research, effective property management, and continual performance evaluation. Each step in James's journey reflects a deliberate and informed approach to real estate investing, providing valuable insights into how you can develop and manage a successful rental portfolio. His story illustrates that building a profitable real estate investment portfolio is within reach with dedication, thorough understanding, and strategic action, even for those starting from scratch.

2.3.9.2 Case Study: Overcoming Investment Challenges

In the dynamic world of real estate, investors often encounter various hurdles that test their resilience and strategic insight. Consider the case of Elena, an investor who had recently expanded her portfolio by acquiring multiple properties in a coastal area known for its robust tourism and real estate market. However, shortly after her investment, the area was struck by a severe hurricane, causing extensive damage to several of her properties and significantly disrupting local economic activities. This scenario posed a dual challenge of physical property damage and a sudden downturn in the local economy, threatening Elena's investment returns and forcing her to reassess her strategies swiftly.

The challenge was first identified through immediate property assessments post-disaster, which revealed substantial structural damage and a sharp decline in property values due to the broader economic impact on the community. Recognizing the situation's urgency, Elena quickly mobilized a team of contractors to evaluate the damage and estimate repair costs. She also engaged with local authorities and her insurance company to understand the extent of coverage and the process for claims. Transparency with tenants, who were equally affected by the disaster, was maintained through regular communication, ensuring they were updated on restoration plans and timelines.

Strategic adjustments were crucial in navigating this tumultuous period. Elena decided to reallocate funds initially earmarked for further property acquisitions towards comprehensive renovations and strengthening existing properties to withstand similar future events. It included upgrading building materials and altering designs to enhance durability against natural disasters. Additionally, recognizing the impact of the economic downturn on her tenants' ability to pay rent, she temporarily adjusted her rental terms to accommodate their circumstances, thereby maintaining occupancy and tenant loyalty.

Another strategic move was refinancing some of her properties to access lower interest rates and better loan terms. That provided her with the necessary liquidity to cover renovation expenses without compromising the quality of repairs. She conducted legal consultations to ensure all renovations and tenant negotiations adhered to local laws and regulations, safeguarding her actions against potential legal repercussions.

The outcomes of these strategic interventions were multifaceted. Once renovations were completed, the properties were better equipped to deal with similar challenges in the future. Still, they also saw increased value due to the enhanced features and renewed investor confidence in the rehabilitated area. Tenant retention rates remained high due to Elena's supportive approach during the crisis, and her quick actions and transparent communication helped maintain a positive reputation among residents and businesses.

Financially, while the initial impact was severe, the recovery and subsequent improvements in property resilience and value mitigated long-term harmful effects, stabilizing her investment returns. The experience significantly improved Elena's crisis management skills and her business's operational resilience, preparing her better for future challenges.

Key takeaways from Elena's experience highlight the importance of rapid response and flexibility in crisis management within real estate investments. Her preventive measures, such as investing in property improvements that contributed to sustainability and resilience, have proven their worth, underscoring the need for proactive rather than reactive management strategies. Maintaining solid relationships with tenants, local businesses, and authorities can provide critical support and information during unforeseen challenges.

This case study compellingly illustrates how adaptive strategies and proactive management can help real estate investors navigate immediate challenges and enhance the long-term value and sustainability of their investments. It emphasizes the necessity of preparedness and the value of resilience, providing practical insights for managing and mitigating risks in real estate investing.

As we close this chapter on overcoming investment challenges, remember that the ability to adapt and respond effectively to unforeseen situations is as crucial as any financial calculation or market analysis in real estate investing. Let these real-world applications and strategies inspire you to build a robust framework for your investment endeavors, equipped to handle the ebbs and flows of the market.

2.3.10 BRRRR Investing

The BRRRR method—Buy, Rehab, Rent, Refinance, Repeat—is a comprehensive real estate investment strategy involving renovating properties, renting them out to generate cash flow, and refinancing to fund additional investments. This method can rapidly expand your real estate portfolio but requires precise financial planning and management.

2.3.10.1 The BRRRR Method Explained

The BRRRR method stands for Buy, Rehab, Rent, Refinance, and Repeat. This powerful investment strategy allows you to leverage your capital to build a substantial real estate portfolio over time. It focuses on recycling your investment dollars by quickly and efficiently moving through these five stages, maximizing your ability to grow your investments exponentially.

Let's break down each step to understand how to implement this strategy effectively. The first step, '**Buy**,' involves purchasing a property significantly under market value, often because it requires repair or is in a distressed sale situation. The key is identifying properties with high After-Repair Value (ARV) potential. This means looking for properties in neighborhoods where renovated homes sell at a premium, ensuring that your investment will grow in value once improvements are made. It's essential to conduct thorough market research, analyzing recent sales of similar properties to estimate the ARV accurately. Additionally, factors like the neighborhood's growth potential, local amenities, and overall market trends should be considered, as these can significantly affect the property's value post-rehab.

Once a suitable property is acquired, the next stage, '**Rehab**,' involves making necessary renovations to increase the property's value and appeal. This stage requires careful planning to ensure that every dollar spent on renovations contributes to an increase in the property's worth and attractiveness to potential tenants. Focus on renovations and improvements that offer the best return on investment, such as updating bathrooms and kitchens, improving curb appeal, or adding features highly valued in your specific market, such as energy-efficient appliances or additional living space. Managing your rehab budget carefully is crucial, ensuring you do not overspend but still achieve high-quality results that will enhance the property's value.

Following renovations, the '**Rent**' stage involves finding tenants for your newly rehabbed property. The goal is to secure reliable tenants to provide a steady rental income stream. This income helps cover your ongoing property expenses and strengthens your financial position when you seek to refinance. Effective property marketing, thorough tenant screening, and setting competitive yet profitable rent prices are crucial. Consider employing professional property management services if you prefer to avoid managing tenant relations and day-to-day property issues directly, as this can save you time and potentially reduce tenant-related risks.

The '**Refinance**' stage is where the BRRRR method starts to leverage your initial investment. After rehabbing and renting the property and assuming its value has increased, you can now approach lenders to refinance at a higher property value. This step is critical as it allows you to pull out most, if not all, of the original capital you invested, plus any additional equity created through renovations and rental income. To ensure you get the best possible terms during refinancing, prepare detailed financial documentation showing the property's income, your overall investment stability, and the increased property value. Choosing the right lender—someone who understands investment properties and offers favorable terms—is vital.

Finally, the '**Repeat**' stage is about taking the capital you've regained from refinancing and using it to start the process with a new property. This is where the compounding effect of the BRRRR method comes into play, allowing you to scale your real estate portfolio more rapidly without continually injecting large amounts of new capital. By effectively repeating this process, you can expand your investment holdings, diversify your portfolio, and significantly increase your passive income over time.

The BRRRR method is not just a tactic but a comprehensive strategy that requires patience, diligence, and a keen understanding of the real estate market. Each step offers opportunities and challenges, but with careful execution, it provides a potent way to build wealth through real estate. As you apply this method, always stay informed about market conditions and remain adaptable to change, ensuring your investment decisions are data-driven and strategically sound. This proactive approach will help you maximize the benefits of the BRRRR method, turning each investment into a stepping stone toward tremendous financial success in the real estate industry.

2.4 FINDING A PROPERTY, MAKING AN OFFER AND NEGOTIATING

Embarking on the process of finding the ideal real estate investment requires meticulous preparation and a strategic approach. Before you even consider placing an offer, a significant amount of groundwork must be laid, ensuring that every step you take is informed and calculated. It begins with a thorough assessment of your financing options. Understanding which loans or credit lines are available and at what terms is critical, as it sets the boundaries for what you can afford. Different financing strategies, whether through traditional banks, private lenders, or creative financing options like lease options, can influence your purchasing power and the types of properties you can consider. (Read more about financing in Chapter 4.1.)

Simultaneously, it is crucial to learn the intricacies of the local market where you intend to invest. This involves analyzing market trends, understanding property values, and identifying the types of properties that are most in demand. A deep dive into the local market helps you spot undervalued properties or those in emerging areas with high growth potential. Additionally, familiarizing yourself with the local regulations, property taxes, and zoning laws is essential, as these factors can significantly impact your investment.

The selection process for potential investment properties should be rigorous. It involves identifying properties listed below market value and conducting a comprehensive review of each property's legal, financial, and technical aspects. This review can include checking the title for any liens, understanding any existing tenant agreements, determining if it's an income property, and assessing the physical condition of the property. A detailed economic analysis is then conducted to calculate the potential value of the investment, considering factors such as renovation costs, potential rental income, and the resale value. This calculated value is then compared against the market value or the seller's price to determine the feasibility and profitability of the investment. Remember that the accuracy and thoroughness of your initial valuation efforts profoundly influence the value you derive from your investments.

2.4.1 The Role of Property Inspections and Appraisals

Understanding the critical roles of property inspections and appraisals is paramount when considering an investment in real estate. These are not just routine steps in the buying process; they are your safeguards, ensuring you know exactly what you're investing in and at what value. Though they seem similar, property inspections and appraisals serve distinct purposes. Professionals with different areas of expertise conduct them.

2.4.2 Property Inspections

A property inspection is a thorough examination of the physical condition of the property. It's typically performed by a licensed inspector who assesses everything from the roof to the foundation, including systems like plumbing and electrical, to identify any existing or potential issues. This process is crucial as it can uncover problems that are not visible to the untrained eye, such as structural damage or outdated wiring, which could lead to significant financial liabilities down the line.

2.4.2.1 Physical Inspection is an Essential Part of the Valuation Process

Physical property inspections are a critical component of the valuation process, revealing issues that may need to be apparent from financial analyses alone. The findings from these inspections can considerably influence the final valuation figures by identifying problems that reduce the property's market value or ensuring that all aspects of the property justify the investment.

Remember that a property consists of land facilities (e.g., parking, garden, swimming pool) and buildings (e.g., main building, garage, storage, garbage house.)

Navigating the inspection process can be more manageable with a comprehensive checklist that examines all critical elements. (Start from the checklists in Chapter 6.4.3.1 and develop to adapt to the current investment object.) This checklist should include an evaluation of ground facilities and building components.

Examples of significant components are:

- Exterior facilities.
- The roof, walls, windows, and doors protect a building from weather-related damage.
- The foundation ensures the structural integrity of the building.
- Internal surfaces include suspended ceilings, walls, floors, windows, doors, and stairs.
- Interior equipment, such as elevators and kitchen equipment.
- Critical systems such as plumbing, electrical, ventilation, cooling, and heating are essential to the property's functionality.
- Additionally, security systems like fire alarms, burglar alarms, and passage systems are crucial, some or all of which may contractually belong to the tenants.

During an inspection, look for signs such as pest infestations, mold, structural damage, and other potential liabilities that could affect the property's value.

Use your eyes, ears, and nose. If you need help understanding the cause of the problem, seek the help of experts who can investigate and tell you what actions are required. When bringing in expert help, clarify that you want to know how to solve the "problem" and not just remove the "symptom." For example, measures may need to be taken externally and internally, depending on how much soil moisture penetrates through the basement wall. Solving the "symptom" would be to install a dehumidifier (to reduce humidity) or an ozone device (to eliminate any odor). Be observant if you find similar machines or whether windows are open. They indicate that the seller knows of a problem but has yet to take long-term action.

However, assessing the condition of a property goes beyond checking off items on a list; it requires a keen understanding of how various factors, like the property's age and the necessity for renovations, could impact your investment. Older properties, for example, might come with a lower upfront cost but could carry higher maintenance expenses, affecting your overall investment returns. Recognizing these factors early on in the inspection process can help you make informed decisions about the feasibility of the investment and the budgeting for future expenses.

2.4.3 Property Appraisal

An appraisal evaluates the property's market value and is conducted by a certified appraiser. It involves examining not only the condition of the property but also considering market trends, the value of similar properties, and other factors like location and future development potential. Appraisals are essential for securing financing, as lenders require them to ensure the property is worth the loan amount. They also play a critical role in negotiations, helping you ensure you're paying a fair price or selling at market value.

Leveraging appraisals effectively is vital in determining the investment value of a property. Appraisers use different approaches to value properties. The sales comparison approach compares the property to similar recently sold properties. The income capitalization approach is used primarily for commercial properties, which bases the property's value on the income it generates. The cost approach considers what it would cost to replace the property minus depreciation. Empower yourself by understanding these methods. (Learn more about them in Chapter 3.4.) This knowledge can help you interpret appraisal reports more effectively and use this information to your advantage, whether buying or selling.

2.4.4 Negotiations

Using the results from inspections and appraisals in negotiations can significantly influence the terms of the deal. Suppose an inspection reveals issues that require substantial investment to fix. In that case, you can request that the seller make repairs before closing or negotiate a lower purchase price. Similarly, an appraisal that comes in lower than the purchase price provides a basis to renegotiate the terms or even withdraw from the deal without penalty, depending on the contingencies outlined in the contract. These strategic uses of inspection and appraisal findings are vital for protecting your investment and ensuring you enter a real estate transaction with full knowledge of the property's condition and value.

2.4.4.1 The Power of Negotiation

When it's time to make an offer, several considerations come into play. Your offer should reflect both the current value of the property and its potential value after any improvements you plan to make. It's also important to consider how quickly properties are moving in the market you're interested in, as this can affect how aggressively you need to make your offer. If you're in a seller's market, you may need to make a more competitive offer close to, if not exceeding, the asking price. However, you might have more leeway to negotiate a lower price in a buyer's market.

Negotiation is where your preparation truly pays off. Armed with your valuation findings, you can enter negotiations with confidence. Presenting your data clearly and professionally to the seller or agent can help justify your offer price. If there are discrepancies between your valuation and the asking price, these should be discussed openly. Perhaps the seller is unaware of specific issues with the property that your inspections uncovered, or they might have overestimated the property's market value.

In negotiating, it's vital to understand and respect what is essential to the other party. The price might be the driving factor for some sellers, while others might value a quicker closing process. Tailoring your negotiations to address the seller's priorities can make your offer more appealing. For instance, if a seller is looking to close quickly, offering a shorter escrow period might make your offer stand out even if it's not the highest.

Finally, mastering basic negotiation techniques can significantly enhance your ability to secure a property at the right price. Potent strategies include building rapport with the seller or agent, being open and honest in your communications, and being prepared to walk away if the deal does not meet your investment criteria. Additionally, always have your financing in order before making an offer to ensure you can move quickly once negotiations begin. It shows the sellers that you are serious and prevents delays in the buying process that could jeopardize the deal.

Navigating the complexities of real estate negotiations with tact and preparedness can transform potential opportunities into successful investments. By thoroughly understanding the financial, legal, and market aspects of the properties you are interested in and approaching negotiations with a respectful yet firm strategy, you can maximize your chances of closing deals that align with your investment goals. This proactive and informed approach is essential for anyone looking to succeed in the competitive world of real estate investing.

2.4.4.2 The Investor's Guide to Real Estate Contracts

Navigating real estate contracts is often perceived as a complex dance of legal terms and conditions. However, understanding these agreements is crucial for safeguarding your investment interests. As an investor, you'll encounter various types of contracts tailored to specific property transaction aspects. Let's first look into the different types of real estate contracts you will likely encounter.

Purchase agreements are the most common and pivotal contracts you will engage with. These are formal agreements between the seller and buyer detailing the terms of the property sale. They outline critical elements such as the property description, purchase price, deposit amount, and any conditions that must be met before the sale is finalized. These conditions can include financing terms and inspections, and the agreement becomes legally binding once both parties sign.

On the other hand, lease agreements govern the relationship between landlords and tenants, detailing terms regarding the lease duration, monthly rent, rules regarding the use of the property, and conditions for the renewal or termination of the lease. Understanding these is vital as they directly affect your cash flow and legal duties as a property owner.

Option contracts offer a unique mechanism in real estate; these agreements give the buyer the right, but not the obligation, to purchase or sell a property at an agreed-upon price within a specific timeframe. They are particularly useful in scenarios where a buyer needs time to arrange financing or assess a project's feasibility before fully committing to the purchase.

Each of these contracts serves a distinct purpose and contains typical provisions designed to protect the interests of all parties involved, ensure clarity in transactions, and provide solutions in case of disputes. For instance, contingencies in purchase agreements are safety nets, allowing parties to back out under predefined conditions without financial penalties. For instance, a contingency for property inspections could reveal issues that could influence the buyer's decision to proceed with the purchase.

Now, when it comes to negotiating these contracts, the ability to secure terms that meet your investment goals can significantly influence your portfolio's performance. Effective negotiation begins with a solid understanding of the property's value, market conditions, and legal implications. Armed with this knowledge, you can negotiate terms that protect your interests and offer flexibility to adapt to changing circumstances. For instance, in a purchase agreement, you might negotiate a lower price in exchange for a quicker closing date if the seller is eager to sell. Alternatively, you might negotiate terms that pass specific property maintenance responsibilities onto the tenants in a lease agreement, reducing your overhead costs.

However, even with meticulous planning and negotiation, real estate contracts can harbor pitfalls that pose risks to your investments. Vague terms, for example, can lead to interpretations that are open to dispute. A contract might stipulate that the seller make a repair before the sale. Still, specifying the standards or timeline for these repairs is necessary to avoid finding yourself in a disagreement about the adequacy of the work completed. Another common pitfall is the failure to include essential contingencies, which could bind you to purchase even if critical financing falls through or an inspection uncovers significant property defects.

To avoid these pitfalls, it is imperative to approach each contract with thoroughness and a keen eye for detail. Ensure that all terms are explicitly defined and the contract leaves no room for ambiguous interpretations. Engage with legal professionals who can provide insights into crafting clauses that protect your interests and comply with applicable laws. They can also review contracts to spot potential issues before you make commitments.

In real estate investing, where significant capital is often at play, understanding and negotiating contracts with precision is not just a skill—it's an essential safeguard that can determine the success of your investments. By mastering this aspect of real estate, you equip yourself with the tools to navigate transactions confidently, minimize risks, and enhance the profitability and stability of your investment portfolio.

2.4.5 Upon Completion of the Purchase

In real estate investing, the moment of closing on a property purchase marks a significant milestone. However, the journey doesn't end there. Finalizing the purchase is just as crucial as any part of the investment process. It involves a detailed handover of all pertinent documents and items associated with the property. This meticulous attention to detail ensures you have all the necessary tools and information to manage your new asset effectively.

The array of documents and items you must collect at closing can be extensive. Keys are just the beginning; you also need access to all relevant documents, which include the title deed, which proves property ownership, and property deeds, which detail the rights and obligations associated with the property. Additionally, obtaining existing lease agreements is crucial if you're purchasing a property with current tenants. These documents outline the terms agreed upon with the tenants and are essential for maintaining continuity and managing tenant relationships effectively.

Mortgage documents are another critical element. Understanding the terms, conditions, and remaining balance is crucial if the property is under a mortgage. This information will help you manage your financial obligations and plan for future financial decisions regarding the property. Similarly, acquiring any existing agreements related to the property, such as maintenance contracts or service agreements, ensures that you are aware of and can continue any ongoing services without interruption.

If available, drawings and blueprints of the property can be invaluable, especially if you plan to make renovations or need to conduct repairs. These documents provide a detailed property layout essential for construction or remodeling work. Ensuring you have paper and digital copies of these documents can safeguard against loss or damage and provide easy access when needed.

All these documents and items should be transferred with the utmost care and attention to detail. A checklist is advisable to ensure that everything is noticed during the handover process. See the draft in the next chapter. Ask the seller questions and add points while reading about the object so the checklist is adapted to the investment object. You should carefully review each item and, if possible, verify with the seller to ensure accuracy and completeness. For instance, confirming that the names and details in the lease agreements match those provided by the seller or ensuring that the property's blueprints are up-to-date can prevent future complications.

In digital times, the electronic management of these documents is becoming increasingly common. Digital copies provide a backup in case of physical damage to paper documents, allowing for more accessible storage and quicker access. Ensuring you have secure digital copies of all necessary documents should be a part of your closing strategy.

Collecting all pertinent documents and items at the close of a property purchase sets a solid foundation for effective property management. It ensures that you are fully prepared to take over the property, understand all associated obligations and rights, and can make informed decisions about the property's future. This thoroughness helps maintain the value of your investment and mitigate potential legal and financial issues that might arise from incomplete or inaccurate documentation.

As you move forward from the closing, these documents become the tools with which you manage your property and shape your investment's future. They provide the clarity and legal grounding necessary to navigate the complexities of real estate ownership and management, allowing you to focus on maximizing your investment's potential. This meticulous approach to the final stages of purchasing protects your investment. It reinforces your capabilities as a prudent and informed real estate investor.

2.4.5.1 Checklist Breakdown

1 Keys and Access

- Main doors
- Mailboxes
- Storage units
- Electronic locks, codes/keycards
- Gate/garage remote controls

2 Contracts and Agreements

- Rental contracts
- Lease agreements
- Supplier/service provider agreements
- HOA agreements (if applicable)

3 Operation and Maintenance

- Equipment operation manuals
- Maintenance instructions
- Warranty documents
- Service records/history

4 Software and Digital Access

- Property management software logins
- Security system access details
- Online account passwords

5 Contact Lists

- Supplier contact list

- Tenant contact list
- Emergency contact numbers
- Sending information about the new owner to suppliers and tenants

6 Financial Documents

- Previous income statements
- Expense reports/receipts
- Recent tax returns
- Utility bills/payment history

7 Inspection and Compliance

- Recent inspection reports
- Certificates of compliance
- Environmental reports (if applicable)

8 Insurance

- Insurance policies
- Proof of insurance payments
- Claims history

9 Miscellaneous

- Blueprints/floor plans
- Property title and deed
- Permits and licenses
- Property tax records
- Utility account numbers/transfer procedures

2.5 BUILDING LONG-TERM WEALTH STRATEGIES

2.5.1 Ethical Investing: Doing Well by Doing Good

Ethical investing in real estate transcends the mere act of buying and selling properties for profit. It involves a commitment to making decisions that yield financial returns, contribute positively to society, and adhere to high standards of integrity and responsibility. This approach centers on sustainability, community impact, and corporate responsibility, turning each investment decision into a stepping stone toward personal wealth, communal well-being, and environmental stewardship. As a real estate investor, embracing ethical practices means you are not just an investor but also a custodian of the community and the environment.

The long-term benefits of ethical investing are profound and multifaceted. By prioritizing ethical behavior in your investment choices, you build trust with stakeholders—tenants, community members, business partners, and financial backers. This trust is invaluable, as it forms the foundation of lasting business relationships and opens doors to future opportunities. Moreover, ethical investing enhances your reputation in the real estate community, distinguishing you as a conscientious investor committed to positive outcomes. This reputation can be a significant asset, attracting like-minded investors and partners who share your values and are eager to support or participate in your projects.

Furthermore, ethical real estate practices contribute to building stronger, healthier communities. Investing in properties and supporting initiatives that improve neighborhood conditions, provide fair housing, and respect tenants' rights helps foster social cohesion and community spirit. These contributions are noticed; they can enhance the area's desirability, leading to increased property values and a more vibrant local economy. Additionally, ethical investing helps you avoid legal problems arising from non-compliance with housing laws and regulations, ensuring smoother operations and protecting your investments from potential legal liabilities.

Balancing profitability with ethical practices is both an art and a science. It requires a strategic approach that integrates ethical considerations into every aspect of the investment process. One effective strategy is investing in green buildings or properties that offer the potential for energy savings. These investments contribute to environmental sustainability and provide economic benefits through lower operating costs and potential tax incentives. Improving existing properties to meet high ethical and environmental standards can also attract a niche market of eco-conscious tenants, allowing you to command higher rents and ensuring your properties stand out in the competitive real estate market.

However, ethical investing can sometimes present dilemmas, such as the challenge of gentrification. While revitalizing distressed areas can yield substantial returns, it may also lead to the displacement of long-time residents if handled more carefully. Navigating such dilemmas requires a nuanced approach that considers both the economic benefits and the social impacts of your investment decisions. Engaging with community stakeholders and seeking win-win solutions that provide both profitability and community benefits is vital. For instance, consider partaking in or initiating community development programs supporting affordable housing or providing local residents with job training.

Building a reputation as an ethical investor is more than adhering to the minimum standards required by law. It involves actively promoting transparency, fairness, and responsibility in every transaction and interaction. Marketing your ethical investments can attract tenants and investors who support your values. Highlighting energy efficiency, community engagement initiatives, or fair housing practices in your marketing materials can differentiate your properties and attract a loyal base of tenants and investors.

In conclusion, ethical investing in real estate offers a pathway to build wealth that is not only financial but also social and environmental. By adhering to fairness, transparency, and community responsibility principles, you create a portfolio that yields returns and contributes positively to society. This approach enriches your investment experience, providing both monetary rewards and the satisfaction of knowing that your investment choices are helping to make the world a better place. As you continue to explore and implement ethical investment strategies, remember that each decision reflects your values and shapes your impact on the world around you.

2.5.2 Sustainability and Green Investments in Real Estate

In the rapidly evolving real estate landscape, sustainability has transitioned from a niche interest to a central property development and management strategy. The growing emphasis on environmental responsibility reflects broader societal changes, where consumers and businesses are increasingly aware of their decisions' impacts on the planet. This shift is not just about goodwill; it's about making strategic investments that ensure long-term profitability and resilience. By integrating sustainable practices into your real estate investments, you contribute to environmental conservation and tap into a market of eco-conscious tenants and buyers, broadening your investment appeal.

Investing in properties with green certifications or potential for energy savings is becoming a surefire strategy to enhance asset value and attract a premium market segment. Certifications such as LEED (Leadership in Energy and Environmental Design) or BREEAM (Building Research Establishment Environmental Assessment Method) serve as badges of efficiency and sustainability that are recognized globally. These certifications involve a rigorous process that assesses a building's performance across several criteria, including energy efficiency, water usage, and material sourcing. Properties that achieve these certifications often benefit from reduced operational costs, higher rental rates, and increased occupancy levels, collectively contributing to a more substantial, stable cash flow.

The benefits of green buildings extend beyond immediate financial gains. They often enjoy higher resale values, reflecting the growing demand among buyers for homes and offices that promise lower utility costs and healthier living environments. For instance, a U.S. Green Building Council study indicated that LEED-certified buildings consistently achieve higher lease rates and have lower vacancy rates than non-certified counterparts. This trend underscores the market's recognition of the value added by sustainable design and technology.

Government incentives play a pivotal role in promoting sustainable investments. Many local, state, and federal programs offer tax benefits, rebates, or grants to property owners who implement energy-efficient upgrades or construct green buildings. These incentives reduce the initial cost burden associated with green initiatives and shorten the payback period, making sustainable investments more attractive. For example, the Energy Efficient Commercial Buildings Tax Deduction in the United States allows property owners to claim a deduction for part of the expenses incurred in enhancing the energy efficiency of buildings. Navigating these incentives requires a proactive approach to staying informed about the latest programs and understanding how to effectively qualify for and capitalize on these opportunities.

As the real estate market continues to develop, integrating sustainability into your investment strategy is not just an ethical decision—it's a financial one. By aligning your investments with the principles of sustainability, you position yourself at the forefront of a growing trend that promises to preserve the environment and enhance the profitability and resilience of your real estate portfolio. Embracing green investments will set the stage for future growth, ensuring your real estate ventures remain viable and valuable in an increasingly eco-conscious market.

2.5.3 Reflecting on Your Real Estate Journey and Preparing for What's Next

As you navigate the often-moving waters of real estate investing, reflecting on your experiences is beneficial and essential for growth and improvement. Reflecting on your investment journey allows you to pause and assess the successes and milestones achieved and the challenges and obstacles encountered along the way. This reflective process is crucial for identifying valuable lessons and strategizing future moves in the dynamic real estate market.

Begin by revisiting the goals you initially set when you first ventured into real estate investing. What were your aspirations? Were they to generate a stable passive income, achieve financial independence, or perhaps restore and flip distressed properties? Assess how closely your achievements align with these objectives. Celebrate the successes, whether your first profitable flip, a fully leased rental property, or simply overcoming your initial apprehensions about entering the market. Equally important, however, is to scrutinize the setbacks. A property didn't sell as quickly as anticipated, or unexpected maintenance issues eroded a significant portion of your profits. Each of these scenarios provides a rich seam of insights that, when carefully analyzed, can fortify your investment strategies moving forward.

Setting new goals is a dynamic process that should adapt to your evolving financial landscape and the broader economic environment. As you gain experience and expand your portfolio, your capacity for more significant or complex investments may increase. Alternatively, shifts in the market, such as changes in mortgage rates or property values, might open new opportunities or necessitate a shift in focus. When setting these new goals, ensure they are Specific, Measurable, Achievable, Relevant, and Time-bound (SMART.) This specificity keeps you focused and makes it easier to track your progress and make adjustments as needed. For instance, if your initial investments were predominantly residential properties, now is the time to explore commercial real estate or delve into Real Estate Investment Trusts (REITs.)

Embracing change and innovation in the real estate sector is vital for maintaining the relevance and profitability of your investments. The real estate market is continually evolving, influenced by technological changes, consumer behavior, and regulatory environments. Staying abreast of these changes and adapting your strategies accordingly is crucial. It might mean investing in Property Technology (PropTech) to enhance operational efficiencies or exploring emerging markets with growth potential. For example, the increasing popularity of remote work has spurred interest in suburban residential properties and office spaces that accommodate new work norms. Being open to such trends and willing to innovate can position you at a competitive advantage.

Planning for succession or preparing for an eventual exit from real estate investing is another critical consideration. Whether you're looking to retire, shift your investment focus, or cash out, having a clear exit strategy is essential. This planning involves several vital decisions—whether to sell your properties outright, pass them on to heirs, or convert them into other forms of investments. Each option has implications for your financial planning, tax obligations, and legacy. For instance, if choosing to pass on your assets to heirs, consider the legal and financial preparations needed, such as establishing trusts or structuring ownership transfers to minimize tax liabilities. If selling, timing the market to maximize returns can be crucial. Also, consider consulting with financial advisors to explore ways of reinvesting the proceeds to ensure continued income post-exit. (Read more in Chapter 2.6.)

2.5.3.1 When to Scale Your Real Estate Investments

Scaling your real estate investments is a pivotal decision that requires careful consideration of both market conditions and your readiness. Initially, the choice between active and passive investment strategies forms the foundation of your investment approach. Active management often involves direct involvement in day-to-day operations, from managing properties to executing renovation projects. This hands-on approach can be advantageous, offering greater control over your investments and the potential for higher returns. However, it demands significant time, effort, and expertise. On the other hand, passive real estate investments, such as investing in Real Estate Investment Trusts (REITs) or using property management companies, provide a less labor-intensive way to access real estate markets. While potentially offering lower returns, this approach allows you to diversify your investments without the need for daily oversight, ideal for those with limited time or desire to manage properties directly.

Identifying the right time to scale your investments is crucial. Key indicators include stabilized cash flow, which suggests that your current investments are generating steady, reliable income, and the presence of new market opportunities, such as emerging neighborhoods or sectors poised for growth. Additionally, reaching specific financial milestones, such as achieving a target return on investment across your portfolio, can signal readiness to expand. It's essential to evaluate both economic conditions—ensuring the market dynamics support expansion—and personal readiness, assessing whether you have the necessary resources and infrastructure to effectively manage a more extensive portfolio.

Long-term financial planning is integral to successful real estate investment, particularly as you scale. Integrating real estate into broader economic planning involves considerations such as estate planning and tax strategies. Real estate can be significant in achieving financial security and independence, providing ongoing income and potential for substantial capital gains. Real estate planning ensures that your assets develop according to your wishes and can provide ongoing benefits to your heirs. Meanwhile, effective tax planning can help maximize the profitability of your investments, taking advantage of any available deductions and credits to minimize liability and enhance returns.

As your portfolio grows, so does its complexity. Managing multiple properties or dealing with diverse types of real estate investments can introduce challenges such as increased administrative duties and higher financial risk. Employing property management services or investing in advanced property management software can mitigate these challenges, helping to streamline operations and maintain efficiency. These tools and services can handle everything from tenant screening and lease management to maintenance scheduling and financial reporting, allowing you to focus on strategic decision-making rather than day-to-day management tasks.

Risk management is another critical aspect of scaling your real estate investments. Maintaining a balanced approach to risk becomes increasingly important as your portfolio expands. Regular risk assessments can help identify potential vulnerabilities within your portfolio, from market fluctuations to property-specific issues such as unexpected maintenance needs or vacancy rates. Revisiting and adjusting your risk management strategies regularly, at least once a year, ensures you are prepared to respond to changes and protect your investments. Techniques such as diversification by property type, geographic location, or investment method can also help spread risk and stabilize returns across your portfolio.

To illustrate successful scaling, consider the case of a real estate investor who began with a single residential rental property and expanded over several years to own multiple commercial buildings. By reinvesting profits from the initial residential rentals into commercial properties in emerging markets, the investor increased the portfolio's value significantly. The investor also implemented advanced property management software to maintain efficiency and employed a professional property management firm to handle day-to-day operations. This allowed the investor to focus on strategic growth and market analysis.

Estate planning and legacy building are also integral to scaling your real estate investments. By establishing legal structures such as trusts or Limited

Liability Companies (LLCs), you can ensure that your real estate assets are managed according to your long-term goals, potentially reducing tax liabilities and facilitating the transfer of assets to heirs. This strategic planning protects your investments and helps build a lasting legacy, ensuring that your real estate success contributes to future generations' financial well-being.

2.5.3.2 Strategies for Achieving Financial Independence through Real Estate

Scaling your real estate investments is akin to nurturing a garden. It requires patience, foresight, and strategic nurturing. As you contemplate expanding your real estate portfolio, several strategies can be implemented to ensure growth that aligns with your financial independence goals. Reinvesting profits, securing additional financing, and forming strategic partnerships are pivotal tactics, each with unique advantages and considerations.

Reinvesting profits is a fundamental strategy that leverages the success of your existing investments to fuel further growth. This approach embodies the principle of compounding returns, where property income is reinvested into purchasing additional assets or upgrading existing ones. For instance, surplus cash from rental income could be used to renovate a property, increasing its value and rental yield. Alternatively, these funds could be used as a down payment for another property, expanding your investment base. The essential advantage here is the use of internal funds, which mitigates the need for external borrowing and the associated debt risks. However, disciplined cash flow management is required to ensure operational expenses and emergency funds are not compromised.

Understanding and leveraging the principles of profit reinvestment can drastically influence the growth trajectory of your portfolio when implementing these strategies. Decisions on when and where to reinvest profits should be guided by thorough market analysis, investment performance assessments, and future financial projections to ensure that each reinvestment contributes to portfolio growth and does not overly expose you to market volatility.

Securing additional financing is another robust strategy to accelerate portfolio growth. It might involve traditional mortgages, lines of credit, or newer financing models such as crowdfunding. Each financing method has its intricacies. For example, a mortgage might offer lower interest rates but typically requires substantial equity and a good credit score. Crowdfunding, while more accessible and flexible, might come with higher costs or profit sharing. It's crucial to assess the terms and conditions of these financing options to ensure they align with your risk tolerance and investment strategy.

Strategic partnerships can also significantly impact your scaling efforts. These partnerships could be with other investors, investment groups, or companies that bring additional resources, expertise, or market access that you might not have independently. For example, partnering with a construction firm could facilitate property development projects. In contrast, a partnership with a property management firm could enhance the operational efficiency of your rental properties. The primary advantage of strategic alliances lies in shared risk and enhanced capacity for larger projects. However, they require aligned interests, clear role delineations, and robust legal agreements to prevent conflicts.

Moreover, leveraging income-generating properties effectively is crucial in building a sustainable and expanding investment portfolio. Rental properties, particularly those in high-demand areas, can provide steady, predictable income streams. To optimize the income-generating potential of these properties, conduct regular market analyses to ensure your rents are competitive yet profitable. Additionally, consider implementing value-add strategies such as property improvements or amenities enhancements to justify higher rents and attract long-term tenants.

Leveraging equity for growth is a strategy employed by many seasoned investors. As your properties increase in value and you pay down mortgage debts, the equity in your portfolio increases. This equity can be accessed through methods such as HELOCs or cash-out refinances, providing you with capital that can be reinvested into buying more properties. While this approach can significantly accelerate portfolio expansion, it also increases your debt exposure, making it imperative to manage this strategy judiciously. Ensure that any debt incurred can be comfortably serviced by your portfolio's cash flow and maintain a buffer against market downturns. (Read more about HELOCs in Chapter 2.6.2.)

Utilizing leverage wisely is the most delicate balance in real estate investing. While leverage can multiply your investment capacity and returns, it also amplifies risks. Develop a clear understanding of how much debt is manageable for your portfolio. Avoid over-leveraging, which could jeopardize your financial stability. Monitor market conditions closely, as shifts in interest rates or economic downturns can impact your debt servicing ability.

Advanced tax strategies also play a crucial role in enhancing your real estate investments' long-term growth and sustainability. Techniques such as depreciation, which allows you to improve a property or deduct the costs of buying, can significantly reduce your tax burden, improving cash flow and profitability. Also, strategies like 1031 exchanges can defer capital gains taxes, freeing up more capital for reinvestment. These tax strategies require careful planning and compliance with complex regulations, so consult with real estate professionals to ensure you maximize your tax benefits while using legal requirements. (Read more in Chapter 4.4.4.4.)

By embracing these strategies, you are not just passively investing in real estate but actively shaping a portfolio that can sustain and grow your wealth, bringing you closer to financial independence. Each decision, from reinvesting profits to leveraging financial instruments, should be made with a strategic vision and an acute awareness of the market dynamics and personal financial goals. This proactive approach ensures that your real estate investments grow and thrive, providing you with a robust economic foundation to support your aspirations and future ventures in real estate.

2.5.4 Diversification Strategies of Your Investment Portfolio

Diversification can be achieved in several ways in real estate investing, and it's a strategy that promises long-term benefits. Proper management, regular reviews of your investment portfolio, and adjustments based on market conditions are necessary to maximize the benefits of diversification.

In real estate investing, diversification is not just a strategy; it's a prudent approach to safeguarding your investments against unforeseen market fluctuations and economic downturns. The benefits of diversifying your real estate portfolio are manifold. By spreading your investments across different investment strategies, geographical locations, types of properties, and markets, you reduce the risk that a single failed investment could adversely affect your overall financial health.

2.5.4.1 Different Investment Strategies

Combining strategies like buy-and-hold, where you invest in properties for long-term appreciation and rental income, with fix-and-flip, where you renovate properties and sell them for a quick profit, can balance your cash flow. While buy-and-hold provides steady, ongoing income, fix-and-flip offers quick returns on investment, which can be particularly useful for funding further investments or covering unexpected expenses. Balancing rental income or flipping properties with equity investments in REITs or real estate funds can provide multiple income streams and reduce reliance on a single source of income. (Read more in Chapter 5.3.)

2.5.4.2 Geographical Diversification

Another layer is geographical diversification, where you invest in properties in different cities or regions. This strategy mitigates risks associated with local economic downturns or property market crashes. For instance, while a town might experience a decline in property values due to a local economic setback, another might thrive and thus balance your portfolio's overall performance. Different markets have varying cycles; a slump in one can be offset by a boom in another, stabilizing your income flow and ensuring continued profitability over the years.

2.5.4.3 Different Types of Properties

One method involves varying the types of properties in your portfolio. It can include a mix of residential, commercial, industrial, and even special-purpose properties like hotels or storage units. Each type of property reacts differently to economic changes. For example, during an economic downturn, residential properties might still perform relatively well due to the constant demand for housing, whereas commercial properties might suffer due to businesses scaling down or shutting down. By including a mix, you can ensure that the underperformance of one type can be balanced by the stable or exemplary performance of another, thereby mitigating risks and maximizing your overall returns.

2.5.4.4 The Need for Careful Planning

However, effective diversification requires careful planning and market research. It's crucial to deeply understand the dynamics of different markets and property types. Engaging with local real estate experts and conducting thorough market analysis are essential steps to identifying lucrative opportunities. This might involve analyzing historical market data, understanding the demographic trends of each area, and staying updated with future development plans that could affect property values.

Implementing a diversification strategy requires a systematic approach. While diversification is a powerful strategy to mitigate risk, it's essential to manage it wisely to avoid overdoing it. The ultimate goal is to enjoy life, manage your investments, and have a good family life and health, inspiring you to make the most of your investments.

Begin by assessing your current real estate holdings to identify any concentrations in specific property types or locations. This assessment will help you understand where there might be potential vulnerabilities or opportunities for diversification. Next, research new markets and property types that complement your portfolio. Consider factors such as economic growth, population trends, and real estate market cycles that could influence the potential success of these investments. Evaluating the risks and returns of each new opportunity. Each investment should be evaluated on its merits, and the overall compatibility with your financial goals and risk tolerance should be considered.

In conclusion, diversification is a powerful strategy for managing risk and enhancing the potential returns of your real estate investment portfolio. By creating multiple income streams through various property types and investment strategies and spreading your investments across different geographic locations, you build a robust portfolio that can withstand market variability and generate sustainable income. As you expand your real estate investments, remember that diversification, continual monitoring, and strategic adjustments are vital to achieving long-term success and financial security in the dynamic world of real estate.

As we close this chapter on diversification strategies, reflect on how these approaches can be integrated into your broader investment plan to build a resilient and profitable real estate portfolio. In the next chapter, we explore exit strategies for real estate investors, providing insights on strategically transitioning out of investments to maximize returns and prepare for future opportunities.

2.6 EXIT STRATEGIES FOR REAL ESTATE INVESTORS

2.6.1 Refinancing

In the complex dance of real estate investing, refinancing is not merely a step but often a strategic leap toward greater financial flexibility and efficiency. Imagine you are several years into a mortgage with high interest rates that were the norm when you secured your initial loan. The market has shifted, and lower rates are now available. It presents a prime opportunity to decrease monthly payments and increase cash flow. Refinancing in such scenarios isn't just beneficial; it's financially astute, allowing you to adapt to new market conditions while better positioning your investment for future growth.

Refinancing can be a pivotal exit strategy from more burdensome financial commitments tied to real estate investments. By renegotiating the terms of your existing mortgage, you can potentially secure lower interest rates, reduce your monthly payment obligations, or alter the loan's term. These adjustments can free up significant monthly cash, providing liquidity for other investments or expenses. For example, suppose you initially secured a mortgage at a 6 % interest rate and refinance to a 4 % rate. In that case, the savings on a substantial loan can be impactful, enhancing your investment's profitability and sustainability.

Beyond immediate cash flow improvements, refinancing can also be strategically used to extract equity from your property, which can be particularly valuable if your property's value has increased significantly since the purchase. This process, often called a cash-out refinance, involves taking out a new mortgage for a more significant amount than what you owe and pocketing the difference in cash. This cash can be used to reinvest in the market by purchasing additional properties or renovating existing ones to boost their value and rental income potential. It's a method seasoned investors often use to leverage their portfolios without selling their assets, continuously cycling their equity into new opportunities.

However, the decision to refinance should be approached meticulously, considering the associated costs and implications. Refinancing is not free; it comes with closing costs, appraisal fees, and potentially other expenses that can add up to a significant amount. Therefore, it's crucial to calculate whether the potential savings outweigh these costs. Typically, a rule of thumb is that refinancing is worthwhile if you can reduce your interest rate by at least 1 %. Yet, every investor's situation varies, and the threshold for refinancing profitability depends on factors such as the remaining loan balance, the new terms being offered, and your strategic financial goals.

Moreover, refinancing offers a strategic avenue to adjust the loan term, which can align more closely with your long-term investment strategies. For example, extending the term of your loan can further reduce your monthly payments, freeing up cash for investments that offer higher returns. Conversely, shortening the loan term while increasing monthly payments can reduce the interest amount significantly over the life of the loan, increasing your equity buildup speed. This strategy can be especially beneficial if you plan to sell the property in the future, as it allows you to maximize your profit by reducing the debt against it.

Navigating the refinancing process requires working with lending professionals who can offer insights and competitive options. The right lender can make the process smoother and more beneficial by providing favorable terms that match your financial outlook and investment strategy. They can also help you navigate the often complex landscape of loan products and terms, ensuring you make choices that align with your immediate financial needs and long-term investment objectives.

Refinancing is not just about finding a way to ease your financial burden in the short term. When used wisely, it is a strategic tool that can reshape your investment portfolio, enhance your property's profitability, and align your real estate holdings with your broader financial landscape. It offers a pathway to transform the equity locked in real estate into capital that can be actively used to pursue further growth opportunities, optimize cash flows, and ensure the sustainability of your investments in the ever-evolving real estate market. As you consider your next moves in the real estate arena, think of refinancing not just as a financial adjustment but as a strategic maneuver that can significantly influence the trajectory of your investment career. (Read more about options and strategies in Chapter 4.1.8.)

2.6.2 Equity Release Options

Another powerful strategy involves the release of equity built up in real estate over the years. Options such as reverse mortgages or Home Equity Lines Of Credit (HELOC) can convert part of your home's equity into cash, providing funds to supplement retirement income. A reverse mortgage, suitable for homeowners who are 62 years or older, allows you to borrow against the equity in your home, with no requirement to pay the loan back until the house is sold or the homeowner passes away. This option can provide monthly payments or a lump sum that can be instrumental in covering living expenses and medical costs, as well as funding leisure activities in retirement.

On the other hand, a HELOC provides a line of credit based on your home's equity, offering flexibility to draw funds as needed. It can be beneficial for covering unexpected expenses or investing in opportunities that arise during retirement. However, it's crucial to consider the implications of such decisions; for instance, a HELOC requires periodic interest payments, and failing to meet these payments can risk home ownership. Each option carries specific benefits and risks, and choosing the right one, considering your financial situation, risk tolerance, and personal preferences, is critical to a successful retirement plan. (Read more about HELOC in Chapter 4.1.1.4.)

2.6.3 Real Estate as a Retirement Strategy

Envisioning your golden years often brings thoughts of relaxation and leisure. Yet, the foundation for a comfortable retirement is built on effective financial planning. Real estate investments are an exceptionally robust vehicle for securing a stable retirement, offering multiple strategies to generate ongoing income or liquidate assets for economic needs. As you approach retirement, understanding how to leverage real estate can ensure that your investments provide financial security when regular employment income ceases.

2.6.3.1 Real Estate for Retirement Income

Real estate investments can create a steady income stream through rental properties, which is invaluable during retirement. The key to success in this strategy lies in meticulous planning and execution. Initially, the focus should be on acquiring properties in locations with strong, long-term rental demand—areas close to hospitals, universities, or major employment centers are typically resilient to market fluctuations. Once these properties are secured, effective property management becomes crucial. It might involve hiring a property management firm to handle day-to-day operations, ensuring you can enjoy retirement without the burden of ongoing property issues. Over time, these properties can not only provide a regular income. Still, they may also appreciate in value, offering the option for a profitable sale in the future.

Many retirees aim to have their properties paid off by the retirement phase, drastically reducing the risk and ensuring that rental income is primarily profit. Consider the scenario where you acquire a rental property during your working years with a 20-year mortgage. By planning strategically, you could align the final mortgage payment with your retirement date, ensuring that the property generates net positive cash flow when you need it most. This kind of forward-thinking approach, where strategic planning aligns the mortgage payment with retirement, exemplifies how real estate can be tailored to meet long-term financial goals, making it a cornerstone of retirement planning.

2.6.3.2 Downsizing or Rightsizing in Retirement

As retirement approaches, you may find that your housing needs have changed. The family home that was once bustling with activity may now be too large, with maintenance becoming more burdensome. Downsizing—or rightsizing—to a smaller home or a different location can reduce these burdens while unlocking equity from your primary residence. This transition involves several critical considerations. Financially, the goal is to maximize the equity from selling your current home, potentially purchasing a less expensive property outright, and using the remaining funds to bolster your retirement savings. It involves selecting a property that meets your current and future needs, considering factors like accessibility, proximity to healthcare, and community activities.

Rightsizing can lead to significant cost savings on utilities, taxes, and upkeep, allowing for a more manageable and financially sustainable lifestyle in retirement. Additionally, moving to a community designed for retirees can offer social opportunities and amenities that enhance the quality of life during your golden years. This strategy optimizes your living situation and adjusts your investment portfolio to better suit your current lifestyle, ensuring that you continue to live comfortably and within your means. The benefits of such a move, including the potential for a more active and engaging lifestyle, should not be overlooked.

2.6.4 Estate Planning and Real Estate

Real estate also plays a vital role in estate planning, ensuring that assets are transferred according to your wishes while potentially minimizing estate taxes. Proper estate planning with real estate involves several important elements. First, understanding the implications of how your properties are titled is crucial. Properties can be owned in ways that allow for the seamless transfer to a spouse or heirs upon your passing, such as through joint tenancy or a living trust. Each method has specific legal and tax implications, affecting how real estate contributions to your overall estate value are calculated and taxed.

Furthermore, real estate can be leveraged to provide for your heirs while minimizing tax liabilities. For instance, gifting real estate assets to heirs during your lifetime can reduce estate taxes while allowing you to see the benefits of your generosity. However, consulting with estate planning professionals is essential to navigate the complex tax regulations and legal structures that best suit your personal and financial circumstances. Properly structured, real estate can be a lasting legacy that supports your family for generations, providing them with economic stability and investment opportunities.

2.6.4.1 Succession Planning for Real Estate Investors

Understanding the importance of succession planning cannot be overstated for real estate investors who view their portfolios as more than just assets but as a long-term wealth-building strategy to secure financial stability for themselves and their families. The essence of this planning lies in its ability to ensure that your investments continue to yield benefits, even when you are no longer at the helm. Through effective succession planning, you can lay a foundation that supports your heirs, ensuring that the wealth accumulated through diligent investment does not dissipate but continues to grow and serve future generations. It is a proactive approach to safeguarding and transferring your life's work, reflecting your vision and care for your family's well-being beyond your lifetime.

When considering options for succession, the choices can vary widely depending on your circumstances and the nature of your real estate holdings. One common approach is directly passing assets to heirs, which might seem straightforward but requires careful handling to mitigate potential conflicts and ensure equitable distribution. Selling the portfolio is another option, particularly appealing if your heirs are not interested in managing real estate or if the market conditions are favorable for a sale. This method converts your investments into liquid capital that can be redistributed according to your estate plans. Alternatively, setting up a trust can offer a structured way to manage and distribute your real estate assets. Trusts can provide tax benefits and greater control over how and when the assets are distributed. It can be crucial for minimizing estate taxes and providing for minors or family members with specific needs.

Each of these options carries its own set of implications, both financially and relationally. Passing assets directly might trigger significant tax liabilities for your heirs, while selling the portfolio could result in capital gains taxes. Trusts, while offering more control and potential tax advantages, require the involvement of legal professionals and incur management fees. These financial implications must be weighed alongside your family's goals and capabilities. Direct transfer or trusts might be preferable if your heirs are keen and capable of continuing your investment endeavors. However, if liquidity or simplicity is a priority, selling the portfolio could be optimal.

The legal and financial preparations necessary for effective succession planning are complex and require meticulous attention to detail. Engaging with experienced legal professionals to draft or update your will and establish any essential trusts is crucial. These legal structures must be carefully designed to comply with state laws and accurately reflect your wishes. Financial considerations include assessing the tax implications of different succession options and planning accordingly to minimize the tax burden on your estate and your heirs. It might involve strategies like utilizing the annual gift tax exclusion or setting up charitable remainder trusts. Additionally, it's essential to keep detailed records of all your real estate transactions, as these will be invaluable in providing clarity and supporting the legal processes involved in transferring ownership.

Preparing your heirs to manage and own your real estate investments is one of the most challenging aspects of succession planning. It involves educating them about the fundamentals of real estate investing and gradually involving them in managing your properties. It could start with small responsibilities, such as assisting with property inspections or tenant communications, and progressively increase to more significant roles, ensuring they gain the confidence and skills needed to manage the portfolio effectively. It's also important to foster open discussions about the future of the investments, aligning the family's goals and expectations. These conversations can provide valuable insights into each heir's interests and capabilities, guiding how responsibilities and assets might be distributed. Moreover, addressing the emotional and relational dynamics that come with wealth transfer is essential. Family meetings, possibly facilitated by a counselor or mediator, can help address any concerns or conflicts, ensuring that the transition strengthens rather than strains family bonds.

In essence, succession planning for real estate investors is not merely a legal or financial process but a holistic approach to ensuring that your investments continue to benefit your loved ones according to your wishes. By carefully considering the options, engaging with professionals, and preparing your heirs, you can create a legacy that supports and enriches your family for future generations.

2.6.5 Knowing When to Sell Your Real Estate Investment

Navigating the decision to sell a real estate investment requires a nuanced understanding of your financial landscape and the broader market environment. It's a decision that can significantly impact your financial well-being, so it's crucial to approach it with a strategic mindset. Reflect on your personal and financial circumstances—changes such as a shift in your risk tolerance, alterations in life circumstances, or a need to liquidate assets for retirement can all influence your decision to sell. For instance, you might find that reallocating assets into less volatile investments becomes more appealing as you approach retirement, prompting the sale of specific properties. Aligning your real estate strategy with your broader financial plan ensures that investment decisions support your overall financial goals, enhancing your economic stability and growth.

Understanding the life cycle of a real estate investment is essential to recognizing when a property has reached its peak potential and is ripe for sale. Typically, a property's life cycle includes acquisition, value addition (through improvements or market appreciation), and eventual sale when the market conditions are favorable or when the property no longer aligns with your investment strategy. Key indicators such as aging infrastructure, escalating maintenance costs, or shifts in neighborhood dynamics can signal that a property may be nearing the optimal point for sale. For example, if an area is experiencing a decline, selling before the market bottoms out can protect you from future losses. On the other hand, recognizing a neighborhood on the rise can allow you to time your sale to maximize returns. This potential for maximizing returns through strategic timing should motivate you to stay informed and make the most of your real estate investments.

Market timing and understanding economic indicators are pivotal in deciding when to sell. Assessing market conditions such as high demand, rising property prices, and favorable interest rates can inform the timing of your sale to optimize financial outcomes. Keeping up to date with local and national real estate trends through reliable real estate market analysis reports and economic forecasts enables you to anticipate market shifts. For instance, if economic indicators suggest an upcoming downturn, selling properties that could lose significant value during a recession might be wise. Conversely, if the market is robust and prices are climbing, holding off on selling to benefit from further appreciation could be advantageous. Recognizing signs of market peaks or impending downturns, such as sudden spikes in property prices or significant increases in interest rates, can also guide your decision-making process.

Evaluating the performance of your property is critical in determining its readiness for sale. Analyze key metrics such as cash flow, capital appreciation, and Return On Investment (ROI) to assess how the property performs against your initial investment goals. For instance, if a property's cash flow has consistently declined despite market appreciation, it might be time to consider selling and reinvesting in a more profitable venture. A structured framework for this analysis involves comparing current performance metrics with the targets set at the investment's inception and with the potential performance of alternative investments. This comprehensive evaluation informs your decision to sell and helps strategize future investments more effectively.

Preparing your property for sale is crucial to attract buyers and secure the best price. Start with enhancing the property's curb appeal through landscaping and exterior improvements, which can significantly influence first impressions. Minor upgrades, such as repainting or updating fixtures, can refresh the property without necessitating substantial investment. Beautifying the interior to highlight its best features can also be important in attracting offers. But it's not just about the property itself-professional photography and strategic marketing are essential to showcase the property effectively to potential buyers. This comprehensive approach will give you confidence in the selling process, knowing that your property is being presented in the best possible light. Employing a mix of online listings, virtual tours, and traditional marketing methods broadens your reach. It increases your chances of a successful sale.

Selecting the right selling strategy is integral to the process. Using a real estate agent can provide expertise and facilitate negotiations. Opting for a sale by auction might attract a quick sale at a competitive price. Alternatively, selling directly to an investor or through For-Sale-by-Owner (FSO) arrangements can reduce commissions and give you more control over the sale process. Each strategy has its merits and should be chosen based on your specific situation, the property type, and market conditions.

Effective negotiation is the final step in securing favorable sale terms. Prepare to negotiate on price, closing costs, and timelines. Being open to negotiation and prepared to make concessions can facilitate a smoother transaction. However, it's essential to have clear boundaries and a minimum acceptable offer in mind. Handling counteroffers with patience and strategic concessions can lead to a successful sale that benefits all parties involved.

Navigating the closing process requires attention to detail and adherence to legal requirements. Ensure all necessary documentation is accurately prepared and that you comply with all legal and regulatory requirements. Transparency with buyers about the property's condition and history can prevent post-sale disputes and foster a positive transaction environment. By meticulously managing these aspects, you can ensure a smooth and successful property sale, paving the way for your next investment opportunity.

In conclusion, real estate offers a versatile and practical suite of strategies for retirement planning. Whether generating passive income, releasing equity for financial flexibility, rightsizing for practical living, or planning your estate, real estate investments can be tailored to support a comfortable and secure retirement. By understanding and utilizing these strategies effectively, you can ensure that your real estate investments continue to provide substantial benefits throughout your retirement years.

2.6.5.1 Lease-to-Own: A Win-Win Exit Strategy

Lease-to-own agreements represent a strategic bridge between renting and owning, providing unique benefits and flexibility to property owners and tenants aspiring to become homeowners. In essence, a lease-to-own agreement is a contract in which you, as the property owner (lessor), allow a tenant (lessee) to rent your property with the option to purchase it at the end of a specified rental period. This agreement typically includes three critical financial components: an option fee, rent premiums, and a set purchase price. The option fee, usually a percentage of the purchase price, is paid upfront by the tenant to secure their purchase option. This fee is often non-refundable but may be credited towards the purchase price if the tenant decides to buy the property. Rent premiums are additional amounts on top of the regular rent, also credited toward the purchase price, contributing to building equity for the tenant over the rental period. Finally, the purchase price is agreed upon at the beginning of the lease, providing price certainty for the tenant and a guaranteed sale price for you as the owner.

From a seller's perspective, lease-to-own arrangements offer several compelling advantages:

- They provide a steady cash flow from rental payments, which can cover mortgage costs or generate income.
- Because tenants interested in eventual ownership will likely maintain the property well, this arrangement can lead to lower maintenance and management costs. Another significant benefit is the potential for a higher sales price, as tenants are often willing to pay a premium for the opportunity to own the home they are renting.
- These agreements can attract a broader pool of potential buyers, including those who may not currently qualify for traditional mortgage financing but are likely to qualify by the end of the lease term.

For buyers, lease-to-own agreements offer the invaluable advantage of locking a purchase price at today's market rate, protecting them against future price increases. This setup allows tenants to build equity through rent premiums while improving their credit scores and saving for a down payment, all while living in the property they may eventually own. Such arrangements also allow buyers to familiarize themselves with the property and the neighborhood before committing to a purchase, reducing the risk of buyer's remorse.

Setting terms that protect both parties' interests is crucial when structuring a lease-to-own agreement. Negotiating a fair option fee and determining realistic rent premiums are essential to ensure equitable agreement. Setting a purchase price that reflects a fair market prediction for the property at the end of the lease term also requires careful consideration and market analysis. Furthermore, including clear legal terms and contingencies in the contract can prevent misunderstandings and protect your interests and the tenants. It is advisable to consult with a real estate attorney to ensure all legalities are appropriately addressed.

While lease-to-own agreements offer numerous benefits, they also come with potential risks. One of the primary concerns is the possibility of the tenant choosing not to exercise the purchase option. This outcome can be due to various factors, such as changes in the market conditions, the tenant's circumstances, or the property's condition. If the tenant opts not to buy, you may need to restart the process of finding another buyer, which could involve additional time and expense. To mitigate this risk, thorough tenant screening and a well-structured agreement are critical. Ensure tenants have a genuine interest in ownership and the financial capability to follow through with the purchase. Clear communication about the terms and conditions of the lease-to-own agreement is essential to align expectations and foster a successful relationship between you and the tenant.

In conclusion, lease-to-own agreements can serve as an effective exit strategy for real estate investors, benefiting both sellers and buyers. For sellers, these agreements offer stable income, the potential for higher sale prices, and quality maintenance from committed tenants. For buyers, they provide a path to homeownership with financial flexibility and the opportunity to lock in purchase prices. When structured and managed carefully, lease-to-own agreements can be a win-win solution, facilitating property sales while helping tenants achieve their homeownership dreams.

In the next chapter, we will explore the crucial aspects of market analysis techniques, further enhancing your ability to make informed investment decisions based on solid, actionable data.

MARKET ANALYSIS TECHNIQUES

"Success in real estate requires learning from the past, adapting to the present, and planning for the future."

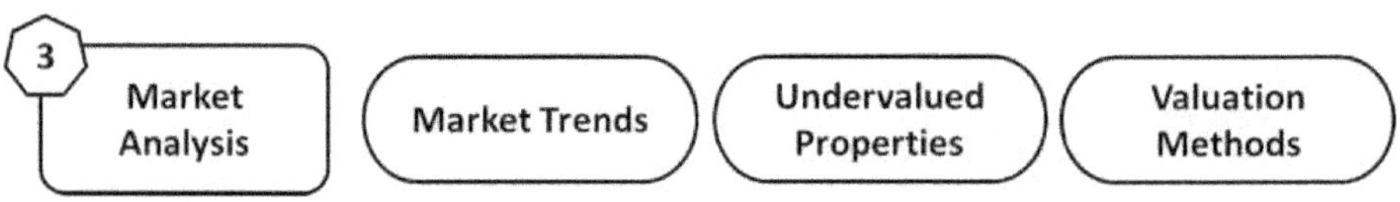

As you embark on your real estate investment path, understanding the terrain through market analysis is not just helpful—it's crucial. This chapter will guide you through the landscapes of economic indicators and market cycles, equipping you with the knowledge to identify the optimal times for investment actions. We will discuss different valuation methods so you can analyze for yourself whether a property is a suitable investment. The chapter concludes with techniques for finding undervalued properties. Just as a seasoned navigator uses a compass to chart the course through unknown waters, you will learn to use market trends, economic signals, and valuation methods to steer your investment decisions wisely and confidently.

3.1 UNDERSTANDING MARKET TRENDS AND ECONOMIC INDICATORS

The real estate industry is profoundly influenced by a spectrum of events ranging from global to local scales. This chapter will explore how these varying levels of influence—from international developments to national policies, regional dynamics, and local activities—impact the market trends. We will begin by examining specific examples that illustrate these effects. Following this, we will provide practical tips on how to stay informed about the latest news and trends. By tailoring these strategies to suit your personal approach and time constraints, you can effectively keep your finger on the pulse of the real estate market.

3.1.1 Global Economic Factors Affecting Real Estate

The global economy is increasingly interconnected, and shifts in one part of the world can have ripple effects across global real estate markets. For example, changes in international trade policies can influence economic activity in various countries, affecting demand for commercial and residential real estate. For instance, a new trade agreement that boosts manufacturing in a particular country could increase demand for industrial real estate in that area. Like any favorable economic policies designed to attract foreign investors might boost the real estate market, international conflicts, financial crises, or political instability can deter foreign investment in a region, potentially leading to a downturn in its real estate market because of capital flight to more stable markets, affecting property demand and prices in those regions.

Understanding these global dynamics is crucial for real estate investors, especially those looking to invest in markets significantly influenced by international investors or global economic trends. Keeping informed about international financial news, consulting global market analysis reports, and studying foreign investment patterns in real estate can provide insights into how global events might impact local markets. It might include subscribing to international economic reports, participating in global real estate conferences, and building networks with investors and analysts with expertise in international real estate markets. This global perspective is beneficial not only for anticipating market downturns but can also help you seize opportunities that arise from international economic developments.

By staying agile and informed, you can better anticipate how global shifts might impact your local investments and adjust your strategies accordingly.

Examples of websites to keep an eye on for the latest updates and insights include

- The U.S. Department of Commerce's International Trade Administration (ITA)[1] offers detailed information on trade policies and economic data.
- The Office of the United States Trade Representative (USTR)[2] is another key resource that provides timely updates on trade agreements and negotiations.

For broader international perspectives:

- The World Trade Organization (WTO)[3] offers extensive reports.
- World Bank[4] provides comprehensive resources on economic policies and development issues globally.

News platforms like Bloomberg.com, Reuters.com, and The Financial Times[5] provide up-to-date coverage on financial markets, economic policies, and geopolitical events. The Economist.com and the BBC News[6] are invaluable for in-depth analyses and comprehensive news coverage. At the same time, the Council on Foreign Relations (CFR)[7] and the International Monetary Fund (IMF)[8] offer expert insights into global economic stability and policy developments.

3.1.2 Identifying Macroeconomic Indicators

The pulse of the real estate market is often synchronized with the broader rhythm of the economy. Key macroeconomic indicators such as GDP growth, unemployment rates, interest rates, and inflation are not just abstract figures reported in the news; they are vital signs that can indicate the real estate market's health. For instance, a rising GDP often signals a strengthening economy, increasing demand for real estate as businesses expand and individuals feel more confident in making significant purchases. Conversely, high unemployment rates indicate a weaker economy, potentially leading to lower demand for real estate as fewer people can afford to buy or invest in property.

Understanding how to source and interpret these indicators is crucial. Start by regularly following releases from reliable sources such as the FederalReserve.gov, the U.S. Bureau of Economic Analysis (BEA)[9], or similar institutions in your country. These organizations provide comprehensive, up-to-date data on these indicators. Reading these reports and extracting relevant information will help you predict market trends and make well-informed investment decisions. For instance, if the reports indicate a trend of decreasing interest rates, it might be a good time to secure financing for a new property since lower rates mean lower borrowing costs, which can improve your investment returns.

3.1.2.1 Utilizing Financial News and Reports

Navigating the vast amount of financial news and reports available can be daunting. Yet, these resources are crucial for keeping abreast of the economic indicators and market trends directly impacting real estate investments. The key is distinguishing between mere noise—irrelevant information to your investment goals—and valuable data that can inform your investment strategies. Start by identifying and following trusted financial news sources and real estate market analysts known for their accuracy and depth of analysis.

Publications like The Wall Street Journal[10], Bloomberg.com, and specialized real estate news outlets like RealtyTrac.com provide reliable information that can help you stay informed about market trends and economic shifts.

When reviewing these sources, focus on articles and reports that relate directly to the markets where you have investments or plan to invest. Pay attention to reports on housing market trends, changes in mortgage rates, employment rates, and any legislative changes affecting property ownership or landlord rights. Consider subscribing to industry reports from market research firms that offer detailed analyses and forecasts for deeper insights. These reports can provide a more detailed view of market conditions and trends, helping you make more informed decisions. Financial models and tools that offer real-time data and analytics can also enhance your ability to quickly interpret market conditions and adjust your investment strategy as needed.

To keep track of interest rates and unemployment figures, subscribing to industry reports from reputable market research firms is essential. Moody's Analytics[11] provides in-depth economic research and analysis, while Bloomberg.com offers comprehensive economic data and detailed reports. Economist Intelligence Unit (EIU)[12] offers expert insights and economic reports. S&P Global[13] provides detailed market insights, and FitchRatings.com offers financial analysis of economic trends. CBRE Research[14] delivers valuable market insights for real estate-focused data. Additionally, the Federal Reserve Economic Data (FRED)[15] from the Federal Reserve Bank of St. Louis offers a comprehensive database of economic indicators, making these sources invaluable for staying informed about key economic trends.

3.1.2.2 Impact of Government Policies

Government policies can significantly impact real estate prices and market dynamics. Tax incentives, zoning laws, and housing regulations can either spur market growth or lead to declines. For instance, a new housing subsidy policy might increase demand for residential properties, pushing prices and benefiting sellers and developers. Conversely, stringent new zoning laws restrict development, limit supply, and slow market growth.

Case studies can illustrate the influence of government policies on real estate markets. For example, consider a region where the government recently increased property taxes significantly. Such a policy might lead to the market cooling, as higher taxes can deter buyers and investors. In contrast, a case where the government introduced tax incentives for green buildings might spur demand in this sector, benefiting investors who focus on sustainable development.

3.1.2.3 Leverage Market Trends

Leveraging market trends is about aligning your investment strategies with the directional flow of the market. This strategic alignment involves not just following the trends but also anticipating them and positioning your investments to benefit from these movements. For example, if you observe a trend towards green living, investing in properties that offer sustainable living options could position you advantageously as demand for such homes increases. Similarly, understanding and acting on trends in property technology, like smart homes, can attract a tech-savvy demographic, enhancing your property's appeal and profitability.

A successful trend analysis application often involves a combination of keen observation, continuous education, and strategic action. Attending industry conferences, participating in real estate investment forums, and conducting regular market reviews are activities that can keep you informed and ready to capitalize on emerging trends. Case studies of past market successes and failures can also provide valuable lessons, helping refine your ability to leverage market trends effectively. By staying adaptable and informed, you can use market trends to guide your investment decisions.

Regarding industry conferences and expos, you can watch the National Association of REALTORS (NAR)[16] and the International Council of Shopping Centers (ICSC) Events[17] and search for this year's Real Estate Wealth Expos.

3.1.2.4 Demographic and Social Changes

Demographic and social changes, such as the rise of remote work and urbanization, continually reshape the landscape of real estate demand. These trends can significantly impact real estate markets, from housing design to preferred locations. For instance, the increased remote work has spurred demand for homes with dedicated office spaces. It has also increased property values in suburban and rural areas as more workers move away from city centers. Similarly, urbanization drives demand for residential and commercial properties in urban areas, influencing property prices and rental rates.

As an investor, staying informed about demographic and social trends is crucial. This knowledge can guide investment decisions, helping you choose properties that align with evolving consumer preferences and needs. Engaging with market research firms, following census reports, and monitoring social trend publications can provide valuable insights into these changes. Additionally, participation in real estate seminars and webinars can offer deeper insights into how these trends will likely affect the market, enabling you to strategize effectively.

Examples of websites to keep an eye on to find seminars and webinars about real estate include **Eventbrite.com** and **Meetup.com**, which list various real estate events nationwide. The National Association of REALTORS (**NAR**) mentioned above, and local REALTOR associations often offer educational events and webinars. **BiggerPockets.com** is another excellent resource known for its forums and event listings focused on real estate investing. The **RealEstateGuysRadioShow.com** also hosts informative seminars and webinars. Many Real Estate Investment Associations (**REIAs**)[18] nationwide offer educational events. Look for local REIA chapters in your area.

Professional organizations' websites, such as the Urban Land Institute (**ULI**)[19], the Institute of Real Estate Management (**IREM**)[20], and the Commercial Real Estate Women (CREW) Network[21], also provide valuable opportunities for learning and networking.

Check the websites of institutions and universities with **real estate programs** (such as the Wharton School, Harvard Business School, and others.) They offer seminars, webinars, and continuing education courses.

LinkedIn is a treasure trove of industry insights. By following and engaging with real estate groups and industry leaders, you can gain valuable knowledge and stay updated on the latest events and webinars. Many of these leaders regularly post about upcoming events, making LinkedIn a key resource for staying informed. You can also find many real estate groups and **Facebook** pages that share information about seminars and webinars. Joining relevant groups can keep you informed.

3.1.2.5 Investor Activities and Market Speculation

Large-scale investors and speculators can significantly influence real estate markets. Their activities can create trends that can either present opportunities or serve as warnings for smaller investors. For instance, if significant investors are moving into a particular market, it might be a sign that the area is poised for growth. However, if not based on fundamental demand, it could also lead to a speculative bubble, which might be risky for latecomers. It's important to be cautious and not blindly follow these trends, as they can lead to potential risks.

Understanding the activities of these large players can provide valuable insights into potential market movements. Engaging with local real estate networks and participating in industry forums is about more than just staying informed. It's about being part of a community that shares your interests and can help you keep track of these activities. Additionally, analyzing market reports and investment news can offer clues about where big investors focus their resources, helping you make more informed decisions about where to allocate your investment capital.

Understanding market trends and economic indicators is vital for successful real estate investing. By staying informed and strategically applying this knowledge, you can enhance your ability to make savvy investment choices that align with market conditions and your personal investment goals. However, it's crucial to be cautious when interpreting these trends, as they can sometimes be misleading. As you continue to explore the depths of real estate market analysis, remember that each piece of data and each economic indicator you learn to interpret is a tool in your investment toolkit, sharpening your edge in a competitive market.

3.1.3 Location Analysis

Analyzing a location goes beyond just understanding its current economic conditions. It involves a deep dive into factors influencing the local real estate market, such as financial stability, employment rates, and population growth. These factors are crucial because they affect the demand for property in the area. A location with a growing job market and increasing population will likely see higher demand for residential and commercial real estate. Conversely, areas with declining economic conditions and population loss might experience reduced demand.

To conduct a thorough location analysis, gather data on the area's economic conditions, demographic trends, and property market performance. This information can often be found in government financial reports, local authority planning documents, and real estate market analysis studies. Additionally, speaking with local real estate agents, economic development officers, and residents can provide on-the-ground insights not captured in official reports.

3.1.3.1 Identify Emerging Markets and Using Local Insights

Identifying emerging markets is akin to discovering hidden gems; these are markets where significant growth is anticipated due to factors like new infrastructure projects, new schools, hospitals, changes in local government policies, or increasing commercial activity. For example, a new industrial park can increase demand for residential and commercial properties, providing a ripe investment opportunity. Recognizing these markets requires a keen eye on economic development plans, real estate development activities, and government announcements.

To identify such opportunities, regularly engage with urban planning and development offices, attend community meetings, and review public records and local news. Subscribe to development news feeds and network with local real estate professionals with intimate knowledge of the area. Analyzing investment patterns and construction activity can also offer clues about emerging markets.

However, the absolute goldmine of local insights lies in your relationships with local agents and community leaders. These connections can provide insider knowledge, often the key to making informed investment decisions. By identifying and investing in these markets early, you can maximize your returns as the demand increases, usually resulting in substantial capital appreciation and robust rental yields.

By combining this local knowledge with broader market data, you can comprehensively understand an area's real estate potential, allowing you to make more precise and potentially profitable investment choices.

3.1.3.2 Identify Key Market Indicators

Key market indicators serve as the compass points guiding real estate investors through the market's ebb and flow. These indicators include housing demand, housing starts, mortgage rates, construction spending, supply levels, and price trends. Each indicator sheds light on different aspects of the real estate market, influencing decision-making processes. For example, a sharp increase in housing starts might indicate a future increase in supply, potentially stabilizing or lowering prices. Conversely, rising mortgage rates could reduce buyer affordability, impacting demand and slowing the market.

Understanding and monitoring these indicators can significantly enhance your ability to forecast market trends. Regularly accessing reports from housing authorities, economic research institutions, and financial news can provide continuous updates on these indicators. (See, among other things, the websites mentioned earlier in this chapter.) Additionally, real estate market analysis tools and platforms offer comprehensive data and trend analysis features that can simplify tracking these indicators. By keeping a finger on the pulse of these key market indicators, you can anticipate changes in the market, allowing you to adjust your investment strategies proactively rather than reactively.

3.1.3.3 The Importance of Understanding Local Events

There is a saying in property valuation: "Location, location, location". It underscores geographical factors' pivotal role in shaping property values and investment viability. Each locale has unique dynamics that can significantly influence the real estate market—from local economic health to community events and development projects. Consequently, gaining a deep understanding of these local nuances is essential for making informed investment decisions. Engaging with local advisors with intimate market knowledge can provide insights often not captured in broader economic reports. These professionals, be they real estate agents, local economists, or property managers, can offer nuanced perspectives on how local events, such as a new municipal development project or changes in local government policies, will likely affect property values and rental demand.

For example, suppose a new commercial complex is slated for construction in a suburb. In that case, local advisors can provide insights into how this development might increase local employment, boost demand for housing, and thereby increase property values. They can also warn about potential downsides, such as increased traffic that might detract from the appeal of residential areas nearby. This kind of localized knowledge is invaluable and can remarkably impact the profitability of your investments. To effectively tap into this wealth of information, consider attending local real estate meetings, participating in community forums, or even engaging in local government sessions. These activities can provide firsthand insights into upcoming projects and policy changes that might impact your investment decisions.

Physically visiting the property can provide valuable information that affects its value. Every house's unique location can significantly influence its market value. Factors tied to the area, location, view, and nearest neighbor can enhance or diminish a property's worth. For instance, a house next to a power line may have a lower market value compared to similar houses in the same area located further away from the power line. The proximity to such infrastructure can impact the perceived desirability of the property due to concerns about aesthetics, noise, and potential health risks. Consequently, even within the same neighborhood, slight differences in a property's location can lead to considerable variations in market value, underscoring the importance of location in real estate valuation.

3.2 ANALYZING AND PREDICTING MARKET TRENDS TO YOUR ADVANTAGE

3.2.1 Analyze Historical Data

Looking back and discerning patterns in historical market data is a skill and a strategic asset in real estate investing. This analysis involves more than a cursory glance at past price fluctuations; it requires a deep dive into various factors that influenced these changes, helping you predict future movements and position your investments accordingly. For instance, examining how property prices in a particular area have reacted to economic downturns, interest rate changes, or infrastructural developments over the decades can provide significant insights. This historical perspective is crucial because it helps establish a pattern of how specific triggers impact property values and rental demand.

Consider a scenario where you are evaluating an investment in a residential area. By analyzing data from the past 20 years, property prices in this area have historically increased following significant infrastructural developments like new highways or transit stations. This pattern not only helps make a current investment decision but also prepares you for similar opportunities in the future. To effectively analyze historical data, utilize resources such as property price indexes, government housing data, and reports from real estate market analysts. Tools like statistical analysis software can also aid in identifying trends and forecasting future movements based on historical data. By mastering this analytical approach, you can make informed predictions about market behaviors, enhancing your investment strategy's effectiveness and responsiveness.

For those interested in license-based software, Argus Enterprise[22] is a robust tool used for asset and portfolio management in commercial real estate. It offers valuation, budgeting, and forecasting tools.

Several top options are available for those seeking subscription-based statistical analysis software for real estate.

- **CoStar.com** is a leading provider offering comprehensive data on commercial properties, transactions, market trends, and demographics.
- **REIS**[23], a division of Moody's Analytics, also provides detailed market reports, forecasts, and property-level analytics on commercial real estates.
- **RealCapitalAnalytics.com** (RCA) provides commercial real estate investment market data and analytics.
- **Zillow Premier Agent□**[24] offers tools for residential real estate agents with extensive market data.
- **CoreLogic.com** offers property data and analytics for valuation, risk management, and market analysis.
- **Esri's ArcGIS**[25] platform provides advanced spatial analysis and mapping capabilities for site selection and urban planning.
- **IBM's SPSS**[26] is widely used for predictive analytics and market research.
- **Tableau.com** allows for interactive data visualization and real-time dashboard creation.
- **Microsoft Power BI**[27] offers interactive visualizations and business intelligence capabilities.

3.2.2 Forecasting Techniques

Predicting the future is a skill reserved for the clairvoyant. Still, real estate investing is rooted in the practical, achievable art of forecasting. Understanding how to anticipate market trends involves combining techniques that analyze past and current data to make educated guesses about future market behaviors. Trend analysis, for instance, looks at historical data to identify patterns that are likely to continue. For example, suppose you observe an area with a steady annual property value increase of 3 % over the past decade. In that case, you might predict that this trend will continue if no significant market changes occur.

Econometric modeling is another sophisticated technique that uses statistical methods to forecast future trends based on various variables. It might involve analyzing how changes in one sector of the economy, like job growth in technology, could affect real estate markets in nearby areas. These models can be instrumental in understanding and predicting the impacts of complex economic interactions on real estate prices. To effectively use these forecasting techniques, one must access historical data from reliable sources such as government housing indices, real estate market reports, and economic research publications. Tools like regression analysis software can also help build and test econometric models, providing a more scientific basis for your predictions.

Several tools stand out for real estate analysis due to their robust data handling, statistical capabilities, and ease of use.

- **Stata.com** stands out with its advanced statistical methods, particularly in econometric analysis, making it a top choice for real estate market studies, price modeling, and investment analysis.
- **IBM SPSS Statistics**[28] provides comprehensive statistical analysis tools with a user-friendly interface suitable for analyzing market trends, property values, and investment returns.
- **SAS**[29] is well-suited for complex analyses. It can handle large datasets and perform detailed regression analysis, useful for property valuation, risk assessment, and market trend analysis.
- **EViews**[30], widely used in econometrics, offers advanced regression tools for time-series analysis and forecasting property prices.
- **JMP**[31] (by SAS) combines robust statistics with dynamic data visualization, making it ideal for exploring and understanding market trends.

3.2.2.1 Leverage Technology and Data Analytics

In today's digital age, technology and data analytics play pivotal roles in enhancing the forecasting abilities of real estate investors. For instance, Geographic Information Systems (GIS) can analyze spatial data related to real estate markets, offering insights into patterns and trends that are not immediately apparent. It could include mapping demographic changes, economic developments, or real estate price movements across different regions. Online real estate platforms provide another valuable resource, offering up-to-date market data and trends that can inform your investment strategies. Many of these platforms feature analytical tools that allow you to visualize data trends, compare market metrics across different areas, and forecast future property values based on current market data.

Embracing these technological tools can significantly enhance your ability to predict future market trends. Regularly using data analytics platforms to monitor market conditions and predict future trends can give you a competitive edge, allowing you to identify investment opportunities and risks before they become apparent to the broader market.

Several organizations offer Geographic Information Systems (GIS) that can analyze spatial data related to real estate markets.

- **Esri□**[32] leads the market with its ArcGIS platform, which provides powerful tools for mapping, spatial analysis, and data visualization. It is ideal for real estate market analysis and urban planning.
- **QGIS.org** is an open-source GIS application widely used for its flexibility and extensive plugin ecosystem.
- **MapInfo Pro□**[33] by Precisely offers advanced spatial analysis capabilities suitable for site selection.
- **Google Earth Pro□**[34] provides comprehensive tools for visualizing property locations and surrounding infrastructure.
- **Carto.com** is a cloud-based GIS platform that offers robust spatial anal-

ysis and visualization tools for analyzing market trends and demographic data.
- **Hexagon Geospatial's**[35] suite of products, including ERDAS IMAGINE and GeoMedia, provide advanced spatial analysis for market analysis.
- **Bentley Systems'**[36] GIS solutions, such as Bentley Map, support spatial data analysis for infrastructure planning.
- **Autodesk InfraWorks**[37] offers GIS and 3D modeling tools useful for development planning.

These GIS platforms enable professionals to make informed decisions through geographic and spatial analysis.

3.2.2.2 Leveraging Social Media for Research

Social media platforms like Facebook, Twitter, and LinkedIn have become powerful tools for real-time market research, offering a treasure trove of data on market trends, consumer behavior, and investment opportunities. Following real estate groups, industry influencers, and professional organizations on these platforms allows you to access various opinions and insights that can inform your investment decisions. For instance, LinkedIn can connect you with industry leaders whose articles and posts provide professional insights into the real estate market. At the same time, Twitter can offer immediate updates on market changes and trends through hashtags such as #RealEstate or #PropertyInvestment.

To effectively leverage social media for research, start by identifying and following accounts offering valuable content relevant to your investment interests. Engage with this content regularly by participating in discussions and asking questions. This interaction can provide additional insights and help build your network of industry contacts.

Tools like **Hootsuite.com**, **TweetDeck**[38], or **BuzzSumo.com** can also help you monitor multiple feeds and hashtags simultaneously, ensuring you get all the essential information. By actively using social media platforms to gather and analyze real-time data, you can enhance your market awareness and responsiveness, giving you an edge in the fast-paced world of real estate investing.

3.2.3 Explore Supply and Demand

The fundamental economic principle of supply and demand also plays a crucial role in real estate markets. When demand for real estate is high and supply is limited, prices tend to rise. Conversely, prices may fall if the market is flooded with properties but demand is weak. For instance, if a new large-scale housing development is completed in an area with dwindling population growth, the increased supply could lead to lower prices. Understanding these dynamics can help you predict price movements and choose the correct investment times and places.

For example, suppose you notice that a particular city is experiencing population growth due to a new industry hub. In that case, demand for residential and commercial properties in that area will likely increase. Investing in properties in this city could yield substantial returns as demand drives up property values.

3.2.3.1 Real Estate Market Cycles

Timing is everything in real estate investment. Staying informed about market trends is crucial for effective market timing.

By understanding market cycles and economic indicators, you can better decide when to buy, sell, or hold real estate assets. Like the economy, real estate markets move in cycles, typically including four phases: recovery, expansion, hyper-supply, and recession. Understanding these phases can significantly impact your investment strategy. During **recovery**, prices are generally low, making it a potentially good time to buy properties. The

expansion phase (boom) sees increased prices and demand, signaling a good time to develop or improve properties to maximize value. Selling during the late expansion or early hyper-supply phase, before the market peaks and begins to decline, can maximize your returns. The **hyper-supply** phase (slow-down) is marked by an oversupply of properties, which could lead to decreased prices and might be a good time to hold off on new investments. Finally, the **recession** phase sees a significant drop in demand and prices, which might seem risky. Still, for the wise investor, it can also be a time to buy premium properties at reduced prices.

Regularly attending industry conferences, subscribing to real estate market newsletters, and participating in investor networks can provide insights and forecasts that help you anticipate market movements. Additionally, maintaining flexibility in your investment strategy is vital, as the market can shift due to unforeseen circumstances, such as changes in government policy or economic disruptions.

Several excellent options are available for those looking to stay updated on the real estate market through subscription-based newsletters.

- **TheRealDeal.com** offers daily updates on market trends, significant deals, and industry insights. Their newsletter provides comprehensive coverage of the commercial and residential real estate sectors.
- **The Urban Land Institute** (ULI)[39] provides in-depth articles and research reports on urban development.
- **CBRE Research□**[40] delivers insights on market trends and economic forecasts across various real estate sectors, including office, industrial, retail, and multifamily real estate.
- **Zillow Research**[41] provides data-driven insights on housing market trends and financial factors. Their analyses are particularly useful for residential real estate professionals and investors.
- **CoreLogic Insights**[42] includes detailed reports on housing market trends, property values, and mortgage performance. Real estate pro-

fessionals widely use its data and insights for strategic planning and market analysis.

- **Redfin's Data Center**[43] newsletter tracks home prices, sales volume, and inventory levels. Their reports are helpful for keeping up with the latest developments in the residential real estate market.
- **The National Association of REALTORS®** (NAR)[44] offers various newsletters with market statistics and policy updates. Their publications provide valuable information for real estate agents, brokers, and industry stakeholders.
- **CoStar Market Insights**[45] provides a detailed analysis of commercial real estate markets. Their reports cover various property types, including office, retail, industrial, and multifamily sectors.

These newsletters collectively offer comprehensive information about the latest trends and developments in the real estate market.

3.2.3.2 Navigating Market Downturns

Recognizing the signs of an impending downturn, such as a significant increase in property supply without corresponding demand, rising interest rates, or economic indicators pointing to a slowing economy, can help you prepare and adjust your strategies accordingly. For instance, a sharp decline in housing starts and permits may be a precursor to a cooling market, signaling that it might be time to consolidate your holdings or brace for lower rental incomes.

Financial preparedness is your first line of defense against the inevitable downturns. Maintaining robust cash reserves ensures you can cover your property expenses and debts even when rental incomes decline or properties are harder to sell. Diversifying your income streams can also buffer against market volatility. It might involve investing in different types of properties (residential, commercial, industrial) or other geographic locations to spread risk. Regularly reassessing your investment strategies is also prudent. This continuous evaluation allows you to adapt to changing market conditions—for example, shifting your focus from acquiring new properties to enhancing the value of your existing ones through renovations or improved management practices.

Downturns, while challenging, can also be ripe with opportunities for the discerning investor. Properties often become undervalued in a downturn due to decreased competition and motivated sellers, providing potential for significant gains when the market recovers. Additionally, you might find more favorable financing options as lenders compete for the reduced pool of borrowers. Adopting a long-term perspective is key here. Real estate investments typically perform best over long periods, smoothing out the peaks and troughs of market cycles. By focusing on and remembering the long-term potential of your investments instead of short-term fluctuations, you can make strategic purchases during downturns that will pay dividends in the future.

Adjusting your investment strategies in response to market downturns might involve several tactical shifts. For example, suppose you predominantly invest in high-end residential properties and foresee a downturn that could hit this market segment particularly hard. In that case, consider diversifying into more recession-resistant sectors, such as multi-family units or properties in less affluent areas where demand remains more stable. Similarly, reassessing your geographic focus to include regions with stronger economic growth can help mitigate risks associated with a local market downturn. Sometimes, liquidating non-performing assets before a full-blown recession hits can preserve capital for more strategic investments.

Analyzing failed investments can provide critical lessons that enhance your resilience in future downturns. Common pitfalls include:

- Poor market entry or exit timing.
- Underestimating the costs of property improvements.

- Inadequate due diligence.

Reflecting on these mistakes helps refine your investment strategies and decision-making processes, ensuring you are better prepared for similar challenges ahead.

Finally, building flexibility into your real estate investments allows you to navigate uncertainty more easily. It could mean securing financing with terms that enable payment adjustments according to cash flow variations or choosing properties that can be easily converted for different uses to respond to changing market demands. Flexibility also involves keeping yourself well-informed and ready to change your strategies in response to new information or emerging trends.

Navigating market downturns requires a blend of strategic foresight, financial prudence, and operational flexibility. By understanding market cycles, preparing financially, seizing opportunities judiciously, and learning from past experiences, you can enhance your ability to withstand downturns and emerge from them stronger and poised for growth. As you continue to build your real estate portfolio, remember that each market cycle phase offers unique challenges and opportunities. The insights and strategies discussed here are designed to empower you to meet these challenges head-on and to capitalize on the opportunities that arise, ensuring your long-term success in the constantly changing world of real estate investing.

3.3 TECHNIQUES FOR FINDING UNDERVALUED PROPERTIES

3.3.1 Real Estate Platforms

In the quest for profitability in real estate investing, one of the most strategic moves you can make is to acquire undervalued properties. These are assets that, for various reasons, are priced below their actual market value. Recognizing such opportunities requires insight, diligence, and, sometimes, creativity. A fundamental way to start is by harnessing the power of online tools and platforms that provide rich data and connectivity to the real estate market. Real estate platforms and Multiple Listing Services (MLS) are replete with listings that, if analyzed correctly, can reveal undervalued properties. These platforms often allow you to set up alerts for new listings that meet specific criteria you've predefined, such as price ranges, locations, or property types, ensuring you are one of the first to know about potential deals.

There are many popular online services, such as **Zillow.com**, which offers extensive property listings, home valuations, and tools for buyers, sellers, and renters, and Realtor.com, operated by the National Association of REALTORS, which provides comprehensive property listings and market insights. **Redfin.com**, a real estate brokerage, offers listings, market analysis, and home valuation tools. At the same time, **Trulia.com**, owned by Zillow Group, provides neighborhood insights and resources for home buyers and renters. **Homes.com** offers property listings and home value estimates.

LoopNet.com and **CoStar.com** provide extensive listings and market data for commercial real estate. **RealtyMogul.com** allows individuals to invest in commercial and residential properties through crowdfunding.

Rental platforms like **Apartments.com** and **Rent.com** offer extensive rental property listings and tools for renters.

Platforms such as **Opendoor.com** and **Offerpad.com** simplify the buying and selling process with instant offers and streamlined transactions. At the same time, **Propertybase.com** helps brokerages manage listings, leads, and transactions with a suite of tools integrated with multiple MLSs. These platforms facilitate various aspects of the real estate market, from property searches and listings to investment opportunities and transaction management.

Multiple Listing Services (MLS) are databases established by cooperating real estate brokers to provide data about properties for sale. There are numerous MLSs in the United States. Search on Google with the keywords MLS and your state.

Exploring platforms like Bigger Pockets Marketplace and Craigslist can also be advantageous. **Bigger Pockets Marketplace**[46] is a hub where real estate investors can find and share investment opportunities, including undervalued properties or distressed sales. While more general, **Craigslist.org** can sometimes yield unexpected gems, especially in the "real estate for sale" section, where private sellers might list their properties at lower prices than the market rate to facilitate a quick sale.

3.3.2 Networking

Networking with local real estate professionals is another invaluable strategy. Real estate agents, brokers, and wholesalers often have first-hand information on off-market deals or properties about to be listed. Building solid relationships with these professionals can give you advanced notice of potential deals, allowing you to act quickly. Moreover, these professionals can provide insights into why specific properties are priced below market value, which is crucial for assessing the investment's potential and associated risks. (Read more about Networking in Chapter 1.7.)

3.3.3 Eviction Records

Understanding the significance of eviction records in this context is crucial. These public records can help identify rental properties where landlords might be experiencing difficulties with tenants, possibly indicating their motivation to sell. Properties with recurring tenant issues might be acquired at a lower price as landlords eager to avoid further hassles might be open to negotiations.

Finding eviction records in America typically involves accessing public records maintained by various government agencies.

County courthouses are the primary repositories for eviction records, which are usually filed within the civil or housing courts. You can visit the courthouse in the county where the property is located and request access to these records. Additionally, many county courts provide online databases where you can search for eviction records by name, case number, or property address. Examples of such online resources include the Los Angeles Superior Court and the Cook County Clerk of the Circuit Court websites.

State judicial websites also offer valuable resources for locating eviction records. Some states have centralized online systems that provide access to court records, including eviction cases. Websites like the Texas Judicial Branch and the New York State Unified Court System offer searchable databases, making it easier to find eviction records across various counties within the state.

Public record websites can also be useful. Platforms like **NETROnline.com** (Nationwide Environmental Title Research Online) and **PublicRecords360.com** provide links to county and state public records, including eviction records, helping you navigate to the appropriate local resources.

Additionally, **tenant screening companies** such as **TransUnion Smart-Move**[47], **RentPrep.com**, and **MyRental.com** offer access to tenant screening reports that often include eviction history. Landlords typically use these services, but they can be useful for checking individual records.

Subscription-based services like **LexisNexis.com**, **CoreLogic.com**, and **Experian RentBureau**[48] offer comprehensive background check services, including eviction records. These services usually require a subscription and are often utilized by landlords, property managers, and real estate professionals.

Local housing authorities can also be a source of eviction records, particularly for public housing or government-subsidized properties. Contacting the local housing authority may provide access to relevant records.

If standard searches do not yield the desired information, filing a **Freedom of Information Act** (FOIA)[49] request with the relevant government agency can be another way to obtain eviction records.

Utilizing these resources allows you to access eviction records in America, ensuring a thorough search for the information you need.

3.3.4 Public Records and Auction Sites

Exploring tax delinquency and auction properties presents another avenue to find undervalued properties. Properties with tax liens due to unpaid property taxes can sometimes be purchased through auctions at lower prices. Accessing public records to identify such properties and attending the auctions can lead to acquisitions at significantly reduced costs. However, it's essential to thoroughly understand the auction process and any potential liabilities attached to the properties, such as outstanding liens or damages.

Accessing public records to find properties that may be sold at auction involves several steps. Start by visiting the county recorder's or clerk's office in the area where you are interested in finding properties. Many offices have online databases to search for property records, foreclosure notices, and tax liens. The county assessor's office also provides records on property ownership and tax assessments, which help identify properties subject to tax sales. Local newspapers publish public notices of upcoming auctions, foreclosures, and tax sales, often as a legal requirement. Many counties provide access to **public records online**, and websites like **NETROnline.com** link to these resources. Title companies and real estate agents specializing in foreclosures can also access public records and offer insights. **Government websites** like U.S. Department of Housing and Urban Development (HUD) and IRS and local government sites provide information on property auctions: court records, accessible at local courthouses or through online databases, document foreclosure proceedings. Additionally, subscription services like **RealtyTrac.com**, **Foreclosure.com**, and **PropertyRadar.com** offer detailed information on properties facing foreclosure and scheduled for auction.

For effective searching, having specific property details (such as the property address or parcel number) and regularly checking for updates is essential because properties scheduled for auction can change frequently. Understanding relevant terminology is also important. Familiarize yourself with terms like "Notice of Default," "Lis Pendens," "Trustee Sale," and "Tax Lien" as they relate to distressed properties.

Several large real estate auction sites in America are well-known for their extensive listings and comprehensive services.

- **Auction.com** is one of the largest, specializing in residential and commercial properties, including foreclosures and bank-owned properties.
- **Hubzu.com** offers a wide range of residential auctions, including foreclosed homes and short sales, with a streamlined bidding process.
- **RealtyBid.com** focuses on online auctions for residential properties like

foreclosures and REOs, providing a user-friendly platform.

- **Xome.com** provides a comprehensive auction platform for various residential properties, complete with detailed property data and integrated services.
- **Williams & Williams**[50] conducts live and online auctions for residential, commercial, and agricultural properties and is known for its extensive marketing.
- **HudsonAndMarshall.com** specializes in residential auctions, including foreclosures and bank-owned properties, offering live and online events.
- **Bid4Assets.com** focuses on online auctions for foreclosed properties, tax deed sales, and government-owned properties, working with various government agencies and financial institutions.

These sites are some of the largest and most reputable platforms for real estate auctions in America, catering to a wide range of buyers' needs.

3.3.5 Driving For Dollars

Another dynamic approach is "driving for dollars," a term used to describe the process of physically exploring neighborhoods to identify properties that appear undervalued. It might include looking for homes that show signs of neglect, such as overgrown lawns, peeling paint, or other disrepair indicators. These properties could be acquired below market value, refurbished, sold for a profit, or rented out. Complementing this physical search with "Direct Mail Marketing for Deals" can significantly increase your chances of success. It involves sending personalized letters or postcards to homeowners in your targeted areas, particularly those who own properties that show signs of neglect or are in pre-foreclosure, expressing your interest in purchasing their homes.

3.3.6 Financial Distress Signals

Lastly, analyzing financial distress signals is critical in identifying undervalued properties. Properties listed as "quick sales" or those that have been on the market for an extended period might indicate that the seller is under financial pressure and may be open to selling at a lower price. Approaching these opportunities requires tact and ethical consideration, ensuring that any transaction is mutually beneficial, transparent, and fair.

By employing these techniques, you can enhance your ability to spot and capitalize on undervalued properties, which is often crucial to successful real estate investing. Each method offers a different perspective and scope, providing a comprehensive toolkit to navigate and thrive in the competitive real estate market. Whether through technological platforms, personal interactions, or strategic marketing, your journey toward uncovering these hidden gems is as rewarding as it is profitable.

3.4 VALUATION METHODS AND TECHNIQUES

Understanding how to value real estate accurately is pivotal for making informed investment decisions. Valuation methods such as Comparative Market Analysis (CMA), Sales Comparison Approach, Income Approach, and Cost Approach are fundamental to this process. Each serves distinct purposes and provides unique insights into property value.

3.4.1 Comparative Market Analysis (CMA)

A Comparative Market Analysis (CMA) is used extensively in the real estate industry to determine the value of a property. It is used mainly by real estate agents to help sellers set a listing price for their property and to help buyers make competitive offers. It is done by comparing it to similar properties recently sold in the same area. This method is beneficial for residential properties with sufficient comparable sales data. A CMA often focuses on factors such as square footage, number of bedrooms and bathrooms, location, and general condition. Adjustments are made for differences between the subject property and comparables. Still, the process is generally less detailed and rigorous than a formal appraisal (like the Sales Comparison Approach).

To conduct a CMA, you would start by selecting properties of similar size, location, condition, and features. Then, adjust the prices of these comparable properties based on differences that might affect their value compared to the subject property. For instance, if the property you are evaluating has a renovated kitchen while the comparable does not, you would adjust the comparable price upwards to reflect this. Or the property in question has one less bedroom. In that case, the agent estimates this difference to $20,000 and adjusts the price downward.

Suppose the properties to be compared differ significantly regarding square feet. Then, calculate the property's "price per square foot." This unit helps to standardize the comparison of different properties by accounting for variations in size. Calculate the Price per Square Foot by dividing a property's sale price by its total square footage.

$$\textbf{Price per Square Foot} = \frac{\textbf{Sale Price}}{\textbf{Total Square Footage}}$$

In the example below, all properties have a price per square foot of $200, indicating a consistent valuation metric across different property sizes.

Subject Property: 2,000 square feet, estimated market value $400,000.

- Price per Square Foot: $400,000 / 2,000 sq ft = $200 per square foot

Comparable Property 1: 1,800 square feet, sold for $360,000.

- Price per Square Foot: $360,000 / 1,800 sq ft = $200 per square foot

Comparable Property 2: 2,200 square feet, sold for $440,000.

- Price per Square Foot: $440,000 / 2,200 sq ft = $200 per square foot

But suppose there are two directly comparable properties in the same block with values of $180 and $230. That would give an average value of (($180+$210) / 2) = $195, indicating that the subject's price ($200 per square foot) is slightly too high.

While price per square foot is the primary unit used, other units or metrics that may be considered in a CMA include:

- Total Sale Price: The overall transaction amount helps understand the total cost.
- Days on Market (DOM): How long was each comparable property listed before selling, indicating market demand?
- Lot Size: Measured in acres or square feet, especially relevant for properties with significant land.

Using these units, a CMA provides a comprehensive picture of the property's value in the current market, aiding in informed decision-making for buyers and sellers.

3.4.2 Sales Comparison Approach

The Sales Comparison Approach, similar to CMA, is a tool for comparing a property with similar properties recently sold in the same area. The Sales Comparison Approach is a formal method used by professional appraisers to determine the market value of a property for various purposes, including financing, taxation, and legal matters. The Sales Comparison Approach considers many factors, such as property condition, age, design, location, and specific market conditions. Adjustments are detailed for each difference between the subject property and the comparables. This method is widely used due to its direct correlation with current market conditions.

Appraisers also use price per square foot as one of several tools to ensure consistency and accuracy in their valuation process. An appraiser might note that comparable homes sold for $200 per square foot on average, but will also adjust for other factors like recent renovations, differences in lot size, and proximity to amenities before finalizing the value estimate. The appraiser must adequately review the property through site visits to calculate a likely market value.

3.4.3 Income Approach

The Income Approach, on the other hand, is often used for commercial properties like office buildings or residential properties with multiple units that generate rental income. It is beneficial for properties that do not have comparable market sales. This method focuses on the potential income that a property can generate, converted into a present value.

To apply this method, you first determine the annual potential rental income and subtract all operational expenses (excluding financing). It is called Net Operation Income (NOI). Then, a capitalization rate (cap rate) will be used to reflect the investor's required rate of return. This rate varies depending on factors like market conditions and property type. The resulting value indicates what an investor might be willing to pay based on the income the property generates.

Net Operation Income (NOI) =
Gross Rental Income – Operating Expenses (excluding financing)

Gross Rental Income, or Gross Income, is the property's total income before any expenses are deducted.

The unit for NOI is "dollars per year" (e.g., $50,000 per year.)

$$\text{Capitalization Rate (Cap Rate)} = \frac{\text{NOI}}{\text{Property Value}}$$

The unit for cap rate is a percentage (e.g., 8 %). Aim for an 8 % or higher cap rate when investing in commercial real estate. Cap Rate helps investors assess the risk and return of a property based on its income. A higher cap rate typically indicates higher risk but also potentially higher returns.

Let's say we want to examine the Cap Rate for our previous examples to find a range for the market value of our subject property. We assume they have a yearly NOI between $50,000 and $55,000.

Subject Property: Estimated market value $400,000.

- Cap Rate: $52,000 / $400,000 = 13.0 %

Comparable Property 1: Sold for $360,000.

- Cap Rate: $50,000 / $360,000 = 13.9 %

Comparable Property 2: Sold for $440,000.

- Cap Rate: $55,000 / $440,000 = 12.5 %

If we use the given percentages of 13.9 % and 12.5 %, the property's market value should be between $374,100 and $416,000.

$$\textbf{Property Value} = \frac{\textbf{NOI}}{\textbf{Cap Rate}}$$

$52,000 / 13.9 % = $374,100 and $52,000 / 12.5 % = $416,000.

Based on this example, the average market value would be $395,050. Average value = ($374,100 + $416,000) / 2 = $395,050

You may also encounter the Gross Rent Multiplier (GRM). This ratio estimates the value of income-producing properties based on their gross rental income, which is the total income generated from the property before any expenses are deducted.

$$\textbf{Gross Rent Multiplier (GRM)} = \frac{\textbf{Property Value}}{\textbf{Gross Rental Income}}$$

The unit for GRM is a numerical value (e.g., 9). In commercial real estate investments, aim for a GRM of 9 or lower. A lower GRM suggests a more valuable investment.

Let's say we want to examine GRM for our previous examples to find a range for the market value of our subject property. We assume they all have a yearly GRM of $80,000.

Subject Property: Estimated market value $400,000.

- Cap Rate: $400,000 / $80,000 = 5

Comparable Property 1: Sold for $360,000.

- Cap Rate: \$360,000 / \$80,000 = 4.5

Comparable Property 2: Sold for \$440,000.

- Cap Rate: \$440,000 / \$80,000 = 5.5

Based on this example, the GRM's average value is five (= (4.5 + 5.5) / 2), which indicates that the value should be around the quoted market value of \$400,000.

A GRM of 5 means the property's purchase price is five times its annual gross rental income. Lower GRMs typically indicate better investment opportunities, as they suggest the property generates more income relative to its price. With GRM, investors can quickly filter through potential properties to identify those worth a closer look and more detailed financial analysis.

When determining the average value, the more values you include, the better. Therefore, it is advisable to find as many comparable properties as possible in your local area. This means looking for properties that are similar in terms of size, location, and condition.

GRM can vary significantly by location and property type. It's helpful to compare GRMs within similar markets and property categories.

GRM does not account for operating expenses, vacancy rates, or financing costs. It's a preliminary measure and should be used alongside other metrics, such as Net Operating Income (NOI) and Capitalization Rate (Cap Rate), for a comprehensive analysis.

Ensure that the Gross Rental Income figure is stable and sustainable over time. Temporary rental income spikes or dips can skew the GRM.

3.4.4 Principles in Commercial Investment

Certain principles guide successful investments in commercial real estate. These include maintaining a positive cash flow, achieving a double-digit cash-on-cash return, and, as mentioned before, aiming for a cap rate of 8 % or higher and seeking properties with a gross rent multiplier of 9 or lower. Positive cash flow guarantees that the property generates more revenue than the costs of operations and mortgage payments, which is crucial for long-term sustainability. A double-digit cash-on-cash return means that the income earned on the money invested in a property is at least 10 %, a strong indicator of a good investment.

3.4.5 Cost Approach

The Cost Approach is based on the premise that a property's value equals the cost of constructing a similar property minus depreciation. This method is particularly relevant for newer properties where the building costs are known or can be accurately estimated. It involves evaluating the land value and the current price of constructing the buildings and other improvements, then subtracting depreciation due to factors like physical wear and tear or functional obsolescence. (Read more about depreciation in Chapter 4.4.3.)

With the cost method, one must determine the cost to replace or reproduce the property's improvements (in buildings and structures.) The cost to construct a building per square foot of gross building area is calculated based on construction costs, including materials, labor, contractor fees, and other expenses. The unit is dollars per square foot (e.g., $150 per square foot.) The cost per square foot is multiplied by the size of the building. The new unit is in dollars.

Total Construction Cost =
Cost Per Square Foot × Total Square Footage

The value of depreciation must be removed from this construction cost before the sum for the land is added. The total property value is now calculated according to the cost method.

Depreciated Cost of Improvements =
Total Construction Cost – Depreciation

Total Property Value =
Land Value + Depreciated Cost of Improvements

A calculation example is shown below:

1. **Cost Per Square Foot**: $150 per square foot.
2. **Total Square Footage**: 2,000 square feet.
3. **Total Construction Cost:** $150/sq ft × 2,000 sq ft = $300,000
4. **Depreciation**: 10 % of $300,000 = $30,000.
5. **Depreciated Cost of Improvements:** $300,000 – $30,000 = $270,000
6. **Land Value**: $100,000.
7. **Total Property Value:** $100,000 + $270,000 = $370,000

3.4.6 Calculating Return on Investment (ROI)

Calculating the Return on Investment (ROI) (also called Yield) is crucial for evaluating the performance of real estate investments and comparing different investment opportunities. You calculate ROI by dividing the net profit of the investment by the cost of the investment. For real estate, this includes factors like cash flow from rental income, potential appreciation, and the impact of tax implications. The unit for ROI is a percentage (e.g., 12 %), and it measures the investment's performance relative to its cost.

Let us take a look at Net ROI.

$$\text{Return on Investment (ROI)} = \frac{\text{Net Profit}}{\text{Cost of Investment}} \text{ X } 100$$

Net Profit = Total Gains – Total Costs

Total Gains =
Rental income + Appreciation + Other income

Total Costs =
Mortgage payments + Taxes + Insurance + Maintenance + Management fees

Costs of Investment =
Purchase price + Renovations + Maintenance + Transaction fees + etc

For instance, if you purchase a property for $220,000 and spend an additional $50,000 on renovations, your total investment cost is $270,000.

Over a year, you earned $30,000 in rental income, and the property appreciated in value by $20,000. Your expenses for the year (including mortgage interest, property taxes, insurance, maintenance, etc.) totaled $15,000.

1. Cost of Investment:

Cost of Investment = $220,000(purchase price) + $50,000(renovations) = $270,000

2. Net Profit:

Total Gains = $30,000(rental income) + $20,000(appreciation) = $50,000
Net Profit = $50,000(total gains) – $15,000(expenses) = $35,000

3. ROI Calculation:

ROI = ($35,000 / $270,000) × 100 = 13 %

An ROI of 13 % means that for every dollar invested in the property, you earn 13 cents in profit over the specified period. It is important to ensure that each calculated value entering the ROI calculation is based on the same time period.

Above was mentioned Net ROI. There is also Gross ROI. Gross ROI considers only the total gains without deducting expenses, while Net ROI deducts expenses from the gains. If we use the same example as above:

1. Cost of Investment:

Cost of Investment = $220,000(purchase price) + $50,000(renovations) = $270,000

2. Net Profit:

Total Gains = $30,000(rental income) + $20,000(appreciation) = $50,000
Net Profit = $50,000(total gains) – 0 = $50,000

3. ROI Calculation:
ROI = ($50,000 / $270,000) × 100 = 19 %

ROI helps compare the profitability of different investments. A higher ROI indicates a more profitable investment.

With Net ROI, you consider your real profit more than using Gross ROI (or the simplified Gross profit. Gross Profit only sees the difference between the purchase and sale values. Based on the example above, this means that if you sell the property later for $350,000, your gross profit is $70,000. (ROI = ($70,000 / $270,000) × 100 = 26 %.) Calculating this simplistically is to deceive yourself. Owning a property will involve costs, so you must ensure that it generates income.)

ROI does not account for the risk associated with the investment. Higher potential returns often come with higher risk. When researching a potential property to invest in, request the income statements for the last three years and calculate the Net ROI for each year. It will increase your knowledge of the object's potential and thus reduce your risk.

3.4.7 Rent-to-Value (RTV) Ratio

The Rent-to-Value (RTV) ratio is a metric used to evaluate the rental income potential of a property relative to its market value. It is calculated by dividing the annual rental income by the property's current market value and expressing the result as a percentage. This ratio helps investors assess how well a property's rental income covers its cost or value.

$$\text{Rent-to-Value Ratio (RVT)} = \frac{\text{Annual Rental Income}}{\text{Property Market Value}} \times 100$$

If we use the same example as above:

1. **Annual Rental Income:**
   Annual Rental Income = $30,000 (rental income)

2. **Property Market Value:**
   Property Market Value = $220,000 (purchase price)

3. **Calculate RVT:**
   Rent-to Value (RVT) = ($30,000 / $220,000) × 100 = 14 %

A higher RTV ratio generally indicates a better return on investment for rental income. In contrast, a lower RTV ratio may indicate that the property's value is high relative to the income it generates. Investors often use the RTV ratio to compare properties and make informed decisions about where to invest for optimal rental income relative to property value.

3.4.8 Development Cost

Understanding the cost of property development or renovation is crucial, as these costs directly affect the total investment needed and the potential returns. Whether developing a new property from the ground up or renovating an existing one, accurately estimating these costs is essential for setting a budget and forecasting the ROI. These costs include construction expenses and fees for permits, design, and landscaping, among others. For example, suppose redevelopment costs are higher than initially projected. In that case, they can significantly reduce the investor's return requirement, affecting the project's overall feasibility.

3.4.9 Evaluating Property Values with AVM

Navigating online valuation tools requires a discerning eye. While tools like Zillow's Zestimate[51] provide a quick appraisal of property values based on public and user-submitted data, it's essential to recognize that these estimates can sometimes be off-mark. To harness these tools effectively, supplement them with additional research. Visit the property, engage with local real estate experts, and compare the online estimates with actual sales data in the area. This holistic approach ensures a more accurate valuation, minimizing risks and enhancing the potential for profitable investments. Moreover, engaging with local experts validates the data. It provides insights into market nuances that online tools might not capture.

Focusing on investment analysis tools, the benefits of integrating these into your evaluation process are manifold. Software solutions that facilitate financial modeling and cash flow analysis can transform raw data into actionable insights, enabling you to predict how well a property will perform as an investment. These tools allow you to simulate different scenarios and assess the potential impact of factors such as market fluctuations, interest rate changes, or alterations in rental income. This capability is invaluable for risk assessment and decision-making, helping you to develop robust investment strategies that withstand market variability. By streamlining the evaluation process, these tools save you time and enhance the accuracy of your investment appraisals, paving the way for more successful real estate ventures.

As technology evolves, the tools available for real estate market analysis and property valuation are becoming increasingly sophisticated. By staying informed about new developments and continuously refining your analytical skills, you can enhance your ability to assess property values accurately and make investment decisions that are informed, strategic, and aligned with your financial goals. Remember, in real estate investing, knowledge is not just power—it's profit.

Several programs and platforms offer automated valuation models (AVMs) for real estate, empowering users with the convenience of quick and accurate property valuations. These AVMs are based on various data sources and algorithms, providing a powerful tool for property evaluation. They have unique features and data sources, so the choice of AVM may depend on specific needs, such as geographic coverage, data updating, and integration capabilities.

- **Zillow's Zestimate**[52] is one of the most well-known AVMs, offering estimated property values for millions of homes across the United States. It uses a proprietary algorithm incorporating public, user-submitted, and MLS data where available.
- Similarly, **Redfin's AVM**[53] offers property value estimates based on MLS data, public records, and Redfin's proprietary data, with updates as often as daily, depending on the availability of new data.
- **CoreLogic's Real AVM**[54] delivers property valuations for lenders, real estate professionals, and other stakeholders, utilizing a comprehensive property and market data and advanced analytics database.
- **HouseCanary.com** provides AVM solutions that offer property valuations and real estate market analytics by combining machine learning with a vast dataset, including public records, MLS data, and proprietary data.
- **Realtor.com**[55] also provides AVM estimates for properties listed on its platform. It uses data from MLS, public records, and other sources to generate property valuations.
- **The RPR**[56] (Realtors Property Resource), a subsidiary of the National Association of Realtors (NAR), offers AVM tools to real estate professionals, providing a Realtor Valuation Model (RVM) that incorporates MLS data and public records.
- **Black Knight**[57] offers AVM solutions through its Collateral Analytics division. It provides property valuation and risk assessment tools that use extensive data sets, including MLS and public records, with advanced analytics.

- **JPMorgan Chase**[58], offers the Chase Home Value Estimator which provides home value estimates for properties across the U.S. using public data and proprietary algorithms.
- **QuickenLoans.com** provides AVM services through its online platform, offering home value estimates using public records, MLS data, and proprietary algorithms.
- Finally, **ATTOM Data Solutions**[59] offers AVM services as part of its comprehensive real estate data solutions, integrating property, tax, and neighborhood data to provide accurate property valuations.

As we transition from exploring valuation methods, our next focus will delve into the financial intricacies of real estate investment, ensuring you are equipped with the knowledge to maximize returns and sustain your investment portfolio.

* * *

The chapter's footnotes

1 *https://www.trade.gov/*
2 *https://ustr.gov/*
3 https://*www.wto.org/*
4 *https://www.worldbank.org/en/home*
5 https://*www.ft.com/*
6 *https://www.bbc.com/news*
7 https://*www.cfr.org/*
8 *https://www.imf.org*
9 *https://www.bea.gov/*
10 *https://www.wsj.com/*
11 *https://www.moodys.com/*
12 *https://www.eiu.com/n/*
13 *https://www.spglobal.com/en*
14 *https://www.cbre.com/insights#overview*

15 *https://fred.stlouisfed.org/*

16 *https://www.nar.realtor/*

17 *https://www.icsc.com/*

18 *https://nationalreia.org*

19 *https://uli.org/*

20 *https://www.irem.org/*

21 *https://crewnetwork.org/*

22 *https://www.altusgroup.com/solutions/argus-enterprise/*

23 *https://cre.moodysanalytics.com/*

24 *https://www.zillow.com/premier-agent/*

25 *https://www.esri.com/en-us/arcgis/geospatial-platform/overview*

26 *https://www.ibm.com/spss*

27 *https://www.microsoft.com/sv-se/power-platform/products/power-bi?market=se*

28 *https://www.ibm.com/spss*

29 *https://www.sas.com/sv_se/home.html*

30 *https://www.eviews.com/home.html*

31 *https://www.jmp.com/en_se/home.html*

32 *https://www.esri.com/en-us/arcgis/geospatial-platform/overview*

33 *https://www.precisely.com/product/precisely-mapinfo/mapinfo-pro*

34 https://www.google.com/earth/about/versions/

35 *https://hexagon.com/company/divisions/safety-infrastructure-geospatial*

36 *https://www.bentley.com/*

37 *https://www.autodesk.com/products/infraworks/*

38 https://*pro.twitter.com/*

39 *https://uli.org/*

40 *https://www.cbre.com/insights*

41 *https://www.zillow.com/research/*

42 *https://www.corelogic.com/subscribe/*

43 *https://www.redfin.com/news/market-tracker/*

44 *https://www.nar.realtor/email*

45 https://*www.costar.com/*

46 *https://www.biggerpockets.com/real-estate-listings*

47 *https://www.mysmartmove.com/*

48 *https://www.experian.com/rental-property-solutions/rentbureau*

49 *https://www.foia.gov/*

50 https://*thewilliamsestates.com/* and *https://www.williamsauction.com/*

51 *https://www.zillow.com/how-much-is-my-home-worth/*

52 https://*www.zillow.com/z/zestimate/*

53 *https://www.redfin.com/redfin-estimate*

54 *https://www.corelogic.com*

55 *https://www.realtor.com/estimates/*

56 *https://www.narrpr.com*

57 *https://blackknightre.com/*

58 *https://www.chase.com/personal/mortgage/calculators-resources/home-value-estimator*

59 *https://www.attomdata.com/data/property-valuation-data/avm/*

MAKE A DIFFERENCE WITH YOUR REVIEW

Unlock the Power of Generosity

"The best way to find yourself is to lose yourself in the service of others."
MAHATMA GANDHI

People who give without expecting anything in return live happier lives. So, let's make a difference together!

Would you help someone like yourself who is curious about real estate investing but needs help figuring out where to start?

My mission is to make real estate investing easy and fun for everyone. But to reach more people, I need your help.

Most people choose books based on reviews. So, I'm asking you to help a fellow beginner investor by leaving a review. It costs nothing and takes less than a minute but could change someone's real estate investing journey.

Your review, which takes no more than a minute, could help...
...one more person take the first step toward financial independence.
...one more family build wealth for future generations.

...one more hard worker secure their financial future.
...one more dreamer make real estate part of their life.

If you enjoyed the book, please consider leaving a review on the site where you purchased it.

If you love helping others, you're my kind of person.

Thank you from the bottom of my heart!
Mari Sellin

FINANCIAL MANAGEMENT

"Every accomplishment starts with the decision to try."
JOHN F. KENNEDY

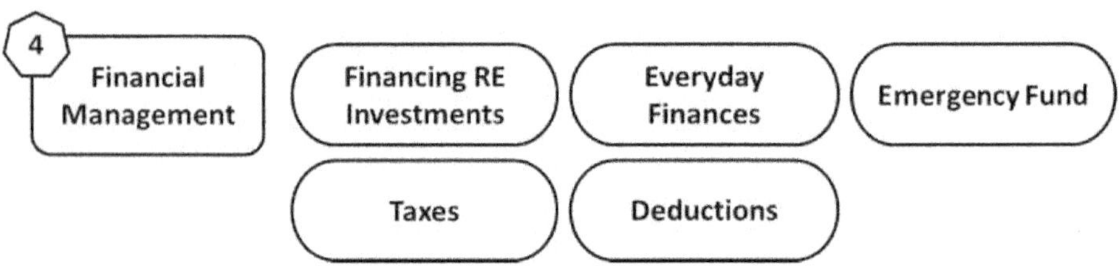

Imagine navigating a ship through a vast ocean, where each financial decision you make adjusts the sails and steers you closer to your treasure—financial independence through real estate. In this vast sea, the currents and winds are the everyday financial tasks that, if managed poorly, can lead you off course. This chapter is your compass, guiding you through the crucial aspects of financial management that solidify your footing in the real estate market, ensuring each decision moves you toward your ultimate goal.

4.1 FINANCING REAL ESTATE INVESTMENTS

4.1.1 How to Invest with Little to No Money Down

Embarking on the path of real estate investment can often seem like a terrain navigated easier by the financially robust—a realm where significant upfront capital is seemingly indispensable. However, let me guide you through a less-trodden yet equally viable path where financial constraints are not a barrier but a challenge to be creatively overcome. This chapter is dedicated to unfolding the myriad of financing options that require little to no money down, making real estate investment accessible to everyone, especially if you're starting and capital is your primary concern.

4.1.1.1 Zero Down Payment with Government Loans

Imagine purchasing a property without the daunting requirement of a hefty down payment. It isn't a fantasy but a reality made possible through specific loan programs to facilitate property ownership. Two notable programs are the VA and USDA loans, which offer zero down payment options under certain conditions. (Read more in Chapter 4.1.3.2.)

VA loans, available to veterans and active military members, not only provide the benefit of no down payment but also do not require Private Mortgage Insurance (PMI), reducing the monthly financial burden on the borrower.

USDA loans, targeting rural property buyers, also offer no down payment and are geared towards promoting homeownership in less densely populated areas. Both programs have specific eligibility requirements, such as satisfactory credit scores and income limits, and properties must meet particular appraisal standards to qualify. Applying for these loans involves a detailed process of examining every financial aspect. Still, they represent a remarkable opportunity to acquire real estate with minimal initial investment.

4.1.1.2 Government and Grant Programs

Leveraging government programs and grants can significantly ease the financial challenges of real estate investing. Numerous federal, state, and local programs offer grants, loans, tax breaks, or other financial assistance for real estate developments, particularly those that enhance economic development or revitalize underdeveloped areas. These programs often have specific criteria and application processes. Still, they can provide substantial financial support without the need to repay funds. For instance, some programs target first-time investors or properties in areas needing economic stimulation, offering lower interest rates or down payment assistance. (Read more in Chapters 4.1.3 and 4.1.4.)

4.1.1.3 Partnerships and Joint Ventures

Forming partnerships or joint ventures presents a practical solution for those who find going solo in real estate investment daunting or financially unfeasible. By unifying resources with one or more partners, you can share the financial burden, responsibilities, and risks of real estate investment. For instance, one partner may bring capital to the table. At the same time, another offers expertise in property management, creating a synergistic relationship that maximizes each participant's strengths. Structuring these partnerships requires clear agreements that outline the contribution of each party, the distribution of profits, roles, and responsibilities, and the terms under which the partnership can be dissolved. These strategic arrangements provide a support system, making the investment journey less isolating.

4.1.1.4 Using Home Equity

For homeowners, the equity built up in their primary residence can be a powerful tool in financing additional real estate investments. Home Equity Lines Of Credit (HELOCs) and home equity loans allow you to borrow against the equity you have accumulated in your home, typically at favorable interest rates. HELOCs offer flexible borrowing and repayment terms that can be particularly advantageous for covering renovation costs or bridging gaps in cash flow. On the other hand, home equity loans provide a lump sum that can be used for more significant investments, such as down payments on additional properties. Both options require careful consideration of your financial stability, as defaulting on these loans can jeopardize your primary residence.

Resources to learn more

Home Equity Lines of Credit (HELOCs) and home equity loans are popular financial products in the United States, and there are numerous resources where you can learn more about them.

To understand HELOCs and home equity loans, you should visit the Consumer Financial Protection Bureau (CFPB)[1], which offers comprehensive guides[2] on HELOCs and home equity loans detailing their benefits, risks, and costs. **Investopedia.com** provides detailed articles explaining how HELOCs[3] and home equity loans[4] work, their advantages and disadvantages, and how to choose between them. Additionally, **NerdWallet.com** offers comparisons of HELOCs[5] and home equity loans[6], advice on the best options available, and calculators to estimate costs.

For more in-depth reading, consider books such as "Mortgages 101: Quick Answers to Over 250 Critical Questions about Your Home Loan" by David Reed.

Examples of lenders

Many banks and financial institutions offer HELOCs and home equity loans. Ask your current bank what options they offer.

Major banks like Wells Fargo, Bank of America, and Chase Bank provide competitive rates and flexible terms for these products. Credit unions such as Navy Federal Credit Union and PenFed Credit Union also offer attractive options for members. Online lenders like LendingTree and Quicken Loans provide easy comparison tools and straightforward application processes. Regional banks, including Regions Bank and SunTrust (now Truist), offer HELOCs with flexible terms and competitive rates.

When choosing a lender, it's essential to compare rates and terms from multiple lenders to find the best interest rates and conditions. Consider the fees associated with each loan, such as application fees, closing costs, and annual fees. Customer service is also crucial; choose a lender with good customer reviews and responsive support. Additionally, look for flexible repayment options, the ability to lock in a fixed rate, and no prepayment penalties.

By exploring these resources and comparing offers from various lenders, you can find the HELOC or home equity loan that best fits your financial needs and goals.

4.1.1.5 Exploring Alternative Funding Sources

Beyond traditional financing routes, the modern investor has access to many alternative funding sources. Below are examples, so investigate if your region has more options.

Peer-to-peer lending (P2P)

Peer-to-peer lending (P2P) platforms allow investors to obtain loans directly from individuals without the intermediation of financial institutions, often at competitive interest rates and with more flexible qualification criteria. Several peer-to-peer lending platforms specialize in real estate financing, offering investors opportunities to fund real estate projects and borrowers access to funds for property purchases, renovations, or developments. Platforms such as:

- **RealtyMogul.com** and **Fundrise.com** allow investors to participate in commercial and residential real estate deals, providing diversified portfolios through equity investments and loans.
- **PeerStreet.com** focuses on real estate-backed loans, enabling investment in short-term, high-yield real estate loans secured by residential and commercial properties.
- **LendingHome.com** targets fix-and-flip properties with short-term bridge loans and also offers rental loans.
- **Groundfloor.us** caters to residential property renovations and new constructions with low minimum investment requirements.
- **CrowdStreet.com** offers commercial real estate investment opportunities for accredited investors, including office, industrial, multifamily, and mixed-use properties.
- **Roofstock.com** is a marketplace for buying and selling single-family rental properties. It offers turnkey investment opportunities with property management in place.
- Lastly, **Mynd Investment**[7] (formerly HomeUnion) provides end-to-end services for single-family rental investments, from acquisition to management and sales, allowing investors to diversify across different markets.

Crowdfunding

Crowdfunding is another innovative approach. It enables investors to raise small amounts of money from many people via online platforms. This method benefits investors who can effectively market their investment projects to potential contributors.

Several crowdfunding platforms offer real estate financing, making it easier for individual investors to participate in the market. Platforms such as:

- **Fundrise.com** is a popular platform that allows investors to access residential and commercial real estate projects through eREITs and eFunds, with low minimum investment requirements.
- **Yieldstreet.com** provides alternative investment opportunities, including real estate, focusing on giving individual investors access to investments typically unavailable to them.
- **EquityMultiple.com** targets accredited investors with commercial real estate investments, offering equity, preferred equity, and senior debt options.
- Some platforms mentioned above regarding P2P also offer crowdfunding solutions: **RealtyMogul.com**, **CrowdStreet.com**, **PeerStreet.com**, **Groundfloor.com**, and lastly, **Roofstock.com**.

These platforms offer diverse investment strategies and risk profiles, providing a wealth of options for real estate investing. This variety makes real estate investing more accessible and diversified through P2P lending and crowdfunding, giving investors the confidence to choose the strategy that best suits their financial goals.

Real Estate Syndications

Additionally, real estate syndications offer a structured way for multiple investors to pool funds and share in the ownership and profits of large properties they might not be able to afford individually.

Real estate syndications provide a method for pooling investor funds to finance real estate projects, and several notable companies offer such opportunities.

- **AshcroftCapital.com** specializes in multifamily real estate investments, focusing on value-add opportunities and offering accredited investors a chance to invest in large apartment communities.

- Similarly, **CardoneCapital.com**, founded by Grant Cardone, targets multifamily properties and provides investment opportunities to accredited and non-accredited investors, aiming to generate passive income and capital appreciation.
- **RealtyShares.com** connects investors with real estate developers for various property types, including residential, commercial, and mixed-use projects. It offers both debt and equity investment opportunities.
- **OriginInvestments.com** focuses on multifamily properties in high-growth markets, offering investment opportunities for accredited investors through its funds aimed at income and growth.
- **MLGCapital.com** specializes in private real estate syndications across multifamily, industrial, retail, and office properties, offering diverse portfolios for accredited investors.
- **NextLevelIncome.com** offers syndication opportunities in multifamily, self-storage, and mobile home park investments, aiming to provide passive income and long-term growth for accredited investors.
- **Verivest.com** provides a platform for investors to discover and invest in real estate syndications. It focuses on transparency and due diligence by offering a directory of vetted real estate sponsors and investment opportunities.
- Some platforms mentioned above also offer real estate syndications, such as **RealtyMogul.com**, **CrowdStreet.com**, and **EquityMultiple.com**.

These real estate syndication companies offer a range of investment opportunities in different property types and markets, enabling accredited and non-accredited investors to participate in large-scale real estate projects and benefit from diversified investment portfolios.

4.1.1.6 Understand Wholesaling

As explained in Chapter 2.3.7 real estate wholesaling is a unique strategy that involves entering into a contract to buy a property and then selling the contract to another buyer before the sale closes. This approach requires little to no money down, as the wholesaler typically does not purchase the property outright but secures it under contract with a deposit. The key to successful wholesaling lies in finding undervalued properties and quickly flipping the contracts for a profit, which demands a deep understanding of the market and strong negotiation skills. While wholesaling can be a lucrative venture, it also carries risks, such as the inability to find a buyer before the contract expires, which necessitates a thorough understanding of the process and market conditions.

Several platforms specialize in real estate wholesaling, offering tools and resources to help investors find, evaluate, and close deals efficiently.

- **PropStream.com** provides comprehensive property data, comparable sales, and marketing tools, making it a popular choice among wholesalers.
- **REIPro**[8] offers a suite of tools specifically designed for wholesaling, including lead generation, deal analysis, and automated marketing.
- **Investor Carrot.com** focuses on helping investors create SEO-optimized websites to attract and manage wholesale leads.
- **Flipster.net** offers deal analysis, property finding, and marketing automation tools.
- **BatchLeads.io** specializes in lead generation and management with features like skip tracing and direct mail marketing.
- **LeadPropeller.com** helps wholesalers generate and manage leads through customizable websites and marketing automation.
- **ConnectedInvestors.com** is a social network and marketplace that provides property listings, deal analysis tools, and investor connections.
- **FreedomSoft.com** offers an all-in-one platform with CRM, lead generation, and deal analysis capabilities.
- **DealMachine.com** provides a driving-for-dollar app, direct mail marketing, and property data access, streamlining the process of finding and managing wholesale deals.
- **Real Estate Worldwide** (REWW)[9] offers tools and educational resources focused on wholesaling, including property data and lead generation.

These platforms cater to the specific needs of real estate wholesalers, providing a range of tools to streamline processes from lead generation to closing deals, enhancing efficiency and effectiveness in the wholesale market.

As you navigate these financing options, remember that each has its intricacies and implications. Your financing choice should align with your long-term investment goals, risk tolerance, and financial situation. By diversifying your funding strategies and leveraging the available resources, you can confidently embark on your real estate investment path, even with minimal initial capital.

4.1.2 Traditional Mortgage Options for Beginners

Navigating the realm of mortgages might initially seem daunting, especially when terms like 'amortization' and 'adjustable rate' come into play. Let's simplify these concepts to ensure you feel confident as you step into this essential aspect of real estate financing. A mortgage is a loan specifically designed to purchase real estate. The principal is the actual loan amount you borrow. On the other hand, interest is the cost you pay for borrowing that money, expressed as a percentage rate. Amortization refers to the schedule by which you pay off this debt, typically through monthly payments over a set period, such as 15 or 30 years. These payments are initially more heavily weighted towards interest, gradually shifting towards principal reduction over time.

Understanding the difference between fixed-rate and Adjustable-Rate Mortgages (ARMs) is crucial. Fixed-rate mortgages lock in your interest rate for the entirety of the loan term, providing predictable monthly payments and shielding you from future interest rate increases. Conversely, ARMs offer a lower initial rate that adjusts over time based on prevailing market rates. While ARMs can provide lower payments early on, they also pose the risk of significant rate increases, making them less predictable than fixed-rate options.

Several types of mortgage loans cater to different needs and financial situations. Fixed-rate and adjustable-rate mortgages are the most traditional. Still, interest-only mortgages present another option, allowing you to pay only the interest on the loan for a certain period before starting to pay off the principal. It can be beneficial if you anticipate a higher income in the future. Still, it can be risky if your financial situation doesn't evolve as expected.

Comparing conventional mortgages with FHA loans offers further insight. Conventional mortgages usually require a higher down payment and better credit score but tend to have lower interest rates and fewer restrictions. FHA loans, backed by the Federal Housing Administration, allow for lower down payments and are more accessible to those with less-than-perfect credit. Still, they require mortgage insurance premiums that can add to the overall cost of the loan.

Shopping around for the best mortgage terms is as crucial as selecting the correct type of loan. Interest rates and terms can vary widely between lenders, and securing a slightly lower rate can save you thousands over the life of the loan. Tools like online mortgage calculators and comparison websites can help you visualize the long-term costs of different mortgage options and decide which is most economical. Always read the fine print and understand all the terms and conditions before committing to a mortgage.

Negotiating with lenders might only sometimes seem straightforward, but knowing a few techniques can help secure better terms. You can negotiate the interest rate, loan length, or specific fees. Understanding what motivates lenders and building solid relationships with them can help in these negotiations. For example, demonstrating a strong credit history or a stable income might convince a lender to offer you better terms.

Qualifying for a mortgage involves several important factors: your credit score, income stability, debt-to-income ratio, down payment size, and the property's valuation. Improving your credit score, increasing your income, or decreasing your debt can all enhance your mortgage eligibility. When applying for a mortgage, you'll need extensive documentation, including tax returns, pay stubs, and bank statements, which lenders will scrutinize to assess your financial stability.

The mortgage application process, from pre-approval to closing, can be intricate. Pre-approval gives you an idea of what you can afford and shows sellers that you are a serious buyer. The final approval comes after thoroughly checking your financial background and the property details. During closing, you'll sign various legal documents to finalize the mortgage, transferring the property ownership to you. Preparing all required documents and understanding each step can make this process smoother.

Finally, always have a contingency plan. Suppose financing falls through at the last minute. In that case, having alternative strategies such as additional loan options, co-signers, or access to private funding can be invaluable. Alternatively, adjusting your investment scope to include less expensive properties or considering partnerships for additional capital might also provide solutions.

By understanding these fundamental concepts and strategies, you can confidently approach mortgage financing, equipped with the knowledge to secure the best possible terms and navigate the process efficiently. This will set a solid financial foundation for your real estate investments.

4.1.3 Exploring Government Loans and Incentives

Navigating the terrain of real estate investment financing can often feel complex and daunting, especially for beginners. However, government loans and incentives are specifically designed to alleviate some of these challenges, offering favorable terms that might not be available through conventional loans. These loans often feature lower down payments, reduced interest rates, and more flexible eligibility criteria, making them particularly appealing to first-time homebuyers or investors looking to expand their portfolios without extensive capital outlay.

Exploring these government loans and incentives opens up a spectrum of possibilities for financing your real estate ventures, offering pathways to investment that accommodate a wide range of financial situations and objectives. By carefully evaluating each option and strategically incorporating these financial tools into your investment planning, you can maximize your potential for success in the real estate market, turning visions of property ownership and profitable investing into tangible realities.

4.1.3.1 Introduction to Government Loans

Government loans differ significantly from conventional loans, primarily because various federal agencies back them. This backing reduces the risk for lenders, enabling them to offer loans with more advantageous terms. For instance, lower down payments and more lenient credit requirements open the door for many individuals who might otherwise be unable to secure financing. Additionally, some government loan programs are designed with specific purposes, such as revitalizing certain areas, assisting veterans, helping rural homeowners, and aligning financial support with broader economic or social goals.

4.1.3.2 Strategic Use of Government Loans in Real Estate Investing

Incorporating government loans into your real estate investment strategy can significantly enhance your purchasing power and expand your portfolio. For example, using an FHA loan to buy and renovate a multi-family property can generate rental income, which can cover mortgage payments and potentially fund additional investments.

Highlight FHA Loans

The Federal Housing Administration (FHA), a part of the U.S. Department of Housing and Urban Development (HUD), offers FHA loans that benefit first-time homebuyers and investors interested in multi-family units. These loans are renowned for their low down payment requirement, sometimes as low as 3.5 % of the purchase price, significantly lower than most conventional mortgage requirements. Additionally, FHA loans are more accessible to individuals with lower credit scores. However, it's essential to consider that FHA loans require borrowers to pay Mortgage Insurance Premiums (MIP), which are added to the total cost of the loan. The eligibility for an FHA loan typically involves providing steady employment and sufficient income to cover monthly mortgage payments and other related expenses.

Introduce VA Loans

VA loans represent a remarkable benefit for veterans and active military members, providing an opportunity to purchase a home with no down payment and no requirement for Private Mortgage Insurance (PMI.) These loans, guaranteed by the Department of Veterans Affairs, are a token of gratitude for military service and a substantial financial advantage. Qualifying for a VA loan involves obtaining a certificate of eligibility from the VA, which confirms the applicant's military service details. VA loans can also be used to purchase investment properties, provided the owner intends to occupy one of the units. It can be particularly advantageous for investors looking to live in one unit while renting out others, effectively building equity and generating income simultaneously.

Explain the 203k Loan

The 203k loan, backed by the Federal Housing Administration (FHA), is tailored explicitly for properties needing rehabilitation or renovation. This type of loan consolidates the home's purchase price and the cost of renovations into a single mortgage, making it easier to manage financially. The key features of a 203k loan include covering a broad range of renovation projects, from structural alterations to aesthetic upgrades. Applicants for a 203k loan must provide a detailed proposal of the work to be done, including cost estimates, which must be evaluated and approved by the lender. This loan is especially beneficial for investors looking to purchase properties at a lower cost due to their need for repairs and improve them for a higher resale value or rental income.

Explore USDA Loans

USDA loans are another government-backed option aimed primarily at aiding rural development. Administered by the United States Department of Agriculture, these loans offer 100 % financing, meaning no down payment is required, which can significantly lower the barrier to property ownership. Compared to other types of loans, reduced mortgage insurance costs make USDA loans financially appealing. According to USDA guidelines, understanding what qualifies as 'rural' is crucial, as these loans are designed to promote development in less densely populated areas. Typically, areas with populations less than 35,000 are eligible. Still, checking the USDA's official site for the most accurate and current eligibility maps is always wise.

4.1.3.3 Application Process for Government Loans

Applying for government-backed loans involves several critical steps. First and foremost, it's essential to meet the eligibility criteria, which vary widely between different programs. Documentation of income, employment, credit history, and other financial details is typically required to demonstrate your ability to repay the loan. Additionally, the property usually must meet specific standards and undergo a thorough appraisal. Preparing for the application process by gathering all necessary documents in advance and possibly consulting with a loan officer specializing in government-backed loans can streamline your experience.

4.1.4 Government Programs and Assistance

Many government programs are specifically designed to support real estate investments that contribute to economic growth, environmental sustainability, or community development. These programs might offer financial assistance, valuable resources, and guidance for new investors. Engaging with local real estate investment groups or attending seminars sponsored by housing authorities can provide further insights into how these programs can be integrated into your investment strategies.

4.1.4.1 Detail State and Local Grants and Incentives

Beyond federal programs, many state and local governments offer additional grants, tax breaks, or incentives to encourage real estate development and investment. These programs often target specific areas for economic revitalization or support particular demographic groups such as first-time homebuyers. For instance, some states offer tax credits for rehabilitating historic properties. In contrast, others might provide grants for installing energy-efficient systems in residential properties. Navigating these opportunities requires research and sometimes the assistance of a real estate professional or legal advisor to fully understand the application process and eligibility criteria.

4.1.4.2 Finding Government Programs and Grants

Start with government websites to find information about leveraging government programs and grants.

- **Grants.gov** is the primary resource for federal grants, listing all available opportunities.
- **The Small Business Administration** (SBA)[10] offers information on loans, grants, and resources for small businesses.
- At the same time, **the U.S. Department of Housing and Urban De-**

velopment (HUD)[11] provides details on housing grants and community development programs.

- **The Economic Development Administration** (EDA)[12] offers grants for economic development projects.
- **State and local resources** are also valuable. Each state has its own economic development agency offering grants, loans, and tax incentives. Local government websites often have information on local grants and funding opportunities.
- Additionally, check out **FoundationCenter.org** for a comprehensive database of grantmakers and grants, and explore resources from **local chambers of commerce and Community Development Financial Institutions** (CDFIs) for additional funding support.
- **Research and networking** play crucial roles. Join industry associations relevant to your field, attend networking events and conferences, and conduct online research to find specific grants and programs.
- **Consulting with experts** such as **grant writers**, **SBA**, and **SCORE.org** mentors can significantly enhance your chances of securing funding.
- Educational resources like **webinars**, **workshops**, and **public libraries** provide valuable information on how to apply for grants and navigate government programs.

These resources and strategies can help you effectively leverage government programs and grants to support your projects and initiatives.

4.1.5 Creative Financing Strategies: Lease Options

Imagine you're presented with an opportunity to invest in real estate that doesn't require the total commitment of an immediate purchase, offering flexibility and a lower financial barrier to entry. It is where lease options come into play—an intriguing strategy for both seasoned investors and beginners. A lease option allows you to rent a property with the exclusive right to purchase it at a later date, typically within a specified period. This arrangement can be particularly advantageous if you're not ready to secure financing immediately or are testing the waters in a new market.

4.1.5.1 Lease Option

The mechanics of a lease option involve two agreements: the lease part, which is similar to any rental agreement, and the option part, which is your right but not the obligation to buy the property later. You pay the seller an option fee, which is usually non-refundable. In exchange, you get the option to buy the property at a predetermined price before the lease expires. This fee compensates the seller for taking the property off the market. In negotiating the terms of a lease option, it's crucial to agree on a purchase price that is locked in, regardless of future market fluctuations. It can be highly beneficial in a rising market.

Using lease options to control a property without owning it outright presents several benefits. It reduces your initial financial outlay, preserves your capital for other investments, and gives you time to assess the property and its potential return on investment. During the lease period, you can also work on improving your creditworthiness or saving for a larger down payment, making it easier to secure a mortgage when you're ready to purchase. Moreover, if the market value of the property increases beyond the agreed-upon purchase price, you stand to gain significant equity when you decide to buy.

Strategizing with lease options requires careful planning and negotiation. To tilt the terms in your favor:

- Focus on negotiating a longer lease term, which gives you more time to secure financing and evaluate the property's performance as an investment.
- Ensure that a portion of each rental payment is credited towards the purchase price, effectively building equity in the property even before you own it.

- Negotiate the right to sublet the property, which will allow you to generate rental income that can be used towards the purchase.

4.1.5.2 Rent-to-Own

Combining insights on lease options with rent-to-own strategies broadens your investment toolkit. Like lease options, rent-to-own agreements provide a path to homeownership for tenants who might not immediately qualify for a mortgage. Tenants pay a higher rent, a portion of which goes towards the down payment on the property, building equity over time. This arrangement can be particularly attractive if you're looking to invest in residential properties where tenants have a vested interest in maintaining and eventually owning the home.

4.1.5.3 Legal Considerations

Legal considerations are crucial in structuring a lease option or rent-to-own agreement. It's essential to have all terms clearly outlined in a contract reviewed by a real estate attorney. This contract should specify the rights and responsibilities of each party, the lease terms, the details of the option to purchase, and the handling of the option fee and rent credits. Proper legal documentation ensures that both parties are protected and that the agreement complies with state and local real estate laws.

By understanding and utilizing lease options and rent-to-own strategies, you can navigate the financial challenges of real estate investing with greater flexibility and lower risk. These strategies facilitate property control and potential ownership under favorable conditions and provide practical pathways for building your real estate portfolio creatively and efficiently. As you explore these options, always consider the long-term implications and ensure each deal aligns with your overall investment goals and financial capabilities.

4.1.6 Creative Financing Strategies: Seller Financing

Imagine a scenario where the barriers of traditional lending institutions are bypassed, and you, as a beginner in real estate, can negotiate directly with the seller to finance your property purchase. It is the essence of seller financing, a powerful yet underutilized strategy that can open doors to numerous investment opportunities. In this arrangement, the seller acts as the property owner and the lender, providing a loan directly to you, the buyer. It means you pay the seller over an agreed period instead of securing a traditional mortgage from a bank.

Seller financing is particularly advantageous when conventional loan approval hurdles are too high or you wish to secure a more flexible repayment plan. Unlike traditional banks that adhere to strict lending criteria, sellers may be more flexible about terms, which can be adjusted to suit both parties' financial situations. For example, suppose you're starting in real estate with limited capital. In that case, a seller might agree to a lower down payment if you agree to a higher interest rate or a balloon payment after a few years. It can make all the difference in enabling you to begin your investment journey.

The benefits of seller financing extend beyond more accessible qualification criteria and flexible terms. For one, the closing process can be significantly faster since you avoid the lengthy bank mortgage approval processes. This speed can be a critical advantage in competitive real estate markets where properties sell quickly. Additionally, closing costs are generally lower without the bank's administrative fees. For sellers, this method can make their property more attractive to a broader pool of buyers, especially those who might struggle to secure traditional financing. It also provides the seller with a steady income stream from the interest on the loan, often at a higher rate than they could achieve through other investments.

When negotiating seller financing, it's crucial to approach sellers with a well-thought-out proposal that outlines your reliability as a borrower and the benefits to the seller. Start by demonstrating your financial stability and commitment to maintaining the property. Be prepared to negotiate terms such as the interest rate, repayment schedule, and loan duration. A typical arrangement is for the seller financing to include a balloon payment, where smaller monthly payments are made for a period before a final lump sum payment completes the purchase. It can be particularly beneficial if you anticipate increased income, allowing you to cover more significant expenses.

Structuring a secure and mutually beneficial agreement is paramount. It's advisable to involve legal counsel to ensure that all aspects of the deal are clearly documented and legally binding. The contract should detail the loan amount, interest rate, repayment schedule, consequences of default, and any other pertinent terms. This legal oversight protects both parties and ensures that the deal complies with all relevant real estate regulations and tax laws, which can sometimes be complex in seller-financed transactions.

Seller financing opens up possibilities for real estate investment, particularly for those just beginning their investment careers. By understanding and leveraging this strategy, you can access property investments that might otherwise be out of reach, accelerating your journey toward becoming a seasoned real estate investor. As you explore this option, remember the importance of thorough due diligence, transparent negotiation, and professional guidance to forge advantageous and secure deals for all parties involved.

4.1.7 Sites for Custom Real Estate Agreements

Several websites offer paid services for writing lease options, seller financing, and customizable agreements for real estate, providing customizable templates and legal advice.

- **RocketLawyer.com** and **LawDepot.com** offer customizable lease option agreements with step-by-step guidance and downloadable documents.

- **Nolo.com** delivers legal documents and resources, including templates and books on lease options.
- **eForms.com** offers an extensive library of customizable legal forms, including lease options, with step-by-step guidance.
- **USLegalForms.com** provides state-specific lease option forms and other legal documents.
- **LegalZoom.com** offers customizable lease option agreements and the option to consult with attorneys for legal advice and document preparation services.

These platforms ensure landlords and real estate investors can create legally sound lease option agreements tailored to their needs.

4.1.8 Refinancing Options and Strategies

Refinancing your mortgage can be a strategic move that pushes your real estate investment forward, offering many benefits that can enhance your financial standing and investment potential. Refinancing involves replacing your existing mortgage with a new one, typically under different terms. This strategy can be particularly beneficial in several scenarios, such as when interest rates have dropped since you first secured your mortgage or when your credit profile has improved, potentially qualifying you for better loan terms. Additionally, refinancing can be a savvy financial move to reduce your monthly payments, thus improving your cash flow, or adjust the loan's term, either shortening it to pay off the debt sooner or extending it to lower monthly payments.

The decision to refinance should be based on a thorough analysis of your current financial situation versus the potential benefits. Key considerations include the amount of equity you have built up in your property, current interest rates compared to your existing rate, and your credit score, which can significantly influence the loan terms. Equity, in particular, plays a critical role as it determines how much you can borrow against your property's value. A substantial amount of equity can provide you with more favorable refinancing options, including the possibility of cash-out refinancing, where you can take out a portion of your equity in cash for further investments or to consolidate higher-interest debt.

Choosing the right refinancing option requires carefully evaluating your long-term financial goals and current economic circumstances. Rate-and-term refinancing, the most common type, involves adjusting either the interest rate or the term of your loan—or both—without changing the principal loan amount. This type of refinancing can help you capitalize on lower interest rates or adjust your monthly budgeting by extending the loan term. On the other hand, cash-out refinancing increases your loan amount by allowing you to borrow against the equity you've built up in your home, providing you with cash that you can use for renovations, investments, or other expenses. Streamline refinancing offers a simplified process for those with government-backed loans, often requiring less paperwork and no appraisal, making it a quicker and less costly option.

The long-term impacts of refinancing on your financial health are significant and should be carefully considered. Refinancing can alter your amortization schedule, potentially leading to higher total interest costs over the life of the loan if the term is extended. However, it can also accelerate your debt repayment if the term is shortened. Understanding these dynamics is crucial in assessing whether refinancing aligns with your financial planning. Moreover, refinancing can temporarily affect your credit score due to the credit check required by lenders and the closing of your old mortgage account. However, consistent payments on your new mortgage can help stabilize and improve your credit score over time.

Evaluating when to refinance involves strategically assessing market conditions and your financial path. Calculating the break-even point, where the savings from lower interest rates offset the cost of refinancing, is essential.

Consider current and projected interest rates, your remaining loan balance, and the costs of closing the new loan. Streamline refinancing options can be particularly attractive when looking to reduce costs and simplify the process, as they often eliminate the need for an appraisal and extensive documentation.

Navigating the refinancing process involves several key steps, starting with choosing the right lender. It's essential to compare offers from multiple lenders to ensure you get the best rates and terms. Consider not only the interest rates but also fees and the flexibility of loan terms.

Numerous websites can help you refinance your property by providing tools, resources, and access to multiple lenders. For example, **LendingTree.com** and **Bankrate.com** offer comprehensive marketplaces for comparing various loan offers. **QuickenLoans.com**, **RocketMortgage.com**, and **Better.com** provide streamlined online refinancing processes. **Zillow.com** and **NerdWallet.com** offer rate comparison tools and educational resources. **SoFi.com** and **Chase.com** provide competitive rates and personalized refinancing options.

Once you've chosen a lender, the application process involves submitting financial documents, undergoing a credit check, and potentially having your property appraised. Being well-prepared with all necessary documentation can expedite this process and improve your chances of approval.

Refinancing can involve several costs, including application fees, appraisal fees, and closing costs. They can add up to several thousand dollars. Understanding these costs and how they impact your financial calculations is crucial. Some lenders may offer no-cost refinancing options where these fees are either waived or rolled into the loan, albeit often at a higher interest rate.

In conclusion, refinancing can be a powerful tool in your real estate investment strategy when used wisely. It offers the potential to reduce your financial burden, improve cash flow, and provide additional capital for investment opportunities. By carefully evaluating your options, assessing the long-term impacts, and navigating the refinancing process with diligence, you can make informed decisions that enhance the profitability and sustainability of your real estate investments. As you move forward, remember that the goal of refinancing should always align with your broader investment objectives, ensuring that each financial decision contributes to your ultimate vision of success in real estate. (Read about refinancing as an exit strategy in Chapter 2.6.1.)

4.1.9 Real Estate Investment Trusts (REITs): A Different Approach

You read an introduction to REITs in Chapter 1.7.2.1. In the diverse world of real estate investment, real estate investment trusts (REITs) stand out as a distinctive and accessible option that allows you to engage with the property market without the need to buy or manage physical properties directly. REITs own, operate, or finance income-generating real estate across various sectors, including retail, healthcare, office, and residential spaces. They offer a unique structure that allows them to pay minimal corporate income tax, provided they meet specific criteria, most notably the requirement to distribute at least 90 % of their taxable income to shareholders as dividends.

Understanding the different REIT types is crucial to discerning which might best align with your investment goals.

- **Equity REITs**, the most common type, directly own properties and generate income through leasing space and collecting rents. These trusts typically invest in specific types of properties such as apartments, shopping centers, or hotels.
- **Mortgage REITs** (mREITs), on the other hand, provide funding for real estate by originating or purchasing mortgages and mortgage-backed securities. They receive income from the interest on these financial assets.

- **Hybrid REITs** combine the strategies of equity and mortgage REITs, holding both physical properties and mortgage loans.

The advantages of investing in REITs are manifold and particularly appealing if you're seeking ways to diversify your investment portfolio beyond direct property ownership. One of the most significant benefits is liquidity; unlike physical real estate, REIT shares can be bought and sold on major stock exchanges, providing flexibility and ease of access that direct real estate investments do not. This liquidity makes REITs an attractive option for those needing to quickly adjust their investment holdings in response to personal financial needs or changing market conditions. Additionally, REITs often offer attractive dividend yields that can provide a steady source of income. This aspect is particularly appealing in a low-interest-rate environment, where other income-generating investments might not offer as competitive returns.

Diversification is another crucial advantage of REITs. Investing in a REIT exposes you to a portfolio of properties across various locations and sectors, spreading out risk more effectively than investing in a single property. This diversification can protect against localized downturns in the real estate market and contribute to more stable returns over time. Moreover, REITs are managed by professional teams with significant industry expertise, providing additional reassurance that the properties and loans are being managed skillfully to maximize shareholder value.

Evaluating REITs' performance involves examining several key metrics that differ slightly from those used in other types of equity investments.

- **Funds From Operations** (FFO), which adjusts for depreciation of property and gains on sales, provides a clearer picture of a REIT's operating performance than traditional earnings metrics.
- **Adjusted Funds From Operations** (AFFO), which further adjusts FFO for rent increases and certain capital expenditures, is often considered

a better indicator of a REIT's ability to generate cash flow and sustain dividends.

- **Dividend yield** is also crucial and can be compared to other income-generating investments to assess a REIT's attractiveness.

When considering REITs versus direct real estate investments, weigh the pros and cons based on your personal investment strategy, and risk tolerance is essential. Direct real estate investments typically offer more control over the property and potentially higher returns, especially if you are skilled in property management or choosing underpriced properties to develop. However, they require more capital upfront, incur higher transaction costs, and demand active management. They also expose you to more localized economic risks. While offering less control, REITs provide ease of entry, lower transaction costs, professional management, and diversification, making them an excellent option for those looking to begin investing in real estate or seeking to spread the risk in their investment portfolios by adding real estate exposure, without the complexities and risks of direct property ownership.

Navigating the world of REITs requires a basic understanding of the underlying real estate market and the specific dynamics of the sectors in which REITs invest. Keeping abreast of market trends, regulatory changes, and economic indicators that influence property values and rent dynamics will enhance your ability to select REITs that are well-positioned to benefit from economic conditions and real estate market trends. As with all investments, a thoughtful approach and ongoing education are vital to leveraging REITs' unique opportunities in real estate investment.

4.1.10 Essential Investment Terms

Understanding the language of real estate investment is akin to learning a new dialect of a foreign language. Mastery of this dialect is not just about enhancing communication; it's crucial for interpreting market conditions, analyzing financial statements, and navigating legal documents effectively. Here, we will explore essential investment terms, helping you understand the language of real estate investment. Also, check Chapter 4.5 Financial Terms, for terms like Amortization, Cash Flow, and Equity.

1. **Appraisal**: An evaluation of a property's value conducted by a professional appraiser.
2. **BRRRR (Buy, Rehab, Rent, Refinance, Repeat):** A strategy for building a portfolio of rental properties.
3. **Buy and Hold**: A long-term investment strategy involving purchasing and holding real estate for a significant period.
4. **Capital Gains** refers to the profit earned from selling a property or investment. They are calculated by subtracting the purchase price from the sales price and adjusting for improvements or additional costs incurred. (Read more in Chapter 4.4.4.4.)
5. **Capitalization rate**, or **cap rate**, assesses a property investment's profitability and return potential. It is calculated by dividing the NOI by the purchase price or the current market value. High cap rates indicate potentially higher returns but also higher risk. (Read more in Chapter 3.4.3.)
6. **Closing Costs** are expenses incurred in transferring property ownership, including attorney fees, title insurance, and taxes.
7. **Commission** is the fee paid to a real estate broker or agent for facilitating a transaction.
8. **Comparative Market Analysis (CMA)** is an estimate of a property's value based on the sales prices of similar properties in the area.
9. **Distressed Property**: Property under foreclosure or being sold by the lender.
10. **Diversification** is the process by which a real estate investor spreads capital to reduce exposure to any particular asset or risk.
11. **Due Diligence** is the process of thoroughly investigating and evaluating a property before finalizing a purchase, including legal, financial, and physical inspection.

12. **Escrow**: Refers to a financial arrangement where a third party holds and regulates the payment of the funds required for two parties involved in a given transaction. It helps make transactions more secure by keeping the payment in a secure escrow account. Escrow is only released when all of the terms of an agreement are fulfilled, as overseen by the escrow company.
13. **Fix-and-Flip or Flipping:** Purchasing, renovating, and selling properties for a profit.
14. **Gross Rent Multiplier (GRM)**: This is a simple measure to estimate the value of an income-producing property. It is calculated by dividing the property's price by gross rental income.
15. **Hard Money Loan**: A loan secured by real property and is provided by private investors or companies. Known for their short approval times and relatively high interest rates, investors often use these loans to renovate and flip properties quickly.
16. **Highest and Best Use**: The reasonable use of property that results in the highest value, typically considered in the appraisal process.
17. **House Hacking** is a strategy in which you live (as your primary residence) in one of the multiple units of your investment property while renting out the others.
18. **Interest Rate**: The proportion of a loan charged as interest by the lender to the borrower. It is expressed as an annual percentage of the loan outstanding.
19. The **income approach** is a valuation method that estimates the value of a property based on its income. The valuation is determined by calculating the present value of future cash flows the property is expected to generate. (Read more in Chapter 3.4.3.)
20. **Joint Venture**: A business arrangement in which two or more parties agree to pool their resources to accomplish a specific task. In real estate, this usually involves investing in a property.
21. **Leverage**: Refers to using borrowed capital to increase the potential return of an investment. In real estate, investors use leverage by using mortgage loans to purchase properties, aiming to increase returns while

using less of their own capital.

22. **LTV (Loan-to-Value) Ratio:** A financial term used by lenders to express the ratio of a loan to the value of an asset purchased.
23. **Market Value**: A property's most probable price should attract buyers in a competitive and open market under all conditions requisite for a fair sale, with the seller and buyer acting prudently and knowledgeably.
24. **MLS (Multiple Listing Service):** A database established and updated by cooperating real estate brokers to provide data about properties for sale.
25. **Mortgage Broker**: It is an intermediary that brings mortgage borrowers and lenders together.
26. **Net Operating Income (NOI)** is a vital calculation used to analyze the profitability of income-generating real estate investments. It represents the total revenue from the property minus necessary operating expenses.
27. **Non-recourse Loan**: This type of loan is secured by collateral, usually property, for which the borrower is not personally liable.
28. **Offering Memorandum**: A document issued to potential investors in a real estate investment that provides details about the property, the terms of the investment, and the risks involved.
29. A **profit and loss account** or **income statement** summarizes your revenues and expenses over a specific period and shows the profit or loss made.
30. **Pre-approval** is a lender's conditional agreement to lend a specific amount based on a preliminary review of the borrower's creditworthiness.
31. **Pro forma** is a method of calculating financial results using specific projections or presumptions. Real estate often uses it to project future cash flows and profits.
32. **PMI (Private Mortgage Insurance) is insurance** that a borrower might be required to buy if their down payment is less than 20 % of the home's value.
33. **Quitclaim Deed**: A legal instrument used to transfer interest in real property. The entity that receives its interests is called the grantee,

and the entity transferring its interest is called the grantor. When the quitclaim deed is executed and delivered, the grantee assumes all the rights to the property.

34. **Rate of Return**: This indicates the return percentage on an investment relative to its cost. For real estate, this could be calculated using various methods, including cash-on-cash return, internal rate of return, or return on investment (ROI.) Read more in Chapters 3.4.3.
35. **Refinance**: This is replacing an existing loan with a new one, typically to reduce interest rates or change the loan terms. Read more in Chapter 2.6.1 and 4.1.8.)
36. A **Real estate investment group (REIG)** is a consortium of investors who pool their resources to invest in properties much more effectively than they could individually. (Read more in Chapter 1.7.2.1.)
37. **Real Estate Investment Trusts (REITs)** are formal entities that own, operate or finance income-producing real estate. They offer investors a chance to own valuable real estate that they might not be able to purchase individually. Modeled after mutual funds, REITs provide investors with regular income streams, diversification, and long-term capital appreciation. (Read more about REITs in Chapters 1.7.2.1 and 4.1.9.)
38. **Rent-to-Value (RTV) Ratio:** A metric used to evaluate the rental potential of a property. It is calculated by dividing the annual rental income by the property's current market value and expressing the result as a percentage. This ratio helps investors assess how well a property's rental income covers its cost or value.
39. **Return on Investment (ROI)** is calculated by dividing the investment's net profit (income return) by its cost or market value. It is also called Yield.
40. **Short Sale**: A sale in which the net proceeds are less than the debts owed on the property, often used as an alternative to foreclosure.
41. **Turnkey Property**: An investor can purchase a fully renovated home or apartment building and immediately rent it to a tenant.
42. **Underwriting** is the process by which a lender or other financial service

provider evaluates the risk of lending money or insuring a property.

43. **Usury**: Refers to the illegal act of lending money at unreasonably high interest rates.
44. **Wholesaling** is a real estate strategy involving contracting a home with a seller and finding an interested party to buy it.

4.2 TAKING CARE OF EVERYDAY FINANCES

4.2.1 Financial Order: The Backbone of Real Estate Investment

The cornerstone of successful real estate investing lies in meticulous financial order. Imagine your investment as a well-oiled machine where each component works seamlessly to ensure efficiency and profitability. Establishing a routine for handling bills, rent receipts, and bookkeeping is not just about keeping track of what you spend and earn; it's about understanding the health of your investment and making informed decisions that enhance its performance.

Regularly updating your financial records helps prevent the accumulation of unaddressed bills and uncollected rent, which can quickly escalate into cash flow problems. This routine also positions you to recognize patterns in income and expenses, enabling you to identify opportunities for cost-saving and areas where your investment is underperforming. For instance, consistent late payments from tenants might indicate a need for a revised collection strategy or a reassessment of tenant selection criteria.

4.2.2 Keeping Accurate Records: Ensuring Tax Compliance

Accurate record-keeping is indispensable in managing your real estate investments, especially regarding tax deductions. Maintaining comprehensive records of all income, expenses, receipts, and invoices is essential. These documents are crucial for preparing your tax returns and substantiating your deductions in case of an IRS audit.

Effective documentation practices include using digital tools to track expenses and store receipts electronically, ensuring they are organized and easily accessible. Regular reviews of your financial records can also help identify discrepancies or missing information, allowing you to address these issues promptly. Such meticulous financial documentation simplifies the process during tax season, ensuring that you can fully capitalize on your entitled deductions without the stress of scrambling for last-minute paperwork.

By understanding and applying these principles of financial management in real estate, you position yourself to take full advantage of the available tax benefits, reduce your liability, and enhance the profitability of your investments. This proactive approach to financial management aligns with best practices in real estate investing. It sets a solid foundation for achieving long-term economic success in this competitive field.

4.2.3 Leveraging Accounting Software in Real Estate

In today's digital age, numerous web-based accounting tools can significantly enhance your financial management practices.

Choosing the right software depends on your specific needs, such as the size of your portfolio, the complexity of your transactions, and your budget. Most platforms offer customizable features so you can tailor the software to fit your unique requirements, enhancing your capability to manage your investments effectively. Whether you handle the bookkeeping yourself or collaborate with external accountants, these tools can facilitate seamless management of your financial tasks, ensuring that you maintain order in your investments and steer clear of potential financial pitfalls.

Some web-based accounting tools are designed specifically for property owners and real estate companies, helping streamline financial management and operations.

- **AppFolio.com** and **Buildium.com** offer property management solutions with robust accounting features such as automated rent collection, expense tracking, and detailed financial reporting.
- **Propertyware.com** focuses on single-family and low-density rental properties, providing tools for rent tracking, expense management, and customizable financial reports.
- **RentecDirect.com** offers similar features, including online rent payments and tenant screening, tailored for landlords and property managers.
- **TenantCloud.com** is a free property management platform with income and expense tracking, financial reporting, and tax preparation tools.
- **Stessa.com** is another free option that automates income and expense tracking for real estate investors. It provides performance dashboards and tax-ready financials.
- **RealPage.com** and **ResMan.com** provide robust accounting and property management solutions with features like automated billing, financial reporting, and compliance tools.

For more general accounting needs that can be adapted for property management, **QuickBooks Online**[13], **FreshBooks.com**, and **Xero.com** offer versatile features such as expense tracking, invoicing, and integration with property management applications. These systems allow for real-time access to economic data, integration with banking and payment systems, and comprehensive reporting features that simplify financial analysis and decision-making. For instance, these tools can automate the generation of income statements and balance sheets, track rent payments, and manage expense receipts, streamlining your financial operations and ensuring accuracy in your financial records.

4.2.4 The Symphony of Financial Statements and Chart of Accounts

The relationship between the income statement, balance sheet, and chart of accounts is akin to a symphony where each instrument plays a critical role. The income statement, or profit and loss statement, captures your property's financial performance over a specific period, showing income generated and expenses incurred. The balance sheet provides a snapshot of your financial standing at a given moment, listing your assets, liabilities, and equity. These documents offer a comprehensive view of your financial health, which is essential for strategic planning and reporting.

The chart of accounts, on the other hand, is the backbone of your financial recording system. It is a categorization tool that organizes financial data into understandable and accessible segments. Each transaction you record in your books, whether a repair expense or rental income, is allocated to a specific account in this chart. This makes aggregating and analyzing data easier, ensuring accuracy and consistency in your financial reporting.

4.2.5 Budget and Forecast: Navigating Future Financial Waters

Understanding the distinction between a budget and a forecast is crucial for steering your real estate investments. A **budget** is your financial plan for the future; it outlines expected income and expenditures based on historical data and planned activities. It is a benchmark, helping you control finances and make strategic decisions.

A **forecast**, however, is an updated version of your budget that incorporates actual financial outcomes as the year progresses. It reflects market changes or investment strategy, providing you with a revised projection of your year-end financial status. These financial tools are essential for maintaining a clear view of your investment's trajectory, allowing you to adjust your strategies in response to real-time financial performance.

Budgeting must be done for all operating accounts, maintenance projects, and investments that you intend to make in the coming years. Update your forecast for each budget line, preferably once a month, to ensure you are on track. Be aware that some invoices may come once a quarter. With a good financial program, you can spread the cost over the three months in question.

4.2.6 Rent versus Costs: Maximizing Property Profitability

The interplay between the rent you charge and the costs you incur directly impacts your investment's profitability. Understanding how operational costs, maintenance expenses, and property management fees affect your rental income is crucial. For example, increasing amenities to justify higher rent might seem beneficial. Still, your net income could diminish if the associated costs disproportionally increase. Analyzing these relationships helps set the rent at a competitive yet profitable rate, ensuring your property remains attractive to tenants while maximizing your financial returns.

4.2.7 Your Annual Financial Compass

Consider implementing a financial year wheel that follows your chosen fiscal year or calendar year—an annual planner that marks significant economic events and obligations throughout the year. This tool can be instrumental in ensuring you never miss tax deadlines, loan repayments, insurance renewals, or scheduled property evaluations. By visually representing when significant financial events will occur, you can prepare adequately, ensuring that these obligations are met without last-minute rushes or missed opportunities for economic optimization.

4.2.7.1 Financial Year Wheel

This financial year wheel helps real estate professionals stay organized and prepared for key economic events and obligations. Make adjustments to improve and adapt to suit your specific business needs and local market conditions.

January

- **Property Tax Payments**: Review and plan for tax payments due in the first quarter.
- **Tax Planning:** Take advantage of all eligible deductions, such as mortgage interest and property taxes.
- **New Year Planning**: Update and set financial and investment goals for the year.
- **Market Analysis**: Review year-end market reports and trends to adjust investment strategies.

February

- **Lease Renewals**: Prepare and send lease renewal notices for mid-year expirations.
- **Tax Preparation**: Start organizing documents for tax season, including income and expense records.
- **Budget Review**: Assess the annual budget and make adjustments based on January's performance.

March

- **Property Maintenance**: Schedule spring maintenance and inspections.
- **Quarterly Taxes**: Prepare and file quarterly estimated tax payments (Q1.)
- **Investment Review**: Evaluate the current property portfolio and consider new acquisitions.

April

- **Tax Filing**: Complete and file federal and state income taxes by April 15.

- **Tenant Engagement**: Plan tenant appreciation events to foster good relationships.
- **Market Trends**: Analyze Q1 market trends and adjust strategies accordingly.

May

- **Property Inspections**: Conduct mid-year property inspections and address any issues.
- **Lease Marketing**: Start marketing for upcoming lease expirations in the summer.
- **Financial Planning**: Review mid-year financial goals and progress.

June

- **Quarterly Taxes**: Prepare and file quarterly estimated tax payments (Q2.)
- **Tax Planning**: re-evaluate your tax strategies based on current market conditions and tax law changes.
- **Budget Adjustment**: Revisit and adjust the budget based on half-year performance.
- **Mid-Year Review**: Conduct a mid-year review of investment performance and market conditions.

July

- **Lease Renewals**: Send out lease renewal notices for year-end expirations.
- **Supplier agreements**: Check supplier agreements and insurance and schedule time to update suppliers or negotiate contract terms.
- **Maintenance Checks**: Perform summer maintenance on properties.
- **Investment Opportunities**: Explore new investment opportunities.

August

- **Tenant Turnover**: Manage tenant turnover and new tenant move-ins for leases ending in summer.
- **Property Improvements**: Plan and execute property improvements before the end of summer.
- **Market Analysis**: Review summer market trends and adjust investment strategies.

September

- **Quarterly Taxes**: Prepare and file quarterly estimated tax payments (Q3.)
- **Budget Planning**: Begin planning the budget for the upcoming year.
- **New Year Planning**: Begin planning financial and investment goals for the upcoming year.
- **Investment Strategy**: Analyze Year-To-Date (YTD) performance and adjust strategies for the final quarter.

October

- **Tax Planning**: Start year-end tax planning to maximize deductions and credits.
- **Lease Negotiations**: Negotiate and finalize lease renewals for the coming year.
- **Property Maintenance**: Schedule fall maintenance and prepare properties for winter.

November

- **Financial Review**: Conduct a financial review and forecast year-end performance.
- **Holiday Preparations**: Plan tenant and client appreciation events for

the holidays.

- **Market Analysis**: Evaluate market conditions and prepare for year-end transactions.

December

- **Year-End Taxes**: Finalize year-end tax planning and make any last-minute adjustments.
- **Quarterly Taxes**: Prepare and file quarterly estimated tax payments (Q4.)
- **Annual Report**: Compile and review the annual financial report, assessing overall performance. Review the size of the emergency fund.

4.3 BUILDING AND MAINTAINING AN EMERGENCY FUND

In the unpredictable realm of real estate investing, preparing for unexpected financial setbacks is not just prudent; it's essential. An emergency fund designated explicitly for your real estate investments acts like a safety net, cushioning you against sudden financial demands that could otherwise compel you to make hasty decisions, such as liquidating assets at a loss. This fund is the financial buffer that allows you to handle unforeseen expenses—emergency repairs due to natural disasters, unexpected vacancy periods that cut off income, or urgent legal issues that require immediate funds—without disrupting your investment's profitability or financial stability.

The size of this emergency fund is not a one-size-fits-all figure. Still, it should be thoughtfully calculated based on several factors to ensure it adequately covers potential risks. Start by evaluating the total value of your properties, as a more extensive portfolio with higher-valued assets may require a more substantial fund to address any significant repairs or legal actions. Consider the condition of each property; older properties or those in areas prone to natural disasters might necessitate a larger fund. The number of properties you manage also plays a crucial role—more properties mean more chances for unexpected costs. Reflect on your typical expenses for each property, including regular maintenance costs and property management fees, and your average monthly rental income, which impacts how quickly you can replenish the fund after it's used.

Developing your emergency fund can be approached through various strategies tailored to fit different financial situations and goals. One effective method is allocating a set percentage of monthly rental income to this fund, treating it as another non-negotiable expense. This method ensures the fund grows consistently and is replenished regularly. Another approach might involve refinancing specific properties to free up some equity that can be directed into your emergency fund, significantly boosting your financial safety net. For those who have recently sold properties or experienced a windfall, allocating a portion of these proceeds to your emergency fund can significantly enhance its size. Additionally, cutting unnecessary expenses from your operations can free up more funds for emergency savings. For real estate investors with diverse investment portfolios, reallocating funds from lower-risk investments can also bolster your real estate emergency fund without exposing you to undue risk.

Once established, the management of your emergency fund requires diligent oversight. Placing the fund in a high-yield savings account or a money market fund can offer liquidity while earning a return on the parked funds, ensuring the money remains accessible and grows over time. Regular reviews of the fund are crucial, ideally aligned with an annual review of your overall investment portfolio or more frequently if your portfolio is extensive or particularly dynamic. This regular scrutiny should assess whether the fund size is still appropriate based on current property values, rental income levels, and expense trends. Adjustments should reflect significant changes, such as property acquisitions or disposals, major rental income shifts, or economic landscape changes that could affect your property's operational costs.

Discipline is critical in terms of usage. Reserve the fund for genuine emergencies only—not for routine expenses or planned improvements. This discipline ensures that when a genuine crisis occurs, the resources are there to handle it. After using funds for an emergency, prioritize replenishing them, treating this replenishment like any other critical investment expense. This strategic approach ensures your emergency fund remains ready to protect your investments from sudden financial demands, allowing you to navigate the ups and downs of real estate investing with confidence and stability.

4.4 TAX IMPLICATIONS AND BENEFITS

Imagine you've just acquired your first rental property. While this is a significant milestone, it's also the point where you must pivot your focus towards maximizing tax benefits, which can substantially enhance your cash flow and overall investment profitability. This chapter aims to demystify the tax aspects of real estate investing, making them accessible and actionable for you.

4.4.1 Tax Issues and How to Navigate Them

4.4.1.1 Staying Informed on Tax Laws

The landscape of tax laws is ever-evolving, with changes that can affect your real estate investments. Staying abreast of these changes is not merely about compliance; it's about seizing opportunities and mitigating risks. For instance, new deductions or credits can significantly reduce your taxable income. Conversely, certain benefits might be phased out, requiring strategic adjustments in your investment approach.

Engaging with professional associations and regularly consulting tax advisors specializing in real estate can provide you with up-to-date information and expert interpretations of complex tax codes. The **IRS.com** website, real estate investment forums, and tax law blogs are invaluable information resources.

Reviewing these resources and scheduling regular updates with your tax advisor ensures that no advantageous tax change passes you unnoticed. (Read about more resources in Chapter 5.4.2.4.)

4.4.1.2 Strategic Tax Planning

Effective tax planning in real estate involves strategic timing and applying various tax-related maneuvers to optimize your financial outcomes.

Consider the concept of depreciation, a non-cash deduction that allows you to reduce your taxable income based on the perceived decrease in the value of your property over time. By strategically planning when and how to leverage depreciation and other deductions, you can significantly lower your tax liability.

Moreover, consider the impact of timing your income. Real estate markets fluctuate, and so do tax rates and regulations. You can achieve considerable savings by strategically recognizing income with lower tax rates in a year. For instance, if you anticipate that tax rates will increase next year, it might be beneficial to accelerate your income into the current year to take advantage of the lower rates.

Strategic planning for deductions is crucial in optimizing these benefits. Timing your expenses also plays a critical role in maximizing deductions. Assume the above example where you expect higher revenues or tax rates in the coming year. In that case, you might accelerate certain deductible expenses, such as property repairs and maintenance, or even pay next year's property tax in advance. This strategy decreases your taxable income during a high-income year, reducing your overall tax burden.

On the flip side, delaying certain expenses to offset the reduced income can be beneficial if you expect a lower income year or lower tax rates in the future. This tactical adjustment requires a keen understanding of your financial landscape and prevailing tax laws, underscoring the importance of continuous financial monitoring and adjustment.

Additionally, strategic tax planning includes understanding how to use the tax benefits of mortgage interest deductions, property tax deductions, and capital gains strategies. By carefully planning these aspects, you can enhance your cash flow and reduce the amount of taxes paid, thereby maximizing the profitability of your investments.

4.4.1.3 Visual Aid: Tax Planning Timeline

To help you visualize the effective timing for various tax-related actions, consider this simplified timeline:

- **January to April**: Review last year's financials and prepare for tax filing. Take advantage of all eligible deductions, such as mortgage interest and property taxes.
- **May to August**: Mid-year financial review; re-evaluate your tax strategies based on current market conditions and tax law changes.
- **September to December**: End-of-year tax planning. Consider strategies to defer income or accelerate expenses to optimize your tax situation for the year.

This timeline serves as a general guide, and your specific circumstances might necessitate a different approach, underscoring the importance of personalized advice from a tax professional.

By embracing strategic tax planning and staying informed about tax laws, you ensure compliance and position yourself to make informed decisions that improve the profitability and sustainability of your real estate investments. This proactive approach to tax management will serve as a cornerstone of your successful real estate investment career, helping you navigate the complexities of tax implications with confidence and strategic insight.

4.4.2 Deductions on Your Real Estate Investments

Navigating the complexities of tax deductions in real estate can significantly impact your financial outcomes, ensuring you maximize returns while staying compliant with tax regulations. Understanding which expenses are deductible and how they are treated can help you plan your financial strategies more effectively. Let's explore the everyday deductible expenses you can leverage as a real estate investor to optimize your tax benefits.

Mortgage interest is one of real estate investors' most substantial deductions. The interest paid on a mortgage for rental properties can be fully deducted from your income, reducing the taxable amount. This deduction is vital as it can significantly decrease the tax burden, especially in the early years of a mortgage when interest constitutes a more significant portion of mortgage payments.

Similarly, **property taxes** paid on real estate investments are fully deductible, providing relief as these taxes can be substantial depending on your property's location and value.

Operating expenses encompass all costs associated with running and maintaining your rental property. These expenses are fully deductible and include advertising, utilities, office supplies, and fees paid to property management companies. Property management fees, in particular, are an ordinary expense for investors who utilize the services of a property management company to handle the day-to-day operations of their rental properties. Deducting these costs effectively lowers the taxable income generated from your investments, thus reducing your overall tax liability.

Repairs and **maintenance** are also crucial deductible expenses. Immediate repairs, like fixing broken windows or doors, are fully deductible in the year they are incurred, offering a direct reduction in taxable income. Maintenance tasks, such as painting or servicing a furnace, also fall under fully deductible expenses, provided they are necessary and reasonable. These deductions help maintain the property value and reduce the amount of taxable rental income.

Insurance premiums, another significant deductible, include standard property insurance and additional coverage like flood insurance. These premiums, necessary for protecting your investment against unforeseen events, are fully deductible, decreasing your taxable income and safeguarding your property.

Depreciation is one of the most beneficial deductions available to real estate investors. It allows you to deduct the costs of purchasing and improving a rental property over its useful life, recognizing its wear and tear over time. The IRS currently allows residential rental property to be depreciated over 27.5 years. This deduction can substantially reduce your taxable income each year, reflecting the property's decreasing value and compensating you for its gradual loss of value due to aging and use.

4.4.2.1 Improvement vs. Repair: Navigating Tax Implications

Distinguishing between improvements and repairs is essential for tax purposes, as each has different tax implications. **Improvements** increase the property's value, prolong its life, or adapt it to new uses. Examples include adding a new roof, installing new windows, or adding an extension. These costs are not immediately deductible; they are capitalized and depreciated over their useful life, providing a prolonged tax benefit.

Repairs, however, are works that keep your property in good operating condition without materially adding value or prolonging its life. Examples include fixing leaks, painting walls, or replacing broken tiles. These expenses are fully deductible in the year they are incurred, offering immediate tax relief. Understanding these distinctions ensures that expenses are categorized correctly, maximizing your potential deductions while adhering to tax regulations.

4.4.2.2 Vacancy Deductions: Managing Non-Rental Periods

Handling deductions related to property vacancies is another area where strategic knowledge can benefit your tax position. Typically, you can deduct expenses incurred when your property is vacant if you actively try to rent it. It includes continued expenses such as mortgage interest, property taxes, and maintenance costs. Effectively, these deductions can offset the lack of rental income during vacancy periods, reducing the financial impact on your overall investment returns.

4.4.2.3 Taking a Deductible Salary Depends on Business Structure

Understanding the deductibility of a salary is not just a matter of tax law; it's a fundamental aspect of your business structure. It's a key that unlocks control over your financial situation. Salary is typically deductible in corporations, while owner distributions are not considered deductible expenses in pass-through entities. This underscores the importance of understanding and choosing the right business structure for your real estate business.

If you take a salary from your real estate business structured as an S Corporation (including LLCs taxed as an S Corporation) or C Corporation, that salary is generally a deductible business expense. It means the business can deduct the salary paid to the owner (or any employee) as an expense, reducing its taxable income.

However, sole proprietorships, partnerships, and LLCs taxed as pass-through entities do not consider the owner's draws or distributions a salary and are therefore not deductible as a business expense. The income generated by the business is taxed as personal income, and the draws do not reduce the taxable income.

4.4.3 Understanding Real Estate Depreciation

In your journey as a real estate investor, grasping the concept of depreciation is akin to discovering a strategic tool that can significantly enhance the profitability of your investments. In real estate, depreciation refers to a systematic deduction that spreads the cost of tangible property over its useful life. It's recognized as a non-cash deduction, reducing your taxable income without impacting your immediate cash flow. This financial mechanism acknowledges that property, much like any physical asset, decreases in value over time due to factors like wear and tear, age, or market conditions.

Depreciation serves a dual purpose: it reflects the decreasing value of your property. It provides a method to recoup part of your investment annually, reducing your tax burden. It can be particularly advantageous, as it allows you to create a buffer against the expenses incurred from maintaining and upgrading your property, thereby improving your cash flow. For example, if you purchase a rental property, you can't deduct the total cost in the year of purchase; however, you can deduct a portion of the cost each year through depreciation, offsetting some of your income from rents and lowering your tax liabilities. By lowering your taxable income, depreciation effectively increases your yearly profits. These deductions can accumulate substantially over a property's lifespan, enhancing the investment's profitability. It's imperative, however, to keep accurate records and calculations, as these will be crucial for tax purposes and potential audits.

4.4.3.1 Different Types of Depreciation

The two most commonly used methods of depreciation in real estate are the straight-line and accelerated depreciation methods. The straight-line method is straightforward: it involves deducting an equal amount of depreciation each year over the property's useful life. The generally accepted useful life for residential rental property is 27.5 years, and for commercial property, it's 39 years. This method is particularly appreciated for its simplicity and predictability, making it a common choice among investors.

Calculating depreciation requires a few key steps:

1. Determine the basis of the property, which is generally the total cost of acquiring the property, including purchase price and any expenses related to the purchase.
2. Select the appropriate depreciation method that aligns with your investment strategy and financial planning.
3. Calculate the annual depreciation expense using the chosen method. For instance, under the straight-line method for a residential property with a basis of $275,000, your yearly depreciation would be $10,000 (= $275,000 / 27.5 years.)

On the other hand, accelerated depreciation, including methods like the Modified Accelerated Cost Recovery System (MACRS), allows for more significant deductions in the earlier years of a property's life. This can be highly beneficial if you anticipate your properties generating higher incomes in the initial years or prefer to recover your investment sooner to reinvest in other opportunities. Accelerated methods are more complex but can be strategically advantageous, depending on your financial goals and cash flow needs.

The Internal Revenue Service[14] provides extensive resources to learn more about MACRS. One key resource is **IRS Publication 946**[15], "How to Depreciate Property," which offers detailed guidance on using MACRS for depreciation. Additionally, tax preparation software websites like **TurboTaxintuit.com** and **H&R Block**[16] offer articles and guides on using MACRS, providing practical advice and step-by-step instructions to help taxpayers understand and apply this depreciation method.

4.4.3.2 Depreciation Recapture

Lastly, when you sell a property that has benefited from depreciation, you face what is known as depreciation recapture. It means that the depreciation claimed over the years is taxed at a specific rate upon the sale of the property. Strategies such as real estate exchange under Section 1031, which allows deferring capital gains tax by reinvesting the proceeds into a similar property, can mitigate the impact of depreciation recapture. This strategy requires careful planning and compliance with specific rules. Still, it can be a powerful tool for deferring taxes and effectively leveraging your investment capital.

By understanding and strategically applying real estate depreciation, you can significantly enhance the financial performance of your investments, ensuring a more stable and profitable portfolio. Another method of depreciation, Cost Segregation, requires more administrative work. It can be used to maximize deductions, which is the topic of the next chapter.

4.4.4 Maximizing Deduction

4.4.4.1 Implementation of Cost Segregation

Every move counts in the intricate dance of real estate investment—especially regarding taxation. Advanced strategies for maximizing deductions can significantly enhance the profitability of your assets. One such strategy is the implementation of cost segregation studies. This sophisticated approach involves a detailed analysis of your property that allows you to accelerate depreciation on certain parts of it. Typically, a building's depreciation is spread over 27.5 years for residential properties or 39 years for commercial ones. However, cost segregation studies can identify property components that can be depreciated over a shorter period, typically 5, 7, or 15 years. These components could include personal property elements like carpets, wall coverings, specialized lighting, or land improvements like sidewalks and landscaping.

Engaging in a cost segregation study involves hiring a qualified professional to dissect your property's acquisition or construction costs and reallocate them into categorically faster-depreciating assets. This front-loaded depreciation results in substantial tax savings in the early years of property ownership, enhancing your cash flow. Instead, you can reinvest the money or use it to strengthen other parts of your portfolio. It's important to note that while cost segregation accelerates depreciation deductions, it does not increase the total amount deducted over the life of the property. It merely shifts these deductions to earlier years, improving your near-term return on investment.

4.4.4.2 Consulting with Tax Professionals

Lastly, engaging with professional associations and consulting with real estate tax professionals is indispensable. These experts help maximize all your deductions and credits and ensure compliance with the latest tax laws and regulations. Their insights can guide you through the complexities of real estate taxation, from conducting cost segregation studies to claiming federal and state-specific credits. The benefits of professional tax planning and preparation cannot be overstated—they provide financial advantages and peace of mind, allowing you to focus more on growing your real estate portfolio and less on navigating its associated tax implications.

4.4.4.3 Tax Credits

Turning our focus to another potent tool in the savvy investor's arsenal—tax credits—real estate offers several attractive opportunities. Tax credits are particularly compelling because they reduce your tax liability on a dollar-for-dollar basis, unlike deductions, which reduce the income subject to tax. For instance, energy efficiency credits are available for properties implementing systems designed to reduce energy consumption. These include solar panels, wind turbines, and specific high-efficiency HVAC systems. Utilizing these credits lowers your operational costs and supports your commitment to sustainable development, an increasingly important criterion for today's environmentally conscious renters and buyers.

Moreover, tax credits for rehabilitating historic buildings can also be a lucrative avenue. Invest in a certified historic structure and undertake renovations that preserve its intrinsic historic character. You might be eligible for credits that can cover a significant portion of your renovation expenses. Rehabilitating a potentially high-maintenance property can help preserve important architectural heritage and turn it into a profitable investment through boosted property values and appeal to tenants drawn to unique historical aesthetics.

4.4.4.4 Capital Gains Tax Strategies You Need to Know

Navigating capital gains tax in real estate can significantly impact your financial outcomes, making a deep understanding of its mechanisms essential. Capital gains tax is levied on the profit from the sale of property or an investment. It's categorized into short-term and long-term gains, with the distinction in the asset's holding period. Short-term capital gains apply to properties held for less than a year. They are taxed at your ordinary income tax rate, which can be considerably higher. On the other hand, long-term capital gains from properties held for more than a year benefit from lower tax rates, typically 0 %, 15 %, or 20 %, depending on your income bracket.

The timing of your property sale is crucial in the amount of capital gains tax you will owe. It is where strategic tax planning becomes invaluable. For instance, if you anticipate a lower tax rate in the following year due to changes in tax laws or a change in your income, it may be beneficial to delay selling your property. Conversely, if you expect higher future tax rates or need to realize losses to offset gains, you might decide to sell sooner.

Several strategies can help minimize capital gains tax. One effective method is holding property for over a year to take advantage of lower long-term capital gains tax rates. Another strategy is using a 1031 exchange, which allows you to defer the payment of capital gains taxes by reinvesting the capital gain, the profit on the sale of a property sale into a new property. This process requires strict adherence to IRS rules, including time limits for identifying and closing on new properties. It is essential to plan meticulously and consult with a tax advisor.

Another method to consider is tax-loss harvesting, where you sell other investments at a loss to offset the gains from your real estate sale. Additionally, strategically choosing when to sell can align with years where you might fall into a lower tax bracket, further reducing the amount owed.

When you sell a property, calculating the capital gains tax due is critical to understanding your net profits. Please start with the original purchase price of your property, adding any associated costs of acquiring it, such as legal fees and transaction fees, which form the cost basis. From this, subtract any depreciation claimed during the period of ownership, as this reduces your cost basis. Then, add the cost of any improvements you've made to the property—these increase your cost basis and can reduce your capital gains tax. The difference between this adjusted cost base and the sale price of your property gives you capital gains, which are subject to tax.

Different rules apply when dealing with investment properties versus personal residences. For individual homes, the IRS offers a generous exclusion—up to $250,000 for single filers and $500,000 for married couples filing jointly—on capital gains from the sale if you've used the property as your primary residence for at least two of the last five years. Investment properties, however, do not qualify for this exclusion, and every dollar of capital gain is taxable. However, real estate investors can use other strategies to mitigate these taxes, which underscores the importance of strategic planning.

By implementing these capital gains tax strategies, you can maximize your investment returns and maintain a robust real estate portfolio. These tactics ensure compliance with tax laws and enhance your ability to reinvest in new opportunities, fostering continued growth and success in your real estate endeavors.

As we conclude this exploration of capital gains tax strategies, it's clear how integral informed tax management is to successful real estate investing. The insights shared here should empower you to navigate capital gains taxes more effectively, ensuring you retain more of your hard-earned investment returns.

4.5 FINANCIAL TERMS

Here, we will explore pivotal economic terms that form the core of real estate accounting and investment analysis, helping you become fluent in the language of real estate.

Remember to look at Chapter 4.1.10 Essential Investment Terms. There, you can find terms you may also need while owning your investment, such as Appraisal, Capital Gains, Capitalization rate, GRM, valuation methods, Leverage, Refinance, ROI, and Rate of Return.

1. **Acquisition Cost** is the total cost that a company recognizes on its books for purchasing property or equipment after adjusting for incentives, discounts, and closing costs but before sales taxes.
2. **Amortization**: This term refers to spreading payments over multiple periods, often used in the context of loan repayments. Real estate typically describes the gradual reduction of the mortgage loan through regular payments that cover both principal and interest components.
3. **Assessment**: The determination of the value of a property for tax purposes.
4. **Appreciation:** The increase in the property value over time.
5. A **balance sheet** is a snapshot of your financial position at a particular point in time, detailing your assets, liabilities, and equity.
6. **Blended Rate**: A rate charged on a loan that changes over time from the initial rate to a different rate.

7. **Capital Expenditure (CapEx)** is the money a company uses to acquire, maintain, and upgrade physical assets such as property, buildings, or equipment.
8. **Cash Flow** is a vital indicator of a property's performance. It represents the net amount of cash generated or spent over a given period. Positive cash flow indicates that a property generates more income than expenses, which is a primary goal for most investors.
9. **Depreciation**: For accounting purposes, this refers to spreading out the cost of a tangible asset over its useful life. Real estate allows investors to deduct a portion of the property's cost each year, reflecting its usage and wear and tear.
10. **Deduction** is an expense that property owners, investors, or landlords can subtract from their income to reduce their taxable income. These deductions lower the overall tax liability and can include various allowable expenses such as mortgage interest, property taxes, operating costs, depreciation, and repairs. (Read more in Chapter 4.4.2.)
11. **Due Diligence** is the process of thoroughly investigating and evaluating a property before finalizing a purchase, including legal, financial, and physical inspection.
12. **Equity** is the difference between a property's current market value and the amount remaining on its mortgage. Equity increases as you pay the mortgage or the property's value appreciates. (Read more in Chapters 2.6.2 and 4.1.1.4.)
13. **Equity Build-up** is the increase in one's equity in a property due to mortgage payments and property value appreciation.
14. **Foreclosure** refers to the process by which a lender takes control of a property from a homeowner who has yet to make the required mortgage payments.
15. **Interest Rate**: The proportion of a loan charged as interest by the lender to the borrower. It is expressed as an annual percentage of the loan outstanding.
16. **Liquidity Crisis**: A situation in which a business or individual can only easily convert assets into cash with a substantial loss in value.

17. **Liquidity**: Refers to how quickly an asset can be converted into cash without significantly affecting its value. Real estate is generally considered a less liquid investment compared to stocks or bonds due to the time and processes involved in selling properties.
18. **Modified Accelerated Cost Recovery System (MACRS)** is the current method of depreciation used in the United States for tax purposes. It allows property owners to recover the cost of certain assets by depreciating them over a specified life span, thus reducing taxable income. Under MACRS, assets are categorized and depreciated over different periods depending on their class life, with key features including various depreciation classes and methods. Assets are classified into different categories, each with a specific recovery period, such as 3, 5, 7, 10, 15, 20, 25, and 39 years. The two primary methods used under MACRS are the General Depreciation System (GDS), which provides accelerated depreciation, and the Alternative Depreciation System (ADS), which uses a straight-line method and longer recovery periods. MACRS also generally applies the half-year convention, meaning assets are assumed to be in service for half of the first year. However, the mid-quarter convention may apply if a significant portion of assets is placed in service during the last quarter of the year. Learn more on irs.com.
19. **Net Operating Income (NOI)** is a vital calculation used to analyze the profitability of income-generating real estate investments. It represents the total revenue from the property minus necessary operating expenses.
20. **Operating Expenses**: Expenses incurred during the regular operation of a business, including property management fees, utilities, repairs, and taxes, in the case of real estate.
21. **Principal**: The amount of money borrowed or the remaining balance of a loan, excluding interest.
22. A **profit and loss account** or **income statement** summarizes your revenues and expenses over a specific period and shows the profit or loss made.
23. **Rent-to-Value (RTV) Ratio:** A metric used to evaluate the rental potential of a property. It is calculated by dividing the annual rental

income by the property's current market value and expressing the result as a percentage. This ratio helps investors assess how well a property's rental income covers its cost or value.

24. **Rental Yield:** The measure of how much cash an income-generating asset produces each year as a percentage of that asset's value.
25. **Variable Rate**: An interest rate on a loan that fluctuates over time. The change is usually based on an underlying reference interest rate or an index that changes periodically.
26. **Year-to-date performance (YTD)** refers to the financial or operational results achieved by a business or investment from the beginning of the current calendar year or fiscal year up to the current date. It is a standard metric used to assess how well a company, investment portfolio, or individual asset has performed over a specific period within the year.
27. **Yield**: The income return on an investment, such as the interest or dividends from holding a particular security. In real estate, it is often used to describe the annual income from a property divided by its cost or market value. See ROI.

* * *

The chapter's footnotes

1 *https://www.consumerfinance.gov/*

2 For example *https://files.consumerfinance.gov/f/documents/cfpb_heloc-brochure.pdf*

3 *https://www.investopedia.com/mortgage/heloc/*

4 *https://www.investopedia.com/terms/h/homeequityloan.asp*

5 *https://www.nerdwallet.com/article/mortgages/heloc-home-equity-line-of-credit*

6 *https://www.nerdwallet.com/article/mortgages/home-equity-loan*

7 *https://www.mynd.co/*

8 https://*www.myreipro.com/*

9 https://*reww.com/*

10 *https://www.sba.gov/*

11 *https://www.hud.gov/*

12 *https://www.eda.gov/*

13 https://*quickbooks.intuit.com/*

14 *https://www.IRS.com*

15 *https://www.irs.gov/publications/p946*

16 https://*www.hrblock.com/*

MINIMIZING FINANCIAL RISKS

"The future belongs to those who believe in the beauty of their dreams."
ELEANOR ROOSEVELT

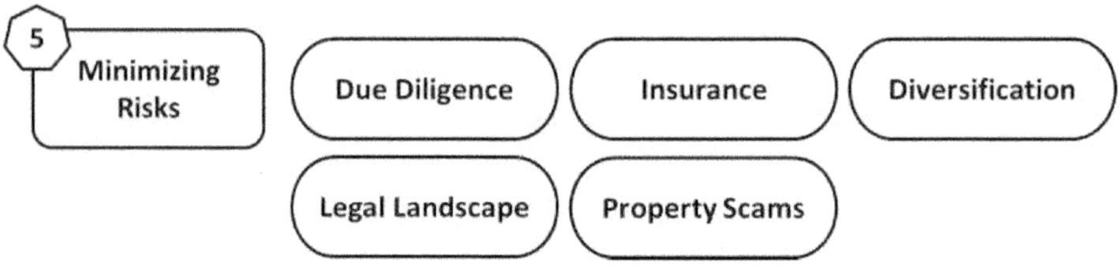

5.1 THE IMPORTANCE OF DUE DILIGENCE IN REAL ESTATE

Imagine standing on the threshold of a significant decision that could pave the way to substantial financial gain or lead to unexpected challenges. It is the daily reality for real estate investors. A crucial component that separates successful investments from regrettable ones is due diligence. It's not just a precaution; it's your best defense against the inherent risks of real estate investment.

Risk vs. Reward Assessment: Navigating real estate investments requires a keen understanding of balancing potential returns with associated risks. For instance, while a property in a rapidly developing area might promise high returns due to appreciation, it also comes with risks like market volatility, which could see property values fluctuating dramatically based on local economic changes. Tenant issues, such as delayed payments and property management challenges, can also affect your cash flow and necessitate a hands-on approach to property management. Assessing these risks against the potential financial returns requires meticulous analysis and strategic planning. You can make informed decisions that align with your investment risk tolerance and goals by evaluating location stability, tenant demographics, and historical market data.

Comprehensive Property Evaluation: A thorough property evaluation is the cornerstone of adequate due diligence. It goes beyond just appreciating the aesthetic aspects of a property or the immediate cost implications. It involves a deep dive into the property's history, a robust inspection of its current condition, and an understanding of the neighborhood dynamics. For example, a physical inspection can reveal issues not immediately apparent in seller disclosures, such as foundational cracks or outdated electrical systems, which could lead to significant repair costs later. Similarly, reviewing the property's historical context—such as past renovations, repairs, and maintenance—can provide insights into its long-term viability and upkeep costs.

Legal and Compliance Checks: Another critical aspect of due diligence is ensuring the property complies with all legal and zoning requirements. Ignorance of the law is not a viable defense, and overlooking this step can lead to severe financial penalties or even the nullification of your investment. Verifying zoning laws is crucial; these laws dictate how a property can be used and what alterations can be made. For instance, purchasing a property intending to convert it into a multi-family dwelling only to discover that zoning laws prohibit such use can be costly. Additionally, ensure there are no existing liens against the property and that all set legal statutes and building codes are met. It protects you from future legal issues and ensures unresolved legal complications do not diminish the property's value.

Implications of Zoning on Investment Decisions: Zoning laws significantly impact real estate investment decisions. They govern the development and use of properties and can affect commercial and residential investments. For example, a zone designated primarily for commercial use would not be suitable for residential developments. Understanding these laws helps select the appropriate property and planning development projects that are legally compliant and aligned with market needs. Performing due diligence to uncover any zoning restrictions before purchasing a property is essential. It involves consulting local planning agencies or zoning boards to get detailed and specific zoning information, which will inform your investment strategy and help avoid potential legal challenges.

Financial Analysis of Investments: An integral part of your due diligence is conducting a thorough financial analysis of the potential investment. It involves detailed cash flow projections, Return On Investment (ROI) calculations, and an understanding of the economic landscape. For instance, cash flow projections help determine if the property will generate enough rental income to cover all expenses and provide profits, while ROI calculations help assess the efficiency of the investment compared to other opportunities. This financial scrutiny ensures that every investment aligns with your financial goals and risk profile, clearly showing expected returns and potential financial exposure.

Conduct Property Inspections and Appraisals: Detailed property inspections and professional appraisals are indispensable elements of due diligence. They objectively assess the property's condition and value, which is crucial for making informed investment decisions. For example, a professional inspector might uncover potential issues like roof damage or old plumbing that could result in significant future expenses. Similarly, an appraiser can accurately estimate the property's market value, ensuring you pay a fair price and understand the investment's potential appreciation.

Utilizing Professional Services: For novice investors, the complexity of due diligence can be daunting. It is where leveraging professional services becomes invaluable. Hiring experienced real estate attorneys, knowledgeable accountants, and skilled property inspectors can provide the expertise needed to navigate the complexities of real estate investments. These professionals help unearth potential issues that may not be obvious to the untrained eye, offering peace of mind and a more secure investment base. Their expertise ensures that all aspects of due diligence are thoroughly covered, from legal compliance checks to financial audits and property inspections, safeguarding your investment against unforeseen risks and challenges.

Engaging in comprehensive due diligence is more than just a step in the investment process; it's a fundamental practice that sets the stage for prosperous and secure real estate investing. By meticulously assessing each potential investment through this multifaceted approach, you minimize risks and position yourself to maximize your returns in the dynamic real estate market.

5.1.1 Conducting Due Diligence: A Step-by-Step Guide

5.1.1.1 Understand Local Market Conditions

In-depth knowledge of local market conditions is essential for any successful real estate investment. It involves more than just understanding broad market trends; it requires a granular analysis of the local dynamics that influence property values and investment viability. Start by researching comparable property prices in the area to gauge the property's market position. Analyze neighborhood occupancy rates to understand the demand dynamics and review average rental prices to estimate potential income.

These insights help assess your property's current value and performance and forecast future trends that could impact your investment. Staying informed about local market conditions enables you to proactively adjust your investment strategy, ensuring your property remains competitive and profitable in a changing market environment. (Revisit Chapter 3.)

5.1.1.2 Review the Property's Strategic Advantages

Understanding the property's strategic advantages involves a comprehensive analysis of what the market demands versus what the property offers. Evaluate if the property features like a garage, ample parking, and well-maintained lawns and gardens meet the expectations of potential tenants or buyers. Also, consider the property's location in relation to high-traffic roads, shopping areas, and access routes to major transportation hubs like airports. While specific locations might be less desirable for residential properties due to noise and pollution, they could be highly advantageous for commercial properties due to higher visibility and accessibility. Ensure functional zoning laws and check the property's building permits.

Analyzing these strategic elements allows you to align the property's attributes with market demands, enhancing its competitiveness and profitability. It also helps make informed decisions about potential modifications or marketing strategies to highlight these advantages, attracting a broader audience and securing better rental or sale terms.

5.1.1.3 Review Property Documentation

Embarking on a real estate investment begins with thoroughly reviewing all available documentation. This foundational step is crucial in identifying underlying issues that might not appear at first glance. Begin by examining the title deeds to ensure no legal insecurity regarding property ownership. Previous sale records offer a historical perspective on the property's market value fluctuations. They can highlight trends or potential issues that have impacted its value over time. Existing lease agreements are also vital documents that need your attention; they can provide insights into the rental operations, tenant consistency, and any ongoing contractual obligations that might carry over post-purchase.

During your review, pay special attention to any liens or disputes linked to the property. A lien, for instance, could indicate a financial liability that could transfer to you upon purchase, impacting your financial planning. Disputes, whether they are between previous owners over property boundaries or with tenants over lease terms, can signal potential legal complications that require resolution before or after your acquisition. Uncovering these issues early on will protect you from unexpected legal troubles and empower you with the leverage to negotiate better purchase terms.

5.1.1.4 Evaluate the Financials

Assessing a property's financial health is as critical as its physical inspection. Start by analyzing the rent rolls, which provide a detailed record of the rental income. Look for patterns of consistent rental income and tenant stability, as these are strong indicators of a property's profitability. Operating expenses also warrant a thorough examination; these include maintenance costs, property management fees, taxes, and insurance. Understanding these expenses is essential for calculating the net operating income (NOI.) This key metric will help you evaluate the investment's potential return.

Consider using templates or tools specifically designed for real estate analysis to simplify this financial examination. These tools can help you organize financial data effectively, making it easier to visualize cash flow scenarios and perform comparative analyses with similar properties in the market. By systematically assessing these financials, you can determine whether the property aligns with your investment goals and delivers a satisfactory financial performance.

5.1.1.5 Assess the Property's Condition

A detailed physical assessment of the property is imperative. Begin with a structural examination to check for any signs of foundational issues or structural damage that may require significant investment to repair. Inspect the roof, walls, and flooring for integrity and durability. Electrical, ventilation, and plumbing systems need careful evaluation to meet safety standards and operational efficiency. Paying close attention to these elements during your visits will help you avoid costly repairs that could deplete your investment returns.

Additionally, consider the property's aesthetic appeal and functional layout, as these factors significantly influence tenant attraction and retention. Features such as the condition of external facades, the functionality of common areas, and the overall curb appeal play critical roles in the property's marketability. By thoroughly assessing these aspects, you can better determine the necessary enhancements to maximize rental income and property value. (Revisit Chapter 3.4.)

5.2 INSURANCE

5.2.1 Protecting Your Investments from Unseen Circumstances

Imagine you've just closed your first investment property. The paint is fresh, the floors gleam underfoot, and every little detail has been meticulously planned. Imagine a storm or an unforeseen plumbing issue suddenly threatening your hard-earned asset. Scenarios like these underscore the critical role of insurance in real estate investing. Insurance is not just a safety net; it's a strategic tool that protects your property and financial well-being.

5.2.2 Assessing Coverage Needs

Determining the right level and type of insurance coverage requires carefully evaluating several factors. The nature of the property—whether a single-family home, a multi-unit residential building, or a commercial property—dictates the basic coverage needs. Moreover, the property's location can significantly influence the risks it faces; properties in flood zones or earthquake-prone areas may require additional policies that standard coverage does not include.

To effectively assess your coverage needs, examine the potential risks associated with the property's location. Properties in flood zones or earthquake-prone areas face unique risks that require special attention. Consult with local authorities or a trusted insurance broker to understand these risks and tailor your insurance coverage accordingly. This proactive approach ensures comprehensive protection and prevents the common pitfall of being under-insured, which can lead to significant out-of-pocket expenses when disaster strikes.

5.2.3 Types of Real Estate Insurance

5.2.3.1 Title Insurances

Title insurance protects against losses due to defects in the title not found during the title search. These defects can include errors or omissions in deeds, mistakes in examining records, forgery, or undisclosed heirs. It also includes defects in liens and encumbrances, such as unpaid taxes, contractor liens, or other encumbrances that may attach to the property and potentially affect ownership, the new owner's financial obligations, or the property's marketability.

Suppose a claim is made against the title. In that case, title insurance covers legal fees and court costs necessary to defend against the claim. Title insurance provides security to buyers and lenders, allowing the transaction to proceed smoothly. Most mortgage lenders require title insurance to protect their interest in the property. It ensures that the lender has a valid first lien on the property.

Unlike other types of insurance that require annual premiums, title insurance involves a one-time premium paid at closing, making it a cost-effective protection measure.

5.2.3.2 During Construction

In the case of construction, it's essential to ensure that there is "Builder's Risk Insurance." This insurance covers buildings, materials, fixtures, and equipment used during construction against damage from fire, theft, vandalism, and other risks.

5.2.3.3 Tenants Insurance

As a landlord, it's crucial to include a clause in the rental contracts and set up a system to remind your tenants to have their insurance when signing the contract and periodically during their tenancy. Residential tenants' insurance covers personal belongings and liability within the rented property. Tenants renting a house should get "Homeowners Insurance," which covers damage to the home and personal belongings due to theft, fire, and certain natural disasters.

Commercial tenants need "Commercial Property Insurance" to cover the buildings and their contents. If the tenant's activities may affect the land, they must have "Environmental Liability Insurance." This type of insurance is essential for properties with potential environmental hazards, such as industrial sites, providing coverage for managing contamination risks and cleanup efforts.

5.2.3.4 Insurance for Property Owners

As a real estate investor, you can access various insurance policies to safeguard various aspects of your investment. Remember that an insurance policy is only valid for damages after the insurance becomes effective.

Property insurance is the most fundamental, covering physical damage to your property from fire, storm, or other disasters. This type of insurance is indispensable, ensuring that your physical asset remains intact and repairable following unexpected events.

Specialized policies, such as **earthquake** or **flood insurance**, become essential in areas prone to specific natural disasters. Standard property insurance often excludes such natural calamities. Hence, assessing the geographical risks and securing additional coverage is a strategic move to protect your investment fully.

Landlord liability insurance is crucial for anyone renting out their property. It protects you against liability claims and lawsuits brought by tenants or visitors who suffer injury on your property due to negligence, such as a fall caused by a loose handrail. This coverage is not just about legal protection; it's about peace of mind, knowing that you are shielded from potentially crippling financial judgments.

Loss of income/rent insurance plays a pivotal role when a property becomes uninhabitable due to damage. For example, suppose a fire or significant plumbing issue forces your tenants to move out. This insurance can compensate you for the lost rental income during repairs, ensuring your cash flow is uninterrupted. This coverage is included in many landlord insurance policies.

Sewer Backup Insurance covers damage caused by sewer or drain backups. This type of insurance is typically an add-on to homeowners or landlord policies, providing specific protection against this damage, which is usually not covered by standard policies.

Umbrella Insurance provides additional liability coverage beyond the limits of underlying policies, such as homeowners and landlords. Its primary purpose is to protect against major claims and lawsuits exceeding the standard policies' coverage limits, ensuring comprehensive protection for significant liabilities.

Ordinance or **Law Insurance**: This insurance covers the additional costs required to bring a building up to current codes after a covered loss. It includes expenses for demolition, increased construction costs, and compliance with building ordinances, ensuring that properties meet modern safety and regulatory standards after damage.

Equipment Breakdown Insurance covers repairing or replacing essential systems and appliances due to mechanical failure. It includes coverage for HVAC systems, electrical equipment, and boilers, ensuring critical building systems are quickly restored to operational status. The equipment dealer usually offers it.

Mortgage Insurance protects the lender if the borrower fails to pay the mortgage. Different types of mortgage insurance, including Private Mortgage Insurance (PMI) for conventional loans and Mortgage Insurance Premium (MIP) for FHA loans, ensure that lenders are safeguarded against borrower default.

5.2.4 Comparing Insurance Providers and Policies

Choosing the right insurance provider is as crucial as selecting the correct type of coverage. When comparing providers, consider coverage limits, which determine the maximum amount the insurer will pay in the event of a claim. Also, consider deductibles, the amount you pay out of pocket before your insurance kicks in, which also play a crucial role in your decision, as they affect both your upfront costs and the cost of premiums.

Premiums, or the regular payment you make to keep the insurance active, are influenced by coverage limits and deductibles, and the provider's assessment of how risky your property is to insure.

While premiums, coverage limits, and deductibles are key factors in choosing an insurance provider, don't overlook the importance of customer service and claim processing efficiency. In times of stress, dealing with a responsive and efficient insurer can make a significant difference, making these aspects equally important in your decision-making process. Ask your network for tips and recommendations on good insurers and options.

5.2.4.1 Cost-Benefit Analysis of Insurance Options

Performing a cost-benefit analysis on different insurance options allows you to balance the cost of premiums and deductibles against your property's potential risks and financial losses. This analysis involves comparing the cost of insurance policies from different providers against their coverage. It's essential to not just look at the price but also consider the comprehensiveness of coverage—cheaper policies might exclude essential risks that could leave you vulnerable.

5.2.4.2 Websites to Compare Insurance Policies

Since there are many insurance companies, finding one that offers what you need at a reasonable cost, good risk coverage, and easy and pleasant customer service is essential.

Platforms for single-family homes, such as **Zillow Insurance Marketplace**[1], **Policygenius.com**, **Insurance.com**, **TheZebra.com**, **NetQuote.com**, **Insureon.com**, and **CoverHound.com**, provide tools to obtain quotes, compare policies from multiple insurers, and access detailed policy information.

Several prominent insurance companies offer customized solutions for commercial property owners, providing comprehensive coverage that protects against various risks. Companies like **Chubb.com, TheHartford.com, LibertyMutual.com, Travelers.com**, and **Nationwide.com**.

LibertyMutual.com and **Nationwide.com** also have insurance policies designed for residential property owners, together with **StateFarm.com** and **Allstate.com**.

5.2.5 Handling Insurance Claims

Effective insurance claim management is pivotal in maximizing the benefits of your coverage. Should an incident occur, prompt and accurate claim filing is crucial. Keep detailed records of documentation and all communications related to the incident and the claim. Photos, repair receipts, and detailed notes can all support your case and ensure a fair assessment by the insurance company.

5.2.6 Integrating Insurance into Risk Management Strategy

Incorporating insurance into your overall risk management strategy for real estate investments involves regular reviews of your policies to adapt to any changes in property values, rental income, or regional risk factors. Annual or bi-annual reviews of your coverage ensure that your insurance protection grows and evolves with your investment portfolio.

By understanding and utilizing the right insurance products, you protect your physical assets and safeguard your financial future against the unpredictable. Innovative insurance strategies are not about cost—they are about value. In the world of real estate investing, they provide a foundation of security that enables you to focus on growing your investments with confidence.

5.3 DIVERSIFICATION TO REDUCE RISK

You may remember that we mentioned the subject diversification in Chapter 2.5.4. In the ever-fluctuating real estate investing market, diversification is a fundamental strategy that minimizes risks and maximizes potential returns across different market conditions. By spreading your investments across various types of properties and other markets, you create a safety net that can absorb shocks in one area while gains in another can compensate. Think of it as not putting all your eggs in one basket; if one basket falls, you still have others intact.

Rebalancing your portfolio is an ongoing process that involves adjusting your investments to maintain alignment with your strategic objectives and risk tolerance. It might mean selling underperforming assets or increasing investments in areas with potential for higher returns. Market conditions can change rapidly, and staying informed through continuous market analysis is vital for timely and effective portfolio adjustments. Use performance metrics like Return On Investment (ROI), capitalization rates, and occupancy rates to monitor the health of your investments and make data-driven decisions.

You can diversify a real estate investment portfolio by creating multiple income streams from diverse assets such as traditional rentals, vacation rentals, Real Estate Investment Trusts (REITs), and real estate funds. Each investment type offers unique advantages and entails specific management nuances that you should consider to optimize your portfolio's performance.

Traditional residential rentals provide a steady source of income and can be a relatively stable investment if chosen wisely. The key to success with conventional rentals lies in selecting the right location, understanding local market demands, and managing properties efficiently. Vacation rentals, on the other hand, tap into the tourism market and can yield higher returns during peak seasons. However, they require dynamic pricing strategies and exceptional customer service to attract short-term tenants. REITs offer a way to invest in real estate without buying or managing the property yourself. By purchasing shares of a REIT, you can receive dividends generated from a diverse portfolio of properties managed by professionals. Lastly, real estate funds pool money from multiple investors to purchase properties, which are managed collectively. It can be an excellent way to gain exposure to more extensive, potentially more profitable projects while sharing the associated risks.

Regularly monitoring and adjusting your diversified portfolio is essential to optimizing its performance and ensuring it continues to meet your financial goals. Set up a schedule to review your portfolio at least annually or whenever significant changes in the market or your financial situation occur. During these reviews, assess whether your investments are performing as expected and explore opportunities to enhance portfolio diversity or adjust your strategy to respond to new market conditions.

In essence, diversification in real estate investing acts as a risk management tool, enabling you to navigate various market conditions effectively. It not only helps protect your portfolio from significant losses but also aids in capturing growth opportunities across different market segments, thus stabilizing and potentially increasing your investment returns over time. By judiciously spreading your investments, you can achieve a more secure and robust financial footing in the volatile world of real estate.

5.4 NAVIGATING THE LEGAL LANDSCAPE OF REAL ESTATE INVESTING

As you step into real estate investing, it's akin to navigating a labyrinth of legalities that unfold with each property transaction. The legal framework surrounding real estate can often seem daunting, especially for those new to the field. However, understanding this framework is not just about adhering to regulations; it's about turning them into strategic advantages. This chapter aims to demystify the legal aspects of real estate investing, ensuring you are well-prepared to manage and protect your investments effectively.

5.4.1 Basic Legal Considerations Every Investor Should Know

5.4.1.1 Overview of Property Rights

At the core of real estate investment is the concept of property rights. These rights are the legal privileges of property ownership, encapsulating the right to possess, control, enjoy, and dispose of a property. These aren't just abstract legal terms; they form the backbone of your powers and responsibilities as a property owner. For instance, the right to control your property means you can decide who rents it within the bounds of fair housing laws and how it's managed. Understanding these rights is crucial before you make any investment, as they affect everything from your ability to lease or sell the property to how you can develop or modify it. Ignorance of these rights can lead to disputes or legal challenges, so having a solid grasp of your ownership is imperative.

5.4.1.2 Keeping Up with Real Estate Laws and Regulations

Navigating the shifting sands of real estate laws and regulations is akin to steering a ship through ever-changing seas. Each adjustment in laws and regulations can significantly impact various aspects of your real estate investments, potentially affecting property values, modifying rental rules, and altering financing options. For instance, a new zoning regulation can either enhance the value of a property by allowing more versatile uses or restrict your development plans, thereby decreasing its potential profitability. Similarly, changes in mortgage interest deduction rules or rental law amendments can affect your property's desirability and profitability, influencing tenant demographics and investment returns.

The necessity of staying compliant with these evolving regulations cannot be overstated. Compliance ensures that your investment remains secure and profitable, shielding you from legal penalties ranging from fines to more severe consequences, such as forced property sales. Federal laws like the Fair Housing Act[2] and the Americans with Disabilities Act (ADA)[3] mandate non-discriminatory practices in renting or selling properties. Local environmental laws may dictate modifications to your property to mitigate impacts on the local ecosystem, and building codes ensure that any construction meets safety standards. Adhering to these regulations protects you legally and financially and boosts your reputation as a responsible investor.

Maintaining compliance, however, requires a proactive approach. Regular consultations with real estate attorneys provide a crucial strategy to stay informed about legal changes that could affect your investments. These legal professionals can offer insights into newly passed legislation or upcoming legal trends that may impact your properties. They are invaluable in interpreting complex legal language and applying it to your specific situation, ensuring that your investment strategies remain compliant and optimal.

Moreover, keeping abreast of legal updates is essential for preemptive management and strategic planning. Various resources can aid in this endeavor. Government websites are primary sources of official legal information, often providing updates on real estate laws directly from regulatory bodies. Legal advisories and professional associations offer more detailed analyses and implications of recent legal changes, helping you understand how they might affect your business operations. Subscribing to industry newsletters and legal databases can provide ongoing updates that might impact your investment areas. Additionally, participating in real estate forums and attending legal workshops can offer interactive ways to gain insights and share experiences regarding navigating real estate laws.

By integrating these practices into your investment operations, you ensure that your real estate ventures are profitable and resilient against legal challenges. Regular updates and legal consultations equip you with the knowledge to adapt to legal changes, safeguard your assets, and ensure that your real estate activities continue to thrive in a compliant and informed manner. Engaging actively with these resources cultivates a robust legal awareness that can distinguish your practices in the competitive real estate investment landscape.

5.4.1.3 Understanding Property Laws

Navigating property laws is fundamental to avoiding costly legal pitfalls. These laws govern everything from the transfer of titles to settling disputes over property boundaries. For example, title laws ensure that you legally own the property you're buying, free from undisclosed encumbrances like liens or other legal burdens. Deeds essential to transferring property ownership must be carefully drafted to include all necessary legal descriptions and comply with local regulations. Real estate investors must also be aware of issues such as easements, which grant others the right to use portions of your property, or adverse possession, where someone else may claim ownership of your property under certain conditions. To navigate these complex situations, strategies such as purchasing title insurance can protect against title disputes, and legal mediation can resolve boundary or right-of-way issues without resorting to costly litigation.

5.4.1.4 Contracts and Agreements

The importance of legally sound documentation must be balanced in real estate transactions. Contracts are the vital lifeblood of real estate transactions, providing a formal agreement that binds parties to their duties and entitlements. Purchase agreements, lease agreements, and service contracts must all be crafted precisely to ensure clarity and enforceability. They should explicitly state the terms of the deal, including descriptions of the property, pricing, timelines, and contingencies that might allow parties to withdraw from the agreement under specific conditions. For example, a purchase agreement might include contingencies that will enable a buyer to back out if a property inspection reveals significant issues or if they cannot secure financing. Any real estate investor must understand how to structure these contracts to protect their interests and anticipate potential problems.

5.4.1.5 Protective Legal Documentation

Every agreement, whether it's a lease with a tenant, a contract with a contractor, or a partnership deal in a joint venture, needs to be meticulously documented. These documents should clearly outline all parties' rights, responsibilities, and expectations to prevent misunderstandings and provide a straightforward course of action in case of disputes. For instance, a well-drafted lease agreement should include terms regarding rent, security deposits, maintenance responsibilities, and conditions for lease termination, among others. Similarly, contractor agreements should specify the scope of work, payment schedules, and standards for the quality of work. Ensuring all contracts are legally binding and enforceable under local laws protects your investments. It establishes a framework for smooth operational management.

5.4.1.6 Navigating Landlord-Tenant Laws

Understanding landlord-tenant laws is critical for real estate investors dealing with rental properties. These laws regulate various aspects of the landlord-tenant relationship, including lease terms, rent regulations, eviction procedures, and security deposits. They vary widely by locality, and non-compliance can lead to legal penalties and damage your reputation as a property owner. For example, eviction laws require landlords to follow strict procedures and timelines when evicting tenants, including providing formal notices and obtaining court orders. Familiarizing yourself with these laws helps you manage your properties effectively and maintain fair and legal interactions with your tenants. (Read more about handling eviction in Chapter 6.3.3.)

5.4.1.7 Dispute Resolution

In the dynamic world of real estate, disputes are not uncommon. They can arise over property boundaries, contract interpretations, or tenancy issues. Having strategies for dispute resolution in place can save you time, money, and stress. Methods such as mediation, arbitration, or litigation can be employed depending on the nature and complexity of the dispute. For instance, mediation can offer a less adversarial approach to resolving tenant disputes, preserving relationships, and reducing legal costs. However, some situations may require more formal resolutions like arbitration or litigation, especially when substantial financial interests or legal rights are at stake.

5.4.1.8 Importance of Legal Compliance in Modifications and Construction

Compliance with legal standards, such as building codes and zoning laws, becomes indispensable when modifying or constructing buildings within your property. These regulations ensure that structures are safe and appropriate for their locations. For instance, building codes dictate standards for electrical systems, fire safety, and structural integrity. On the other hand, zoning laws determine what types of buildings and activities are allowed in specific areas. Non-compliance can lead to fines, forced removal of non-conforming structures, or a halt in development processes. Thus, obtaining the necessary permits before beginning any construction or significant renovations is crucial. It not only helps in adhering to legal standards but also in maintaining the validity of your insurance and reducing the risk of challenges from community members or local authorities.

5.4.1.9 Consulting with Legal Professionals

Finally, while this guide provides a foundational understanding, consulting with legal professionals is paramount in handling more complex transactions or disputes. Real estate attorneys can offer tailored advice and representation, ensuring compliance with the law and protecting your investments from legal threats. They can help draft and review contracts, negotiate deals, and represent you in court if necessary. Finding a competent lawyer with experience in real estate is invaluable. Look for professionals with proven track records who come highly recommended by industry peers. Establishing a relationship with a trusted legal advisor can provide ongoing support and guidance as your real estate investment portfolio grows.

5.4.2 Navigating Zoning Laws and Regulations

5.4.2.1 Zoning laws

Zoning laws serve as the blueprint for urban development, shaping the environment in which we live, work, and invest. These regulations are organized into distinct categories, such as residential, commercial, and industrial, each dictating the activities and constructions permissible in specific areas. For instance, residential zones are designated primarily for housing, commercial zones for businesses, and industrial zones for manufacturing and distribution facilities. Understanding these distinctions is crucial for real estate investors, as zoning laws can significantly influence property values, potential uses, and the scope of development projects.

When you aim to modify the use of your property or develop it in a way that current zoning laws do not permit, you may need to navigate the process of applying for a zoning change or exception. This process generally involves submitting detailed plans and justifications for the change to local planning commissions or zoning boards, who will assess the potential impact on the community and the environment. The necessary documentation often includes site plans, architectural drawings, traffic impact studies, and sometimes environmental assessments. Successful applications typically address how the change adheres to or enhances the community's long-term planning goals.

Presenting your case effectively to the zoning board is more art than science. It requires a clear, persuasive argument that aligns with community development goals and addresses the commission's and local residents' potential concerns. Community support can play a pivotal role in the approval process. Engaging with neighborhood groups and stakeholders early in the process to solicit their input and address their concerns can build a coalition of support that sways board members. Demonstrating how your project can bring benefits like job creation, improved infrastructure, or enhanced community services can also strengthen your case.

Real-world examples of zoning challenges abound, highlighting different aspects of the complexities involved. Consider the case of a developer who purchased land for a new residential development only to discover that the zoning classification required a more significant percentage of open space than planned. The developer successfully petitioned the city to modify the zoning ordinance by demonstrating how the development included public amenities that benefited the community, such as a park and a community center. On the other hand, a real estate investor faced significant setbacks when a zoning board denied a request to convert an old warehouse into a residential loft complex. The board cited concerns about insufficient infrastructure and the project's fit within the existing neighborhood character. These cases illustrate the importance of thorough preparation, community engagement, and flexibility in real estate development.

5.4.2.2 State and Local Regulations

Beyond zoning, state and local regulations can also impact your real estate investments. These may govern everything from property tax assessments to environmental regulations and building safety standards. Each layer of regulation adds complexity to property management and development. For instance, local building codes ensure that structures meet safety standards, which are crucial during renovations or new construction. Failing to comply with these codes can result in fines, project delays, or legal action. Similarly, environmental regulations might restrict your development plans if your property is in a sensitive area, such as near wetlands or a coastal zone.

5.4.2.3 Building Permits

Obtaining building permits is a fundamental step in ensuring that your real estate projects comply with local regulations and codes. Permits are official approvals from local authorities that allow you to proceed with construction or significant renovations. The permitting process varies by location but generally requires submitting detailed plans for review by city or county officials. These plans must demonstrate compliance with building codes, zoning laws, and sometimes even aesthetic guidelines set by the community. Navigating this process efficiently requires thoroughly understanding the specific requirements and timelines involved. Delays in obtaining permits can lead to significant costs because of project hold-ups, so proactive planning and engagement with permitting offices are advisable.

5.4.2.4 Stay Updated on Zoning Laws, Regulations, and Tax

When it comes to staying updated on federal tax credits, zoning laws, and housing regulations, the websites of key government bodies are indispensable.

- **The Internal Revenue Service** (IRS)[4] is a comprehensive resource for federal tax credits, including those related to real estate and housing.
- **The U.S. Department of Housing and Urban Development** (HUD)[5] is a go-to for federal housing regulations, programs, and resources updates.
- **The Federal Housing Finance Agency** (FHFA)[6] is another essential source that provides news and updates on housing finance and regulations.

Each state government plays a crucial role in providing state-specific information on housing, taxation, and regulations through its dedicated website. For instance, the California Department of Housing and Community

Development (HCD) provides updates specific to California. Similarly, state housing finance agencies offer detailed information on state-specific tax credits, zoning laws, and housing regulations. An example is the New York State Homes and Community Renewal agency, which provides extensive resources for New York State.

Understanding city and county-specific zoning laws and housing regulations is crucial, and local resources are the best place to find this information. City and county government websites, such as the City of Los Angeles Department of City Planning, offer comprehensive details on the city's zoning and planning. Local housing authorities, such as the Chicago Housing Authority, also play a significant role in providing updates on local housing regulations and initiatives.

In addition to government resources, several news websites and industry publications offer valuable insights into real estate regulations.

- **The National Real Estate Investor** (NREI)[7] provides news and analysis on real estate, including tax credits and zoning laws.
- **TheRealDeal.com** offers real estate news on regulatory changes and market trends.
- **The Urban Land Institute** (ULI)[8] publishes articles and reports on housing regulations and zoning laws, making these publications essential for industry professionals.

Professional organizations also serve as essential sources of information.

- **The National Association of REALTORS** (NAR)[9] updates real estate industry regulations, offering resources and advocacy for real estate professionals.
- **The American Planning Association** (APA)[10] provides resources and insights on planning and zoning laws across the United States, making these organizations valuable for staying informed on industry

developments.

Navigating zoning laws and regulations is a critical skill for real estate investors. Understanding these legal frameworks helps make informed investment decisions, plan development projects, and manage properties effectively. Engaging with the community, adhering to local guidelines, and seeking proper permits can enhance the likelihood of successful real estate ventures. As we close this chapter, remember that the complexities of real estate law are navigable with the proper knowledge and strategies.

5.5 PROPERTY SCAMS

5.5.1 Protect Yourself from Scams

In real estate investing, the excitement of finding a new property or securing a lucrative rental can sometimes be overshadowed by the less palatable aspect of the industry: scams. As a beginner, navigating these waters with a keen eye and an informed mind is crucial. Unfortunately, the variety and complexity of fraudulent schemes in the real estate sector can be daunting. By understanding the common types of scams and learning how to spot them, you can protect your investments and avoid potential financial pitfalls. You will also better understand your potential tenant, who asks you to verify yourself and your existence.

5.5.2 Different Kinds of Property Buying Scams

One prevalent scam is escrow wire fraud, where scammers posing as the escrow company or real estate agents instruct you to wire funds to a fraudulent account. Loan flipping scams involve lenders enticing property owners to repeatedly refinance their mortgage, drawing equity from the property under the guise of financial benefit, which leads to excessive fees and higher loan balances. Foreclosure relief scams target homeowners in distress, offering fake legal services to save their homes from foreclosure in exchange for upfront fees and, in some cases, tricking them into signing over the title of their home. Moving scams may occur when unscrubbed movers hold your belongings hostage to extort higher fees than previously agreed upon. In commercial real estate scams, fraudsters might present non-existent properties or developments to investors, often showcasing impressive returns that are entirely fabricated. Home inspection scams arise when inspectors, sometimes colluding with sellers, downplay property defects to hasten sales. Title or deed scams involve the illegal appropriation of property titles, where scammers forge documents to claim ownership of properties they do not legally own. Lastly, companies that promise to help you when you've fallen victim to a scam.

5.5.3 Different Kinds of Rental Property Scams

Rental scams frequently target unsuspecting tenants and sometimes even property owners. Fake property listings lure individuals with attractive rental rates for properties that the scammer does not manage or, in some cases, do not exist. Scammers posing as fake letting agents or landlords may collect deposits and the first month's rent without having the authority to rent out the property. In the case of fake overseas landlords, scammers claim to be out of the country and request funds or personal information before showing the property. Phishing scams involve fraudsters attempting to gather sensitive personal information under the guise of rental applications. These applications look legitimate but are designed solely to steal identities. Fake printed listings can also be a tool for scammers, who advertise properties at attractive prices to lure potential renters into fraudulent schemes.

5.5.4 Different Kinds of Property Scams Online

The digital landscape has given rise to various online property scams. Facebook property scams involve fake ads for rental properties or homes for sale, which lead to phishing websites designed to steal personal information or financial details. Rental property scams on Craigslist are common, where scammers post attractive rental listings to solicit security deposits and rent for properties they do not own. Fake property scam websites may appear professional and legitimate, offering investment opportunities or rental properties at below-market rates to entice victims into fraudulent transactions.

5.5.5 Look Out for These Signs

To protect yourself from these scams, vigilance is essential. Be wary of transactions that require you to act quickly with little time for due diligence. Always verify the identity of the person you are dealing with, and be cautious of requests for wire transfers or payments via non-traditional methods. Unusually low prices can also be a red flag for potential scams, as they are often used to attract attention and lure in victims. Review property documents and transaction histories regularly, and consider hiring a reputable lawyer to review all contracts and agreements. Utilizing professional real estate platforms and services that verify listings and landlords can also provide an additional layer of security.

By educating yourself about these common scams and maintaining a cautious and informed approach to your real estate transactions, you can significantly reduce the risk of falling victim to fraud. Remember, if an offer seems too good to be true, it probably is. Always conduct thorough research and seek professional advice when necessary. Your vigilance is not just about protecting your investments—it's about securing your financial future in the ever-evolving real estate landscape.

5.6 LEGAL TERMS

Understanding the language of real estate investment is akin to learning a new dialect of a foreign language. Mastery of this dialect is not just about enhancing communication; it's crucial for interpreting market conditions, analyzing financial statements, and navigating legal documents effectively.

Here, we will explore pivotal legal terms that form the core of real estate law and investment.

1. **Abstract of Title**: A summary of the legal history of a property, including ownership, claims, and liens.
2. **Acceleration Clause**: A contract provision that allows a lender to require immediate repayment of the loan if certain conditions are met.
3. **Bill of Sale**: A document that transfers ownership of personal property from one party to another.
4. **Breach of Contract**: The failure to perform a legal obligation as agreed in a contract.
5. **Broker**: A licensed individual or firm arranges real estate transactions between buyers and sellers.
6. **Closing**: The final step in a real estate transaction where the transfer of ownership occurs.
7. **Cloud on Title**: Any claim or encumbrance that may impair the title to a property.
8. **Collateral**: Property pledged as security for a loan.
9. **Condominium**: A type of property ownership where individuals own individual units within a larger complex.
10. **Covenant**: A written agreement or restriction on the use of land.
11. **Deed**: A legal document that transfers ownership of real property from one party to another.
12. **Due Diligence** is the process of thoroughly investigating and evaluating a property before finalizing a purchase, including legal, financial, and physical inspection.
13. **Easement**: A right to cross or use someone else's land for a specified purpose.
14. **Encroachment**: An intrusion onto another person's property, such as a building or fence.
15. **Encumbrance** refers to any claim or liability attached to a property, such as liens or easements, that may affect the property's transferability and free use until dismissed.

16. **Fiduciary**: A person or entity that acts on behalf of another, with a duty to act in their best interest.
17. **Fixture**: Personal property attached to land or a building regarded as an irremovable part of the real property.
18. **Foreclosure** is the legal process by which a lender takes possession of a property due to the borrower's failure to repay the loan.
19. **Grantee**: The person receiving title to a property.
20. **Grantor**: The person transferring title to a property.
21. **Joint Tenancy**: A form of property ownership where two or more parties own equal shares and have equal rights to the property.
22. **Landlord**: The owner of a property leased or rented to another party, known as the tenant.
23. **Lease**: A contract granting the use or occupation of property for a specified period in exchange for rent.
24. **Lien**: A legal right a lender has in the borrower's property, granted until the debt obligation is satisfied.
25. **Option to Purchase**: A contract giving a buyer the right to purchase a property at a specified price within a specified time frame.
26. **Plat**: A map showing dividing a piece of land into lots, often used in subdivisions.
27. **Quitclaim Deed**: A deed that transfers whatever interest the grantor has in the property without warranties or guarantees.
28. **Right of First Refusal**: The right to purchase a property before it is offered to others.
29. **Tenant**: A person who, in return for a rental payment, has the right to occupy land, building, or part of a building located on property owned by the landlord.
30. **Title**: A legal document evidencing a person's right to or ownership of a property.
31. **Title Insurance**: Insurance that protects against losses due to defects in the title not discovered during the title search.
32. **Warranty Deed**: A legal document that guarantees that the seller holds a clear title to real estate. Only the person with ownership rights can

sell a property to a buyer.

33. **Zoning** is a regulation established by local governments to control land use and properties within their jurisdiction. Zoning laws dictate how properties can be used, significantly affecting property values and investment strategies.
34. **Zoning Ordinance**: A written regulation or law that defines how a real estate in its specific geographic zone may be used by its owner.

* * *

The chapter's footnotes

1 *https://www.zillow.com/brands/home-insurance-coverage/*

2 *https://www.hud.gov/program_offices/fair_housing_equal_opp/sexual_harassment*

3 *https://www.ada.gov/*

4 *https://www.irs.gov/*

5 *https://www.hud.gov/*

6 *https://www.fhfa.gov/*

7 *https://www.nreionline.com* (*https://www.wealthmanagement.com/real-estate*)

8 *https://uli.org/*

9 *https://www.nar.realtor/*

10 *https://www.planning.org/*

EFFECTIVE PROPERTY MANAGEMENT

"The real investment in real estate is not just in property but in the growth and development of one's capabilities and understanding."

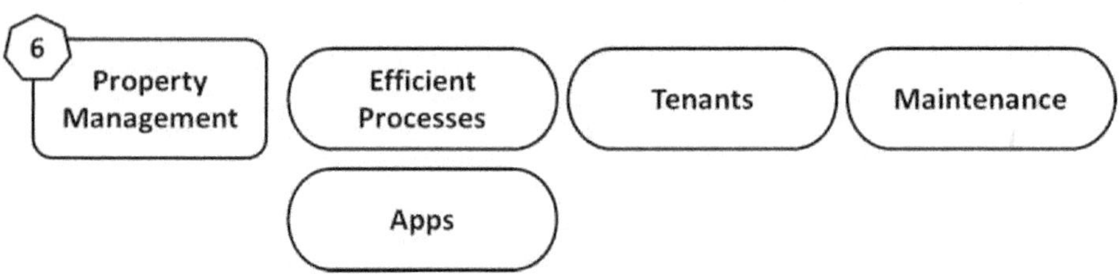

Imagine stepping into the role of a conductor, where each property in your portfolio represents an instrument in your orchestra. Just as a conductor ensures each note is played at the right time and tone, effective property management requires you to orchestrate various tasks seamlessly. This chapter is dedicated to helping you master the art of property management by establishing efficient processes and understanding the intricate dance between being a property owner and a business strategist.

6.1 EFFICIENT PROCESSES

In real estate investment, efficiency isn't just about saving time—it's about enhancing profitability and stability. Efficient processes serve as your best defense against the unpredictable challenges that can arise. For instance, imagine a scenario where an unexpected plumbing issue occurs in one of your properties. Suppose you have an efficient system in place. In that case, this problem can be addressed swiftly, minimizing discomfort for your tenants and costs for you. This proactive approach saves you money and protects your reputation as a reliable landlord.

The key to developing efficient processes is understanding that real estate management is as much about business acumen as property know-how. Each property you own is like a mini-business; the apartments or premises you lease are the products you offer. Therefore, your approach should be systematic and goal-oriented. Start by setting clear objectives for what you want to achieve with each property: maximizing occupancy, increasing rental income, or maintaining low maintenance costs.

For example, a regular maintenance schedule can prevent minor issues from escalating into costly repairs. It saves money in the long run, keeps tenants satisfied, and reduces turnover rates. Additionally, utilizing digital tools to automate rent collection and tenant communications can significantly reduce administrative burdens, allowing you to focus on strategic growth initiatives. By viewing your properties through the lens of operational efficiency and strategic planning, you position yourself to maximize returns and sustain long-term growth.

Understanding that real estate is a business will transform how you approach property management. It requires a shift from merely overseeing properties to actively managing a business. This perspective encourages implementing systems and processes that enhance operational efficiency, drive financial performance, and improve tenant satisfaction. By adopting this business-minded approach, you successfully equip yourself with the tools to navigate the complexities of real estate investment and management.

In essence, effective property management is about foresight and planning. It's about being prepared for the challenges and opportunities of owning real estate. By establishing efficient, goal-oriented processes from the outset, you safeguard your investments and pave the way for a flourishing real estate business. Remember, in real estate investing, being proactive isn't just a strategy—it's a necessity.

6.2 FINDING AND VETTING TENANTS

6.2.1 Marketing

6.2.1.1 Residential Tenants

In real estate investing, finding and vetting tenants is akin to selecting the right ingredients for a gourmet recipe. Each choice significantly impacts the overall success of your investment. Effective marketing of your rental properties forms the cornerstone of attracting desirable tenants who respect your property and pay their rent on time.

To begin, consider the power of online listings. Utilizing platforms such as **Zillow.com**, **Apartments.com**, or even **Craigslist.org** offers extensive visibility among prospective residential tenants. However, the key to genuinely captivating an audience lies in the presentation. High-quality photographs that showcase well-lit, clean, and attractive spaces are crucial. Coupled with detailed descriptions highlighting unique features or amenities of your property, such as newly renovated kitchens, proximity to public transport, or included utilities, these listings can draw significant interest.

Shifting gears to social media, platforms like Facebook, Instagram, and Twitter serve as dynamic tools for advertising your rental properties. The interactive nature of these platforms allows for real-time engagement with potential tenants. By targeting your ads to specific demographics within the vicinity of your property or those displaying interest in real estate, you enhance the efficiency of your marketing efforts. Budgeting for these campaigns should be strategic; allocate funds based on projected reach and conversion rates, always aiming for the highest return on investment. Measuring the effectiveness of these campaigns through metrics such as engagement rates, click-through rates, and conversion analytics will help you refine your strategies over time.

6.2.1.2 Commercial and Industrial Tenants

When advertising vacant commercial premises, several top-tier websites offer robust platforms for reaching potential tenants. **LoopNet.com** is among the most popular choices, providing extensive networks and comprehensive tools that cater to a broad audience of commercial real estate professionals, including brokers, investors, and tenants. **CREXi.com** (Commercial Real Estate Exchange) is another robust marketplace that simplifies leasing with user-friendly tools for listing and managing properties.

At the same time, **OfficeSpace.com** is particularly useful for advertising office spaces and other commercial units. **CityFeet.com** is ideal for urban commercial listings, and Zillow Commercial Real Estate leverages its large user base to reach a broad audience, making it a versatile option for property owners. These websites collectively offer comprehensive solutions for effectively marketing and filling vacant commercial properties.

For those looking for more specialized platforms, **CommercialSearch.com** and **Brevitas.com** offer targeted services, with Brevitas focusing on connecting property owners with qualified tenants globally. **Catylist.com** provides localized listing services integrated with commercial real estate boards. Finally, **CoStar.com** and **42Floors.com** may also be interesting to examine more closely.

6.2.2 Screening Process

Once you've captured the interest of potential tenants, the next crucial step is developing a robust screening process. It begins with establishing clear, non-discriminatory criteria that align with fair housing laws. Essential elements of this screening include verifying credit scores, which reflect financial responsibility, and income verification to ensure potential tenants can comfortably afford the rent. Also, delving into rental history can reveal any past evictions or disputes, and criminal background checks help ensure your property's and its occupants' safety and security. Employing professional tenant screening services can streamline this process, providing comprehensive reports and allowing you to make informed decisions swiftly.

Chapter 3.3.3 mentions three residential tenant screening companies: **TransUnion SmartMove**[1], **RentPrep.com**, and **MyRental.com**. Other providers are TurboTenant.com, **Apartments.com**, **TenantAlert.com**, **Experian.com**, **TenantBackgroundSearch.com**, and **Zillow.com**.

Several specialized screening companies and services are available to help landlords and property managers evaluate commercial tenants. **CoStar.com's Tenant, Dun & Bradstreet** (D&B)[2], and **LexisNexis.com's Risk Solutions** offer comprehensive tools to assess potential tenants' financial health, creditworthiness, and business history. **Experian.com's Business Credit Reports** and **Equifax.com's Commercial Information Solutions** provide detailed credit reports and financial stability assessments.

At the same time, **TransUnion SmartMove for Business** tailors its services to small businesses, offering credit and background checks. **Sperry Van Ness (SVN) Tenant Screening**[3] and **CoreLogic.com's Credco** delivers specialized commercial tenant screening solutions, including lease history reviews and risk assessments. **TenantAlert.com** and **Credit.net** offer credit and background checks designed explicitly for commercial properties, ensuring landlords can make informed decisions when selecting tenants.

These services collectively provide the necessary insights to mitigate risk and ensure reliable, financially stable tenants for commercial real estate.

6.2.3 Having Fair Housing Laws

The legal landscape of tenant selection must be considered. Adhering to fair housing laws is not merely a legal obligation but a moral one, ensuring all potential tenants are treated equitably regardless of race, religion, gender, familial status, or national origin. Familiarizing yourself with these laws protects you from legal repercussions. It fosters a reputation of integrity and fairness in your business practices. When interviewing candidates, focus on questions that relate directly to their reliability and compatibility with your property's rules and community standards. Queries about their reasons for moving, expectations of the rental experience, and long-term living plans can provide deeper insights into their suitability.

6.2.4 Accurate Documentation

Documenting every step of the screening process is imperative. Maintaining records of all interactions, application forms, screening reports, and the rationale behind tenant selections guards against potential disputes. This documentation is invaluable as evidence for any legal questions regarding your screening practices and decisions. By meticulously following these steps, you protect your investment and create a stable and respectful tenant base, which is the bedrock of successful property management.

6.3 HANDLING TENANT ISSUES AND EVICTIONS

6.3.1 Lease Agreements

One of the foundational elements of successful property management is the establishment of clear, comprehensive lease agreements. These documents are not merely formalities but essential tools that clarify landlords' and tenants' expectations and responsibilities. A well-crafted lease agreement serves as a reference point that can prevent many common tenant issues from arising. For instance, by explicitly outlining payment terms, you set firm deadlines for rent submissions, which helps maintain consistent cash flow and reduce payment-related disputes. Additionally, incorporating detailed behavior policies can help maintain harmony within the property; for example, rules regarding pet ownership, noise levels, and use of common areas ensure that all tenants understand what is expected of them, thereby minimizing conflicts. Check the Chapter Resources to find websites offering contract proposals you can copy and improve.

6.3.1.1 Policies

Pet policies are crucial aspects of residential rentals, especially given the increasing number of tenants with pets. Outline what types of pets are allowed, if any, along with rules regarding pet size, breed, or number. This protects your property and ensures comfort and safety for all tenants.

For commercial premises, ventilation or the ability to create a safe fire escape may limit the number of people allowed on the premises. Also, the need to have a policy for how many people are expected to live in a home of a specific size must be considered. Ventilation is most often adapted for a particular number of people. The more people stay in a space, showering, cooking, and so on, the greater the risk of moisture damage in the bathroom, for example.

6.3.1.2 Maintenance Responsibilities

Moreover, maintenance responsibilities should be clearly divided between the landlord and tenants. This clarity helps keep the property in good condition and avoids misunderstandings related to repair duties. It's beneficial to include clauses that obligate tenants to report maintenance issues promptly, which allows you to address these issues before they escalate into more significant problems. To enhance the effectiveness of your lease agreements, consider including a clause that requires tenants to acknowledge having read and understood the terms. It can be crucial in legal contexts to prove that the tenants were fully informed.

6.3.1.3 Tenant Adaption

The aspect of tenant adaptation in the lease agreement, mainly when tenants request modifications or remodeling, is crucial. Ensure that any modification requests by tenants are formally agreed upon in writing. This agreement should specify the scope of the work, who will carry it out, and how the rent will be adjusted to reflect these changes. Engage several contractors to provide quotes for the proposed modifications to ensure cost-effectiveness. Review these estimates carefully and include them in the negotiation process with your tenant. Once agreed upon, it is important that all parties are included in signing this agreement before work commences to avoid future disputes.

6.3.1.4 Setting Rents

As already stated, drafting a comprehensive lease agreement is akin to laying the foundation for a sturdy building—it sets the stage for a reliable, conflict-free relationship between you and your tenants. In your lease agreements, including clear clauses protecting your interests and tenants is paramount. Start with payment terms, which should specify the rent amount, due dates, and acceptable payment methods. This clarity prevents misunderstandings and ensures a smooth financial operation. Equally important are security deposit details, which protect you against potential property damage. Specify the amount, conditions for deductions, and the process for return upon lease termination.

Setting competitive yet profitable rent prices is a delicate balancing act that requires a thorough analysis of several factors. Start by examining the current market rates in your property's locality to ensure your pricing is competitive.

Utilize online real estate platforms and local market reports to gather this information. Consider and specify the unique features and location of your property. Amenities such as modern appliances, convenient parking, and proximity to public transit can justify higher rent prices. Economic conditions play a role, too; during economic downturns, you might need to adjust prices to maintain tenant occupancy. Ensure the rent exceeds your estimated costs, including long-term maintenance.

Lastly, addressing rent increases and lease renewals requires a balance between maintaining competitive pricing and recognizing the value of long-term, reliable tenants. Legally, rent can typically be increased at the end of a lease term. Still, local regulations may dictate how much notice must be given and the maximum allowable percentage increase. When negotiating lease renewals, consider the tenant's payment history and care of the property. Good tenants warrant flexible terms as an incentive for renewal, which helps maintain occupancy and reduces turnover costs. Ensure all negotiations and agreed terms are documented and included in the renewed lease agreement to avoid future misunderstandings.

6.3.1.5 Managing Payments

Implementing effective payment systems is essential for maintaining a steady cash flow. Offer multiple convenient payment options, including online payment systems, which decrease the likelihood of late payments. Platforms like PayPal.com, Venmo.com, or direct bank transfers provide secure and traceable payment methods. Each method has its benefits; for instance, online payments provide instant transfers and digital records of transactions, making financial management more manageable. However, be aware of potential drawbacks such as transaction fees or technical issues that could delay payments.

Managing late payments and defaults tactfully is crucial. Establish clear policies regarding late payments, including any fees and the grace period before these fees are applied. Communicate these policies clearly at the beginning of the lease term and include them in the lease agreement. If a tenant frequently pays late, engage them in a discussion to understand their situation and explore solutions like adjusting payment dates. If non-payment persists, have a legal process for handling defaults to protect your investment. This process should comply with local laws and include issuing a formal notice before taking further legal action.

6.3.2 Open Communication

Effective communication is another pillar crucial to managing tenant relations smoothly. Establishing open communication lines with tenants can preempt many issues and aid in their quick resolution. Regularly scheduled check-ins can be a proactive way to catch potential problems early. It is easier to have recurring reconciliation meetings with your commercial tenants than with your residential tenants. With residential buildings, it is easiest to spontaneously contact the tenants in connection with maintenance visits, fault reports, or other visits to the property.

Moreover, strong communication skills can be invaluable when conflicts arise. Conflict resolution techniques, such as active listening, empathetic engagement, and clear, respectful expression of perspectives, can help defuse tensions and foster a cooperative environment. Always maintaining professionalism, regardless of the circumstances, reinforces your reputation as a fair and responsible landlord.

6.3.3 Evictions and Preventive Measures

However, even with the best preventive measures, situations may arise where evictions become necessary. It's crucial to handle evictions strictly according to legal procedures to avoid potential legal repercussions. Start by familiarizing yourself with local laws and regulations concerning eviction, as these can vary significantly by location. The process generally begins with a formal notice to the tenant, which must be drafted according to legal standards and delivered in a manner prescribed by law. Following this, if the issue remains unresolved, you may need to file for eviction with the courts. This legal process might involve hearings and require law enforcement to be involved in enforcing an eviction order. Throughout this process, meticulous documentation of all communications and actions is imperative to support your case.

Implementing preventive measures can significantly reduce the frequency and severity of tenant issues. Thorough tenant screening is your first defense line, helping ensure that you select tenants who are likely to be reliable and cooperative. Regular property inspections allow you to monitor the condition of your property and address maintenance needs proactively. Building a positive landlord-tenant relationship can also lead to more cooperative interactions and make tenants more likely to respect property rules and communicate openly about any issues they encounter. Establishing and maintaining these practices enhances your properties' operation and contributes to a stable, profitable real estate investment business.

By embracing these strategies, you will be equipped to manage your properties effectively, ensuring that your tenants and investment portfolio can thrive.

6.3.4 Valuable and Free Information from Online Resources

Various online resources provide valuable and free information on real estate legislation, legal forms, rental laws, and eviction procedures.

- **Nolo.com** provides a wealth of information on legal topics, including landlord-tenant law[4], real estate legislation, and eviction procedures. It offers articles, legal guides, books[5], and DIY legal forms[6] tailored for landlords.
- Similarly, **the American-Apartment-Owners-Association.org** (AAOA) offers resources and tools for landlords, including information

on rental laws, tenant screening, and eviction processes, with legal forms, state-specific law summaries, articles, and webinars.

- **FindLaw.com** offers extensive legal information on real estate and landlord-tenant law through legal articles, case law summaries, and a lawyer directory. For example, read their article about "Eviction Notices and the Eviction Process"[7].
- **LegalZoom.com** provides legal documents and resources, including information on landlord-tenant laws and property management. It also features DIY legal forms, legal advice, and attorney access. The Business, Personal, Forms, and Support tabs contain useful information.
- **Avvo.com** connects users with attorneys specializing in real estate and landlord-tenant law. It provides legal guides, Q&A forums, and a lawyer directory. Find "Legal Guides" under the "Legal Topics and Q&A" tab.
- **The U.S. Department of Housing and Urban Development** (HUD) offers information on federal housing laws[8]. HUD Regulations are on the "Code of Federal Regulations"[9] page. Rental assistance programs and tenant rights are also available, with articles, guidelines, and resources on fair housing and tenant protections. The easiest way is to use the search function.
- **The American Bar Association** (ABA)[10] provides resources and articles on landlord-tenant law and real estate legislation, offering legal guides, articles, and access to legal professionals.
- **LawInfo.com**[11] offers legal information on various topics, including landlord-tenant law and eviction processes. It features state-specific legal guides, articles, and a lawyer directory.
- Lastly, **RentPrep.com** provides resources for landlords, including information on tenant screening, rental laws, eviction procedures, and tenant screening services. It also offers free rental application forms[12], articles, and podcasts.

6.4 MAINTENANCE AND UPKEEP: KEEPING YOUR PROPERTY IN TOP SHAPE

Navigating property maintenance responsibilities involves carefully balancing compliance with various legal standards and enhancing the value of your investments. As a landlord, you are tasked with maintaining your properties and adhering to stringent health and safety standards, building codes, and environmental regulations. These legal obligations are designed to ensure the safety and well-being of your tenants and the community. Ignoring these responsibilities can lead to substantial financial penalties and severe damage to your reputation.

For instance, staying compliant involves regular checks to ensure all electrical and plumbing systems meet local building codes, conducting lead-based paint inspections in older properties, and adhering to energy efficiency requirements. It's advisable to familiarize yourself with these regulations by consulting with local housing authorities or hiring a property compliance specialist. This proactive approach mitigates the risk of legal issues. It ensures that your properties remain safe and appealing places to live.

6.4.1 Budgeting for Maintenance and Repairs

Budgeting for maintenance and repairs is another fundamental aspect that requires careful planning. Establish a budget that accounts for both expected costs, based on your maintenance plan, and unexpected repairs. Setting aside a portion of the rental income into an emergency fund dedicated to property upkeep is beneficial. This fund can cover sudden expenses, such as emergency plumbing repairs or storm damage, ensuring you can address these issues without financial strain. Regularly review and adjust your maintenance budget based on actual expenses and changes in property conditions to ensure it remains accurate and sufficient.

When repairs are necessary, having a streamlined process for handling repair requests is vital. Prioritize requests based on their urgency and impact on tenant safety and property integrity. Establish a network of reliable, qualified contractors who can handle various repair needs.

6.4.2 Using Professional Services

When choosing service providers, consider their expertise, availability, and cost-effectiveness. Communicating effectively with tenants during repair processes is crucial to managing their expectations and minimizing inconvenience. Prompt and professional handling of repairs can greatly enhance tenant satisfaction and retention.

Sometimes, the most effective approach is to use professional maintenance and repair services. This is particularly true for specialized tasks requiring specific skills or handling multiple properties. Thorough vetting, including checking their credentials, references, and insurance coverage, is essential when selecting professional service providers. Negotiate contracts that clearly outline the scope of work, compensation terms, and timelines. Maintaining good relationships with these providers can lead to better service and discounted rates for ongoing work.

Working with contractors requires careful selection and effective management to ensure quality workmanship and adherence to timelines. Always obtain multiple quotes to ensure competitive pricing and request detailed proposals to clarify what each contractor will provide. Regularly inspect their work to ensure it meets your standards and the legal requirements. By establishing clear communication, setting expectations upfront, and fostering professional rapport, you can create partnerships that contribute significantly to the upkeep and enhancement of your properties.

6.4.3 Develop Useful Maintenance and Investment Plans

Enhancing the value of your properties through regular maintenance and timely upgrades is a critical aspect of property management that goes hand in hand with legal compliance. By keeping your properties in top condition, you not only prevent the natural wear and tear that can lead to more costly repairs down the line but also boost their marketability. Upgrading appliances, refreshing the paint, and improving landscaping are just a few enhancements that can increase the perceived value of your properties. These improvements can increase rental rates and attract tenants willing to pay a premium for well-maintained and aesthetically pleasing living spaces.

Developing a robust maintenance plan is essential to managing these tasks effectively. Start by thoroughly assessing each property to identify potential issues, from structural integrity to appliance functionality. Based on this assessment, create a detailed maintenance schedule addressing routine upkeep and more significant periodic repairs. This schedule should prioritize tasks based on their urgency and impact on tenant safety and property value, ensuring that critical issues are addressed promptly.

A regular maintenance schedule not only helps in budgeting but also plays a crucial role in preserving the value of your properties and ensuring tenant satisfaction. Establish a checklist of routine maintenance tasks, such as inspecting roofs and gutters, servicing heating and cooling systems, and checking smoke detectors. These tasks should be performed at set intervals—monthly, quarterly, or annually—to prevent problems before they arise. For example, scheduling HVAC inspections before the onset of extreme weather conditions can prevent system failures when tenants most need heating or cooling, thereby avoiding discomfort and potential complaints.

6.4.3.1 A Seasonal Maintenance Plan for Regular Checks

Using comprehensive property maintenance plan checklists, property owners and managers can ensure that all building components and grounds are adequately maintained, reducing the risk of costly repairs and improving the property's overall value and safety. To cover what needs to be done on each property, an annual seasonal maintenance plan and a long-term maintenance and investment plan are required. The yearly maintenance plan helps identify urgent action needs and updates the long-term maintenance and investment plan.

As each property is unique, the checklists below need to be adapted.

1 Spring

- Inspect for winter damage and make necessary repairs.
- Prepare landscaping for the growing season.
- Clean gutters and downspouts.
- Property inspection (use 5. Property Maintenance Plan Checklist)
- Are there repairs that the tenant has not reported?
- Are there maintenance needs that need to be planned and carried out?

2 Summer

- Maintain cooling systems and inspect for proper operation.
- Check irrigation systems and water usage.
- Inspect and maintain outdoor recreational areas.
- Property inspection (use "5. Property Maintenance Plan Checklist" below)
- Are there repairs that the tenant has not reported?
- Are there maintenance needs that need to be planned and carried out?

3 Fall

- Prepare heating systems for winter.
- Clean and inspect gutters and downspouts.
- Winterize landscaping and outdoor plumbing.
- Property inspection (use 5. "Property Maintenance Plan Checklist")
- Are there repairs that the tenant has not reported?
- Are there maintenance needs that need to be planned and carried out?

4 Winter

- Inspect for icicles and ice dams, and remove snow from roofs and walkways.
- Maintain heating systems and check for efficiency.
- Ensure all safety systems are functioning correctly.
- Property inspection (use 5. Property Maintenance Plan Checklist)
- Are there repairs that the tenant has not reported?
- Are there maintenance needs that need to be planned and carried out

5 Property Maintenance Plan Checklist

Exterior Building Maintenance

1 Roof

- Inspect for leaks, damage, or missing shingles.
- Clean gutters and downspouts.
- Check for moss or algae growth.
- Inspect flashing around vents, chimneys, and skylights.

2 Walls and Siding

- Inspect for cracks, holes, or damage.

- Clean and power wash as needed.
- Check for signs of water damage or rot.
- Inspect and repair caulking around windows and doors.

3 Windows and Doors

- Check for broken or cracked glass.
- Inspect seals and weatherstripping.
- Lubricate hinges and locks.
- Clean windows and screens.

4 Foundation

- Inspect for cracks or signs of settling.
- Check for water pooling around the foundation.
- Ensure proper grading to direct water away from the building.
- Inspect the basement or crawl space for moisture.

Interior Building Maintenance

1 Walls and Ceilings

- Inspect for cracks, holes, or water stains.
- Repair and repaint as needed.
- Check for signs of mold or mildew.

2 Floors and Carpets

- Inspect for damage or wear.
- Clean and maintain according to material type (e.g., carpet, tile, hardwood.)
- Check for loose or squeaky floorboards.

3 Electrical & Security System

- Test all outlets and switches.
- Inspect electrical panels and breakers.
- Check for exposed wiring or frayed cords.
- Check all alarm systems.
- Test smoke and carbon monoxide detectors.

4 Plumbing System

- Inspect for leaks in pipes, faucets, and fixtures.
- Check water pressure and drainage.
- Inspect water heaters for rust or sediment buildup.
- Test sump pumps and backflow valves.

5 HVAC System

- Replace or clean air filters regularly.
- Inspect and clean ducts and vents.
- Schedule professional HVAC servicing.
- Check for proper operation of thermostats.

6 Appliances

- Inspect and clean kitchen and laundry appliances.
- Test for proper operation and efficiency.
- Schedule maintenance for significant appliances as needed.

Common Areas and Amenities

1 Hallways and Stairwells

- Inspect for damage or wear.

- Ensure proper lighting and emergency lighting.
- Check handrails and railings for stability.

2 Elevators

- Schedule regular inspections and maintenance.
- Test emergency features and alarms.
- Inspect for smooth operation and leveling.

3 Fire Safety Systems

- Test fire alarms and sprinkler systems.
- Inspect fire extinguishers and replace them as needed.
- Ensure clear access to fire exits and signage.

Exterior Grounds Maintenance

1 Landscaping

- Mow lawns, trim bushes, and prune trees.
- Remove weeds and maintain flower beds.
- Inspect irrigation systems for leaks or blockages.
- Apply mulch or fertilizer as needed.

2 Driveways and Parking Lots

- Inspect for cracks, potholes, or damage.
- Clean and seal asphalt or concrete surfaces.
- Ensure proper signage and striping.

3 Walkways and Pathways

- Check for cracks, uneven surfaces, or trip hazards.

- Clean and maintain surfaces.
- Ensure adequate lighting for safety.

4 Fencing and Gates

- Inspect for damage, rust, or loose components.
- Repair or replace as needed.
- Ensure gates are functioning correctly and securely.

5 Outdoor Lighting

- Test all exterior lights and replace bulbs as needed.
- Inspect for damaged fixtures or wiring.
- Adjust timers or sensors for optimal operation.

6 Playgrounds and Recreational Areas

- Inspect equipment for damage or wear.
- Ensure proper surfacing and safety measures.
- Clean and maintain areas regularly.

6.4.3.2 Long-Term Maintenance and Investment Plan

Hiring a professional to inspect and establish a long-term maintenance and investment plan can be highly beneficial. Maintenance involves restoring a function, such as repainting a wooden window and is a predictable need. It transitions into an investment when you aim to enhance or upgrade to a higher standard, such as replacing wooden windows with more energy-efficient ones. Planned maintenance, when mismanaged, can lead to urgent and more expensive repairs.

To keep yourself updated in the future, consider finding a professional who uses a software program for which you can purchase a license. Alternatively, you can create your maintenance plan using a tool like Microsoft Excel. Doing it yourself gives you better control over your property's status. However, you might miss something, especially as a beginner. With professional help, with or without a software program, the likelihood of missing important information is reduced.

When creating your maintenance plan, specify what needs maintenance and its location (e.g., south window), the required tasks (e.g., repainting), the quantity or size, the year when it needs to be done, and the estimated cost. Include a column to track when the action was last performed. To create a long-term cost review, add another column to indicate how often the maintenance needs to be done. For example, suppose the roof was last maintained 30 years ago, and you estimate it needs maintenance in about ten years. In that case, this information is invaluable for future budgeting.

The more detailed your plan, the better control you'll have over long-term maintenance and investment costs. This comprehensive information will aid in accurate budgeting for this year's and future years' costs.

6.5 APPS FOR PROPERTY MANAGEMENT

Throughout this book, we've discussed various providers of different apps and programs. Many of these providers have been mentioned multiple times across different sections because they offer various services that property owners may find beneficial.

Leveraging technology can significantly enhance efficiency and accuracy in the dynamic realm of real estate management. Many apps have emerged, revolutionizing market research, property inspections, tenant screening, rent collection, etc. These apps streamline property management tasks and significantly reduce the likelihood of human error, allowing for more precise management and forecasting.

Consider, for example, property management software such as **AppFolio.com** or **Buildium.com**, which offers an all-in-one solution for property managers. These platforms integrate functions like advertising rental properties, collecting rent online, screening tenants, and managing maintenance requests. Integrating these functions into a single platform eliminates the need to juggle multiple systems, saving time and reducing errors. Furthermore, features like automated rent collection not only simplify administrative tasks but also help maintain consistent cash flow—a crucial aspect of successful property management.

Maintenance management can also be significantly enhanced through apps like **PropertyMeld.com** or **MaintenanceCare.com**, which allow you to schedule and track maintenance tasks efficiently. These tools ensure timely responses to maintenance issues, improving tenant satisfaction and extending the lifespan of your property's assets. The ability to schedule regular maintenance checks and track them through these apps helps prevent minor issues from escalating into major repairs, saving significant costs in the long run.

Customer Relationship Management (CRM) systems, such as **Salesforce.com** and **HubSpot.com**, are invaluable for maintaining relationships with tenants and potential tenants as they become numerous. They help organize contact information, track interactions, and automate communications, ensuring every opportunity for engagement is noticed.

Financial analysis tools are crucial for making informed investment decisions. Platforms like **Quicken.com** and **Propertyware.com** provide robust functionalities for tracking expenses, managing budgets, and generating detailed financial reports. On the other hand, investment evaluation platforms offer deeper insights into the viability of investment opportunities by considering various economic and market indicators.

Integrating these apps into your day-to-day operations can be a game-changer. Most property management apps offer cloud-based platforms that ensure data syncing across multiple devices, allowing you to manage your properties anytime, anywhere. This mobile accessibility is particularly beneficial for real estate managers who must be on-site frequently or manage properties in multiple locations. However, while these apps offer convenience and efficiency, it is crucial to consider security measures. Ensuring that the apps comply with data protection regulations and using strong, unique passwords are essential to protect your and your tenants' information.

By embracing these technological tools, you can significantly improve the effectiveness of your property management practices. From simplifying daily tasks to improving financial management and boosting tenant relations, integrating these apps into your business operations can transform your approach to real estate management, setting a new standard for success in the industry.

Remember that integrating technology in property management aims to streamline operations, enhance accuracy, and improve tenant satisfaction. Each app or technological advancement mentioned or discussed in the book offers unique benefits to help you achieve these objectives. Choose the ones you need to manage your properties.

6.5.1 Reflecting on Real Estate Tech Startups

The real estate sector has rapidly transformed with the influx of technology startups, enhancing interactions with properties and refining financial and operational processes. Innovations like virtual property tours allow buyers and renters to explore properties remotely. At the same time, automated investment analysis tools provide data-driven insights accessible to all investors. The only certainty is that technological developments will continue to change the real estate industry in all areas.

6.5.1.1 The Role of AI in Predicting Real Estate Trends

Artificial Intelligence (AI) in real estate investing is becoming increasingly pivotal as it reshapes how investments are analyzed, managed, and optimized. AI technologies like machine learning, predictive analytics, and natural language processing enable algorithms to learn from data and make predictions. A critical application is Automated Valuation Models (AVMs), which use data and mathematical modeling to provide quick and accurate property valuations. (Read more about AVM in Chapter 3.4.9.)

AI automates complex processes and offers deeper insights into market trends and property values. AVMs can appraise properties faster and more accurately than traditional methods, expediting decision-making. AI-driven market analysis tools aggregate data to highlight trends, predict future movements, and identify opportunities, allowing for well-informed decisions in competitive markets.

AI also enhances customer service and operational efficiency through chatbots, which handle inquiries, schedule viewings, and provide instant responses. It improves client experiences and frees up human resources for complex tasks.

The predictive power of AI offers significant advantages by forecasting changes in property prices, rental yields, and market demand. AI can analyze demographic data, economic indicators, and consumer behavior to identify emerging markets, opening up exciting new investment opportunities and enabling strategic investments before price increases.

However, AI in real estate presents ethical considerations and challenges, such as data privacy and algorithmic bias. Be observant so that this data is handled securely and complies with privacy laws, which is crucial. If the data used to train AI models is biased, the predictions and decisions made by AI will also be biased. With biased data, AI provides unfair pricing strategies or recommendations, emphasizing the need for human oversight to maintain ethical standards.

Human judgment, a cornerstone of the real estate industry, remains essential in interpreting AI insights and making nuanced decisions. While AI provides valuable data processing and analysis, human expertise ensures the integrity and reliability of investment strategies, reassuring investors of their continued significance in the industry.

In summary, AI transforms real estate investing by offering robust data analysis, predictive modeling, and operational efficiency. Addressing its challenges requires careful consideration of ethical implications, data security, and the value of human oversight. By integrating AI thoughtfully, investors can enhance decision-making, stay ahead of market trends, and succeed in real estate ventures. AI is undoubtedly shaping the future of the industry.

6.5.1.2 Blockchain Technology

Blockchain technology is beginning to redefine property transactions with its ability to offer transparent, secure, and efficient contract processes and title management. Blockchain can be used to create smart contracts that automatically execute transactions when certain conditions are met, such as transferring property ownership upon receipt of payment. This technology not only speeds up transactions but also minimizes the risk of fraud, as the records on the blockchain are immutable and transparent. Several case studies, such as Propy.com, which conducted the first-ever real estate transaction on a blockchain in the United States, highlight the potential of this technology to streamline real estate operations.

6.5.1.3 Internet of Things (IoT)

The Internet of Things (IoT) introduces smart home technologies for remote energy consumption monitoring and automated maintenance requests, improving property appeal, management efficiency, and operational costs. IoT devices can monitor energy usage and secure properties through smart locks and security systems. For instance, installing smart thermostats can help manage energy costs more efficiently. At the same time, IoT water sensors can provide immediate alerts about leaks, preventing extensive water damage. These technologies improve properties' operational efficiency and enhance tenants' safety and satisfaction, contributing positively to the value of your real estate investments.

6.5.1.4 Have a Strategic Approach

Engaging with real estate tech startups can be immensely beneficial, yet it requires a strategic approach. One effective method is through direct partnerships, where real estate professionals and tech startups collaborate on specific projects or innovations. This could involve co-developing a new property management platform or integrating IoT technology into new developments.

Investing in startup ventures is another avenue. This not only potentially offers lucrative returns but also provides early access to innovative tools and products that could give you a competitive edge in the real estate market. However, it's important to approach these opportunities with a well-thought-out plan, ensuring you're prepared for the potential risks and rewards. Alternatively, adopting new technologies early—even those still in the beta testing phase—can position you as a leader in adopting cutting-edge solutions, setting you apart from competitors.

However, navigating these collaborations with an awareness of the associated risks is crucial. Startups, by nature, can be volatile. Their products are often in continuous development, with features and functionalities evolving. It can pose challenges if the tools or technologies do not integrate well with existing systems or develop in a direction that no longer aligns with your needs.

Another consideration is the startup's financial stability; the risk of a startup folding could leave you with unsupported software or incomplete projects. Moreover, the rapid pace of technological advancement means continuous learning and adaptation. Staying updated with the latest developments and training your team to adapt to new tools can require significant time and resources.

Around the world, real estate tech focuses on sustainability and energy efficiency through technologies that reduce carbon footprints and improve energy efficiency. Virtual Reality (VR) is expected to become more mainstream, offering even more immersive and interactive ways for potential buyers to experience properties. As these technologies continue to develop, they promise to profoundly reshape the landscape of real estate investing, inspiring a new wave of innovation and transformation.

As you navigate this dynamic junction of real estate and technology, your ability to adapt and innovate will be crucial. Embrace the opportunities real estate tech startups present, but approach them with a strategic mindset that balances potential benefits against inherent risks. By staying informed and adaptable, you can leverage these innovations to enhance your investment portfolio and lead the transformation of the real estate industry.

In embracing the innovations brought by real estate tech startups, you've explored how virtual tours, blockchain, AI, and IoT are transforming the industry. You've also navigated potential collaborations and considered the risks involved. As this chapter closes, remember that the landscape of real estate technology is ever-evolving. The tools and strategies that are cutting-edge today may be the standard tomorrow, and staying ahead requires not just adaptation but a proactive approach to technology adoption. As you continue your journey through real estate investing, remember that integrating technology is not just about keeping up with trends—it's about setting them.

6.5.2 Evaluating App Effectiveness through Trials and Reviews

Before committing to any real estate software, it's wise to conduct thorough evaluations through trials and user reviews. Most reputable software providers offer trial periods during which you can test the functionalities and determine if they align with your needs. During these trials, assess everything from ease of use to the responsiveness of customer support.

User reviews and feedback provide invaluable insights into the software's practical use and reliability. Platforms such as Capterra.com and G2.com's crowdsource user reviews offer a spectrum of user experiences that can highlight potential strengths and weaknesses not immediately apparent in a trial. Consider reviews from users with similar business models or needs as yours.

When evaluating the effectiveness of a real estate app or software, several criteria should be considered to ensure it meets your specific needs. User-friendliness is paramount; the software should be intuitive and easy to navigate, even for those not particularly tech-savvy. Its ability to integrate with other tools, such as accounting software or email systems, can significantly enhance productivity by creating a seamless workflow. Mobile access is another critical factor, as the ability to manage your investments on the go is essential in today's fast-paced world.

Customer support is also a vital consideration. Reliable support can make a significant difference, especially when dealing with complex issues or troubleshooting technical problems. Additionally, consider your specific needs, budget, and the scale of your operations. A cost versus benefit analysis can help determine if the investment in a particular tool is justifiable based on its efficiencies and advantages.

Finally, always be prepared to reassess your technological tools as your business needs evolve. The dynamic nature of real estate investing might require you to upgrade or switch to different software that better suits your growing needs. Keeping abreast of technological advancements and continuously evaluating the tools at your disposal ensures that your real estate venture remains competitive and efficient.

In harnessing the power of technology in real estate investing, you are simplifying complex processes and gaining a significant competitive edge. The right technological tools can enhance operational efficiency, improve decision-making processes, and ultimately contribute to a more profitable investment portfolio. As we continue to explore the impact of technology in real estate, remember that these tools are here to serve your goals and should be utilized in ways that best align with your strategic vision and operational style.

6.6 MANAGEMENT TERMS

Here, we will explore a few **management terms** that form the core of real estate management, helping you become fluent in the language of real estate.

1. **Accessibility**: The design of buildings or environments is accessible and usable by people with disabilities.
2. **Air Conditioning** in buildings refers to the system or process used to control and regulate the temperature, humidity, and air quality within an indoor space. It primarily involves cooling the air but can also include heating, ventilation, and humidity control to ensure a comfortable and safe environment.
3. **Amenities** are features or services provided at a property that enhance its appeal and comfort, such as a gym or pool.
4. **Builder**: A person or company that constructs buildings or structures.

5. **Building**: A structure with walls and a roof, such as a house, office, or factory.
6. **Building codes** are regulations that determine the design, construction, and maintenance standards for buildings to ensure safety and health.
7. **Caretaker**: A person responsible for the general maintenance and care of a building or property.
8. **Common areas** are areas of a property shared by all tenants or owners, such as lobbies, hallways, and recreational facilities.
9. **Curb appeal**: The attractiveness of a property when viewed from the street, which influences its initial impression on potential buyers or tenants.
10. **Due Diligence** is the process of thoroughly investigating and evaluating a property before finalizing a purchase, including legal, financial, and physical inspection.
11. **Emergency plan**: A strategy and procedures for responding to fires, natural disasters, or security threats.
12. **Energy consumption**: The amount of energy used by a building or property.
13. **Energy efficiency**: Using less energy to provide the same service or achieve the same result in a building. For example, ensure that all HVAC systems cooperate optimally with each other.
14. **Facility management** is the coordination of the physical workplace with tenant operations, encompassing maintenance, safety, and services.
15. **Fire safety**: Measures and practices in place to prevent and respond to fires in a building.
16. **Floor**: A level or story within a building.
17. **Garbage disposal**: The process and systems for collecting and removing waste from a property.
18. **Garden architect**: A professional who designs and plans the layout and planting of gardens and landscapes.
19. **Heating system**: The system provides heat to a building, such as a furnace or boiler, geothermal heat, district heating, air source heat pump, or solar energy.

20. **Homeowners Association (HOA)**: An organization that manages and regulates properties within a community.
21. **HVAC (Heating, Ventilation, and Air Conditioning)**: Systems regulate indoor temperature, air quality, and comfort.
22. **Ice removal**: Remove icicles from roofs, gutters, and downpipes.
23. **Inspection**: An examination of a property to assess its condition and identify any issues or needed repairs before purchase and annually.
24. **Janitorial**: Services related to cleaning and maintaining a building's interior spaces.
25. **Land**: A parcel of earth considered property, including its natural resources.
26. **Landlord**: The owner of a property who rents it out to tenants.
27. **Landscaping** is the process of making a yard or piece of land more attractive by altering the existing design, planting trees and shrubs, and adding ornamental features,
28. **Lease agreement**: A contract between a landlord and tenant outlining the terms of the rental arrangement.
29. **Lighting**: The arrangement or provision of light in a building or area.
30. **Maintenance**: Planned maintenance and incurred repairs to a building or site to ensure they remain in good condition.
31. **Maintenance plan**: A scheduled plan for performing routine maintenance and inspections on a property.
32. **Move-in/move-out procedures**: The standardized processes followed when tenants move into or out of a property.
33. **Occupancy**: The state of being occupied or the number of units or spaces currently rented in a property.
34. **Parking**: Designated areas where vehicles can be parked at a property.
35. **Pest control**: The management and regulation of pests within a property to prevent damage and health hazards.
36. **Preventive maintenance**: Regular and planned maintenance actions to prevent unexpected failures and prolong the life of building systems.
37. **Project manager**: A person responsible for planning, executing, and overseeing a project to ensure completion.

38. **Property**: A piece of real estate, including land and its buildings.
39. **Property Management** is the administration, operation, control, and supervision of properties carried out by or on behalf of the owner.
40. **Property manager**: A person or company responsible for managing a real estate property, including renting, maintenance, and tenant relations.
41. **Repair**: The action of fixing or restoring something that is broken or damaged.
42. **Security**: Measures and systems in place to protect a property from unauthorized access and harm.
43. **Signage**: Signs and symbols used to identify, direct, or inform people within a property.
44. **Slip prevention in winter**: Sand or salty icy surfaces.
45. **Snow removal**: Clearing snow from areas such as driveways, sidewalks, and parking lots.
46. **Sub-central**: Systems or equipment that support the main utility systems in a property, often located centrally within the building.
47. **Staging**: This term usually refers to "preparing a private residence for sale on the property market." In this book, staging aims to make a home or an entire property (with land and buildings) appealing to tenants or, when selling, to attract the most potential buyers, selling a property faster and for more money.
48. **Tenant**: A person or entity renting or leasing a property from a landlord.
49. **Terrace**: A level, paved area or platform next to a building, often used for outdoor activities.
50. **Utilities**: Essential services provided to a property, such as water, electricity, gas, and sewage.
51. **Vacancy Rate**: It represents the percentage of all available units, or square feet, in a rental property that is vacant or unrented at a particular time.
52. **Ventilation** refers to circulating fresh air throughout a space to maintain indoor air quality, control temperature, and remove excess moisture, odors, and pollutants. Ventilation can be achieved naturally, using

self-draft and thermal forces, or mechanically, with the help of fans and ventilation systems. It's essential to maintain a healthy indoor environment.

53. **Waste management**: The collection, transportation, and disposal or recycling of waste materials from a property.
54. **Zoning regulations** are local laws governing land use and property development, specifying the types of buildings allowed in certain areas.

* * *

The chapter's footnotes

1 *https://www.mysmartmove.com/*

2 *https://www.dnb.com/*

3 *https://svn.com/*

4 *https://www.nolo.com/legal-encyclopedia/landlords*

5 *https://store.nolo.com/products*

6 *https://store.nolo.com/products/online-legal-forms*

7 *https://www.findlaw.com/realestate/landlord-tenant-law/rules-for-landlords-and-property-managers-when-evicting-a-tenant.html*

8 *https://www.hud.gov/program_offices/general_counsel/lawsandregulations*

9 *https://www.ecfr.gov/*

10 *https://www.americanbar.org/topics/realestate/*

11 *https://www.lawinfo.com/resources/real-estate/*

12 *https://rentprep.com/resources/landlord-forms/*

READY TO MAKE AN IMPACT?

PASS THE KNOWLEDGE ON TO A LIKE-MINDED PERSON

Now that you have everything you need to start your real estate investing journey, it's time to pass on your newfound knowledge and show other readers where they can find the same help.

Simply by leaving your honest opinion of *A Practical Guide to Real Estate Investing for Beginners* on the site where you purchased it, you'll show other beginner investors where they can find the information they're looking for and promote their passion for real estate forward.

Thank you for being so helpful. When we share our knowledge, real estate investing can become a reality for everyday people—and you help me do just that.

Thank you for being a part of this journey!
Mari Sellin

CONCLUSION

As we conclude our journey through the comprehensive landscape of real estate investing, we must reflect on the path we've traversed together. From the foundational basics of understanding financial analysis and market dynamics to the complexities of strategic planning, legal considerations, and effective property management, each step has been a building block toward your mastery of real estate investing. We've explored diverse financing options, delved into rigorous market analysis, emphasized the importance of risk management, and highlighted the critical role of continuous learning and adaptation in this dynamic field.

As we've discussed, the essence of real estate investing for beginners is acquiring properties and developing a robust understanding of the market trends, financial intricacies, and legal frameworks governing this domain. Your journey started with grasping these fundamentals, which are crucial for making informed decisions that are both profitable and sustainable.

Strategic planning and meticulous risk management have been recurring themes in our discussions. They are the bedrock upon which successful real estate investing is built. By carefully assessing potential risks and planning investment strategies, you safeguard your assets and ensure enduring success.

Real estate is a field that thrives on foresight and adaptability. The market will continue to evolve, influenced by economic shifts, technological advancements, and regulatory changes. Therefore, a commitment to ongoing education and a keen eye on market conditions are indispensable tools for any investor. Remember, the learning never stops. Embrace it as a continuous journey, where each piece of new knowledge and every experience, whether a success or a learning moment, shapes your path forward.

Looking ahead, the future of real estate investing holds remarkable potential for growth and expansion. Despite the challenges and fluctuations of economic cycles, real estate remains a resilient sector, offering tangible assets and opportunities for well-prepared and informed people. Your journey in real estate investing will be filled with challenges and rewards. Approach each with a strategic mindset and ethical practices, and you will build wealth and a reputable legacy in the real estate world.

I sincerely thank you for investing your time and effort in navigating the complexities of real estate with this book. Your commitment to enhancing your understanding and skills is commendable, and it's an honor to have shared this knowledge with you.

As you move forward, I urge you to leverage the insights and strategies we've discussed. Set clear, actionable goals such as conducting your first market analysis, attending a networking event, or reviewing your investment strategy with new perspectives. Take proactive steps toward realizing your real estate ambitions. Remember, the real estate market is ripe with opportunities for those prepared to seek them out and act upon them diligently.

While working on this book, I found more websites than are mentioned in any chapter that contained information or templates that might be helpful to you. Check out the references below.

In closing, remember that the path to financial independence through real estate investing requires perseverance, strategic planning, and ethical integrity. Embrace the challenges as opportunities to learn and grow. Your journey toward achieving your real estate goals and building lasting wealth is just beginning, and the possibilities are as expansive as your commitment to exploring them.

Every journey, including your real estate investment, begins with a single step. Take one small step every day, and in a year, you'll look back and see how far you've come. This is the power of progress. Remember that every expert was once a beginner.

Step forward with confidence and determination, and strive for excellence in every transaction and investment decision. Here's to your success in real estate investing – may it be as fulfilling as it is prosperous.

With love,
Mari Sellin

Check out my site here: *marisellin.com*

Join my newsletter at https://bf.marisellin.com/cy03odh5gk and receive the **Checklist for Real Estate Investing for Beginners**. This checklist is the ideal companion to this book. It's crafted to help you implement the book's strategies step by step, making the process clear and achievable.

REFERENCES

To make it easy for you as a reader to find good tools on web pages, you will find the URLs directly in the text or as footnotes. Below are references to sources. Under "More," you will find more information and tools that may interest you.

LAYING THE FOUNDATION

Davis, G. B. (2023). *Real estate vs. stocks (What 145 years of returns tells us)*. BiggerPockets. *https://www.biggerpockets.com/blog/real-estate-vs-stocks-performance*

Croce, D. (2024). *3 benefits of leverage in real estate*. Birgo Insights. *https://www.birgo.com/blog/3-benefits-of-leverage-in-real-estate*

LAYING THE FOUNDATION - MORE

BigBoppers Finance News. (2023). *Real estate vs. stocks: Where should you invest your money in 2024?* *https://bigboppers.net/real-estate-vs-stocks-where-should-you-invest-your-money-in-2024/*

RTI Bridge Loans. (n.d.). *Reasons why you should invest in real estate over stocks*. *https://rtibridgeloans.com/learn/reasons-why-you-should-invest-in-real-estate-over-stocks/*

USHUD. (2024). *Real estate news*. *https://blog.ushud.com/*

Real Estate Knowledge Institute. (n.d.). *REKI*. *https://realestateki.com/*

Kiavi. (2023). *6 steps to effective networking for real estate investors*. *https://www.kiavi.com/blog/network-effectively-in-real-estate-investing*

Slaughter Graham, N. (n.d.). *Maximize LinkedIn's networking potential*.

National Association of Realtors. https://www.nar.realtor/magazine/broker-news/network/maximize-linkedin-s-networking-potential

INVESTMENT STRATEGIES

The Equity Report. (2024). *The top 5 practices for ethical investing in real estate.* https://equity.report/the-top-5-practices-for-ethical-investing-in-real-estate/

INVESTMENT STRATEGIES - MORE

Investopedia. (n.d.). *Investopedia.* https://www.investopedia.com

Arabella Capital. (2024). *Real estate investing terms explained.* https://arabellacapital.com/glossary-of-real-estate-investing-terms/

Upside Avenue Multifamily REIT. (n.d.). *Glossary.* https://upsideavenue.com/

Stewart. (2024). *Real estate dictionary.* https://www.stewart.com/en/real-estate-dictionary

The Nick Borrero Team. (n.d.). *Generational homebuying trends: How different generations approach buying homes.* https://thenickborreroteam.com/generational-homebuying-trends-how-different-generations-approach-buying-homes/

40plusfinance. (2024). https://40plusfinance.com/

Aday, S. (2024). *What is the difference between active and passive real estate investing?* Doorloop. https://www.doorloop.com/blog/active-passive-investing

Sina Solutions, LLC. (2024). *Why selling to investors can be beneficial.* https://www.sinasolutionsllc.com/why-selling-to-investors-can-be-beneficial/

Property Flip or Hold. (2024). *Property flip or hold for real estate investors.* https://propertyfliporhold.com/

Olya, G. (2019). *How to make big bucks by flipping your house.* GO Banking Rates. https://www.gobankingrates.com/investing/real-estate/real-life-house-flipping-success-stories-and-how-to-do-it-yourself/

Blankenship, R. (2018). *The top 10 risk factors in flipping houses (and what to do about them).* Forbes. https://www.forbes.com/sites/forbesrealestatecouncil/2018/02/20/the-top-10-risk-factors-in-flipping-houses-and-what-to-do-about-them/

PR_Finance. (2023). *Residential vs commercial properties.* Max Property

Finance. https://maxpropertyfinance.co.uk/residential-vs-commercial-properties/

Orr, J. (2024). *House hacking vs Nomad™*. Real Estate Financial Planner™. https://realestatefinancialplanner.com/house-hacking-versus-nomad/

Lecko, D. (2024). *Wholesale real estate: Full guide & profit calculator*. DealMachine. https://www.dealmachine.com/blog/wholesale-real-estate

Corporate Finance Institute. (n.d.). *Real estate development model*. https://corporatefinanceinstitute.com/resources/financial-modeling/real-estate-development-model/

Struyk, T. (2023). *The factors of a "good" location*. Investopedia. https://www.investopedia.com/financial-edge/0410/the-5-factors-of-a-good-location.aspx

Harper, Z. (2024). *Effective strategies for increasing rental property value*. Steadily. https://www.steadily.com/blog/effective-strategies-for-increasing-rental-property-value

Porter, K. (2024). *How to negotiate after a home inspection*. Credible. https://www.credible.com/mortgage/negotiate-after-home-inspection

Allred, C. (n.d.). *10 real estate investment exit strategies to consider*. Invest. https://invest.net/real-estate/exit-strategies

MARKET ANALYSIS TECHNIQUES

Moore, P. (n.d.). *How to do a real estate market analysis*. Bigger Pockets. https://www.biggerpockets.com/guides/real-estate-market-analysis

Placer.ai. (2023). *Complete guide to efficient real estate market analysis*. https://www.placer.ai/guides/real-estate-market-analysis

Freeze, P. (2023). *How to navigate the four stages of the real estate cycle*. Bay Management Group. https://www.baymgmtgroup.com/blog/real-estate-cycle/

Folger, J. (2024). *What you should know about real estate valuation*. Investopedia. https://www.investopedia.com/articles/realestate/12/real-estate-valuation.asp

MARKET ANALYSIS TECHNIQUES - MORE

Formigle, I. (n.d.). *The four phases of the real estate cycle*. Crowd Street. https://www.crowdstreet.com/resources/investment-fundamentals/real-estate-cy

cle-phases

Swiftland. (2023). *A cooling multifamily market in 2023.* *https://swiftlane.com/newsletter-archive/cooling-multifamily-market-2023/*

Garage21. (2024). *How to navigate real estate investment in high-inflation environments?* *https://garage21.org/how-to-navigate-real-estate-investment-in-high-inflation-environments/*

Cartier, B. (n.d.). *10 things real estate investors should do during economic downturns.* Stessa. *https://www.stessa.com/blog/10-things-real-estate-investors-do-during-downturn/*

Syndication Pro, Sponsor Cloud. (2023). *Understanding cap rate: The key to evaluating real estate investments.* *https://syndicationpro.com/glossary-definitions/cap-rate*

Nikhil. (n.d.). *Exploring cheap houses for sale: Affordable abodes.* ExoFeeds. *https://exofeeds.com/cheap-houses-for-sale/*

Beattie, A. (2024). *10 factors to consider when buying an income property.* Investopedia. *https://www.investopedia.com/articles/mortgages-real-estate/08/buy-rental-property.asp*

FINANCIAL MANAGEMENT

Santarelli, M. (2024). *How to invest in real estate with no or little money?* Norada. *https://www.noradarealestate.com/blog/invest-in-real-estate-with-no-money/*

Fontinelle, A. (2024). *The ins and outs of seller-financed real estate deals.* Investopedia. *https://www.investopedia.com/articles/mortgages-real-estate/10/should-you-use-seller-financing.asp*

Lake, R. (2024). *The complete guide to financing an investment property.* Investopedia. *https://www.investopedia.com/articles/investing/021016/complete-guide-financing-investment-property.asp*

Best Ever Commercial Real Estate. (2021). *Cash flow vs appreciation: 5 expert investors share their insights.* *https://www.bestevercre.com/blog/cash-flow-vs-appreciation-5-expert-investors-share-their-insights*

JMZ Management. (2023). *Understanding emergency fund for rental property owners.* *https://www.jmzmanagement.com/jmz-blog/emergency-fund-for-rental-*

property-owners

Harper, Z. (2024). *How to calculate depreciation on a rental property.* Steadily. *https://www.steadily.com/blog/how-to-calculate-depreciation-on-a-rental-property*

FINANCIAL MANAGEMENT - MORE

Truinvest.com. (n.d.). *Beginner's guide to investing in real estate investment trusts (REITs). https://truinvest.com/beginners-guide-to-investing-in-real-estate-investment-trusts-reits/*

Freeman, G. (2024). *How to buy a house with low income.* The Mortgage Reports. *https://themortgagereports.com/24603/how-to-buy-a-house-with-low-income-in-2017*

Davis, G. B. (2024). *Minimum down payment for an investment property: 9 ways to invest with less.* Spark Rental. *https://sparkrental.com/minimum-down-payment-for-an-investment-property/*

Carson, C. (2023). *Creative financing: How to use it in real estate.* Bigger Pockets. *https://www.biggerpockets.com/blog/creative-financing*

1031 Specialists. (n.d.). *Building a tax-efficient legacy: Exploring 1031 exchange rules. https://www.1031specialists.com/blog-posts/building-a-tax-efficient-legacy-exploring-1031-exchange-rules*

Simpson, K. (n.d.). *Benefits of a VA loan for an investment property.* The Simpson Team, West Capital Lending. *https://simpson-team.com/benefits-of-a-va-loan-for-an-investment-property/*

Grossman, M. (2024). *Closing the deal: Guide to finding the right gap lender for real estate investors.* Azzets. *https://azzets.com/finding-the-right-gap-lender-for-real-estate-investors*

Depersio, G. (2022). *Can FHA loans be used for investment property?* Investopedia. *https://www.investopedia.com/ask/answers/112515/can-fha-loans-be-used-investment-property.asp*

Gotter, A. (2024). *5 grants for real estate investing in 2024.* Bigger Pockets. *https://www.biggerpockets.com/blog/grants-for-real-estate-investing*

Brumer-Smith, L. (2023). *How REIGs work and if they're right for you.* The Motley Fool. *https://www.fool.com/investing/stock-market/market-sectors/real-*

estate-investing/basics/real-estate-investment-group/

Hard Money Mike. (2022). *How to calculate your hard money loan amount.* *https://hardmoneymike.com/2022/11/25/how-to-calculate-your-hard-money-loan-amount/*

Tansy. (2024). *Amortizations.* *https://usetansy.com/amortizations*

Apartments.com. (2024). *How to build an emergency fund for your rental property.* *https://www.apartments.com/rental-manager/resources/expenses/how-build-emergency-fund-your-rental-property*

Araj, V. (2024). *The pros and cons of refinancing your home loan.* Quicken Loans. *https://www.quickenloans.com/learn/pros-and-cons-of-refinancing*

Martin, E. J. (2024). *Mortgage refinance: What is it and how does it work?* Bankrate. *https://www.bankrate.com/mortgages/how-does-refinancing-a-mortgage-work/*

Internal Revenue Service. (2024). Self-employed individuals tax center. U.S. Department of the Treasury. *https://www.irs.gov/businesses/small-businesses-self-employed/self-employed-individuals-tax-center*

Internal Revenue Service. (2024). S corporations. U.S. Department of the Treasury. *https://www.irs.gov/businesses/small-businesses-self-employed/s-corporations*

Internal Revenue Service. (2024). Corporations. U.S. Department of the Treasury. *https://www.irs.gov/businesses/corporations*

Internal Revenue Service. (2023). Publication 334: Tax guide for small business (Cat. No. 11063U). U.S. Department of the Treasury. *https://www.irs.gov/publications/p334*

Internal Revenue Service. (2023). Publication 15 (Circular E): Employer's tax guide (Cat. No. 11949F). U.S. Department of the Treasury. *https://www.irs.gov/publications/p15*

MINIMIZING RISK

Stohler, N. (2024). *10 risks of real estate investing to know before you buy.* Azibo. *https://www.azibo.com/blog/risks-of-real-estate-investing*

DiLallo, M. (2023). *Real estate due diligence checklist.* The Motley Fool. *https://www.fool.com/investing/stock-market/market-sectors/real-estate-investi*

ng/commercial-real-estate/due-diligence/

Wealth VP. (2023). *Risk management in real estate: Tools and strategies for modern investors*. LinkedIn. *https://www.linkedin.com/pulse/risk-management-real-estate-tools-strategies-modern-investor*

Rohde, J. (n.d.). *14 most common types of insurance for real estate investors*. Roofstock. *https://learn.roofstock.com/blog/insurance-for-real-estate-investors*

Pitt Law Online Blog. (2023). *Introduction to property law: Understanding the basics*. *https://online.law.pitt.edu/blog/introduction-to-property-law-understanding-the-basics*

Nerlinger, S. (2024). *Real estate dispute resolution methods*. Legal Match. *https://www.legalmatch.com/law-library/article/real-estate-dispute-resolution-methods.html*

IRS. (2023). *Like-kind exchanges - Real estate tax tips*. *https://www.irs.gov/businesses/small-businesses-self-employed/like-kind-exchanges-real-estate-tax-tips*

Mathis, T. (n.d.). *Strategies to optimize your real estate tax deductions*. Anderson. *https://andersonadvisors.com/strategies-to-optimize-your-real-estate-tax-deductions/*

Tuovila, A. (2024). *Preventing a tax hit when selling rental property*. Investopedia. *https://www.investopedia.com/articles/personal-finance/121415/how-prevent-tax-hit-when-selling-rental-property.asp*

Frankel, L. (2024). *A Wave of Zoning Law Changes Could Have Huge Impacts for Investors and Housing- Here's What you Need to Know*. Bigger Pockets. *https://www.biggerpockets.com/blog/wave-of-zoning-law-changes-could-have-major-impacts-on-investors*

MINIMIZING RISK - MORE

Embroker. (2024). *Real estate risk management: Threats facing the industry*. *https://www.embroker.com/blog/real-estate-risk-management/*

Texas Signature Inspections. (2023). *How to inspect a barn*. Houston Home Inspections. *https://texassignatureinspections.com/how-to-inspect-a-barn/*

Addicott, A. (n.d.). *How to get insurance to pay for roof replacement*. Arch Articulate. *https://archarticulate.com/how-to-get-insurance-to-pay-for-roof-re*

placement/

Insurance file. (2024). *Homeowners insurance vs mortgage insurance: Understanding the key differences.* https://insurancefile.com.ng/homeowners-insurance-vs-mortgage-insurance/

Highfile. (n.d.). *Simple commercial lease agreement - Word | PDF | Google Docs.* https://www.highfile.com/simple-commercial-lease-agreement/

IRS. (2023). *Publication 530: Tax information for homeowners.* https://www.irs.gov/publications/p530

Luxon, B. (2023). *Rental property tax deductions checklist.* Landlord Studio. https://www.landlordstudio.com/blog/rental-property-deductions-checklist

The Entrust Group. (2024). *7 tax benefits of real estate investing.* https://www.theentrustgroup.com/blog/tax-benefits-real-estate-investing

Coons, C. (n.d.). *Guide: How to avoid capital gains tax on real estate.* Anderson. https://andersonadvisors.com/guide-how-to-avoid-capital-gains-tax-on-real-estate/

EFFECTIVE MANAGEMENT

Gohil, S. (2023). *The ultimate guide to marketing your rental property.* Styldod. https://www.styldod.com/blog/rental-property-marketing

Manolas, K. (n.d.). *The complete guide to tenant screening.* Avail. https://www.avail.co/education/guides/complete-guide-to-tenant-screening

Deming, M. (2022). *The landlord's preventative property maintenance checklist.* Realtor.com, Avail. https://www.avail.co/education/guides/complete-guide-to-rental-property-maintenance/preventative-maintenance-checklist

EFFECTIVE MANAGEMENT - MORE

ATS. (n.d.). *Enhance your property listings with ATS's virtual reality staging solutions.* American Technology Services. https://networkats.com/enhance-your-property-listings-with-atss-virtual-reality-staging-solutions/

Landicho, T. (2024). *How to screen tenants in 7 steps (+ free checklist & flowchart).* Fit Small Business. https://fitsmallbusiness.com/how-to-screen-tenants-for-rental-property/

Bitton, D. (2024). *The top 7 most important tips for better tenant management.*

Doorloop. https://www.doorloop.com/blog/tenant-management-tips

Landicho, T. (2023). *The essential rental property maintenance checklist for landlords*. Fit Small Business. https://fitsmallbusiness.com/rental-property-maintenance-checklist/

Smith, J. (2024). *Setting your home up for successful selling - Katana*. Webflow HTML Website Template. https://www.ntagusa.com/blog-article/setting-your-home-up-for-successful-selling

Ericson, C. (2023). *Home-selling checklist: 12 things to do before selling your house*. Realtor. https://www.realtor.com/advice/sell/home-selling-checklist-things-to-do-before-selling/

Arrivo. (n.d.). https://arrivo.ai/

Yarotska, Y. (2024). *Best software for real estate investors: Top 13 tools you will want to use*. Ascendix. https://ascendixtech.com/best-real-estate-investment-software/

Kumar, A. (2023). *13 best real estate investing software for 2023.* LinkedIn. https://www.linkedin.com/pulse/best-real-estate-investing-software-amit-biwaal

About the Author

Mari Sellin is a renowned property consultant with a rich background in helping property owners manage, develop, and optimize their properties from financial and technical perspectives. With extensive experience in project management and operational efficiency, Mari has become a trusted advisor in the property industry. She primarily focuses on helping companies streamline their operations, enhancing productivity and effectiveness.

Mari, an entrepreneur, educator, and author, believes in every individual's untapped potential. She is passionate about helping people achieve more by offering the proper support and direction.

Mari is also the founder of Admiranda Publishing, a company committed to publishing insightful and practical books.

https://marisellin.com
https://www.facebook.com/MariSellin4
https://www.facebook.com/AdmirandaPublishing
https://www.instagram.com/mari.sellin
https://bf.marisellin.com/cy03odh5gk

www.ingramcontent.com/pod-product-compliance
Lightning Source LLC
Chambersburg PA
CBHW072243240926
51846CB00012B/156
9789198961676